YALE CLASSICAL MONOGRAPHS, 6

THE

BLACK AND WHITE

STYLE

———

ATHENS AND AIGINA
IN THE
ORIENTALIZING
PERIOD

———

SARAH P. MORRIS

YALE UNIVERSITY PRESS
NEW HAVEN AND LONDON

Published with assistance from the Stern Memorial Fund.

Designed by James J. Johnson and set in Bodoni type by Waldman Graphics, Inc.
Printed in the United States of America by Murray Printing Company, Westford, Mass.

Library of Congress Cataloging in Publication Data

Morris, Sarah P., 1954–
  The black and white style.

  (Yale classical monographs; 6)
  Bibliography: p.
  Includes index.
  1. Vase-painting, Greek—Greece—Aigina Island.
2. Vase-painting, Greek—Greece—Athens. I. Title.
II. Series.
NK4647.M67 1984 738.3′82′09385 83–21660
ISBN 0–300–03064–9

Illustration Credits

American School of Classical Studies at Athens, Agora Excavations: Plate 5.
Antikenmuseum, Staatliche Museen Preussischer Kulturbesitz, Berlin: Plates 2, 8 (A 44), 9, 12, 18, 19, 21 (A 33), 22 (A 46).
Antiken-Sammlung, Staatliche Museen zu Berlin, Hauptstadt der DDR: Plates 7, 8 (A 41), 13, 20, 21 (A 31).
Deutsches Archäologisches Institut, Athens: Plates 4, 6, 10, 11 (357 a and b, 554, 577, 584, 585, unnumbered fragment), 14, 22 (484), 25, 26, 27.
Hirmer Fotoarchiv, München: Plate 24.
Metropolitan Museum of Art, New York: Plates 1 (Anonymous Gift, 1949), 15.
Museum of Fine Arts, Boston: Plate 16.
Staatliche Antikensammlungen und Glyptothek München: Plate 3.

10 9 8 7 6 5 4 3 2 1

TO MY MOTHER AND FATHER
FOR THEIR SUPPORT AND INSPIRATION

CONTENTS

CONTENTS

PREFACE

This is not a book about all of Protoattic pottery, or even strictly about all of the Black and White style. The focus of this monograph is the work of several eccentric yet critical artists of Middle Protoattic pottery whose activity spans the crucial years of the Orientalizing period. Within their lifetimes, one can witness the transition from a developed Subgeometric style to mature archaic via an original, if sometimes awkward, series of experiments. Through an examination of these artists, whose works were found mainly on Aigina, an association with Aigina as place of manufacture was confirmed. Hence the role of Aigina, or at least of an Aiginetan workshop, is maintained throughout the text, without the intention of renaming Protoattic.

The interpretation is neither novel nor radical: the Ram Jug (Pl. 10) was assumed to be local when it first appeared, and scholars like Pfuhl, Payne, Beazley, and Dunbabin have doubted whether it is Attic. Arguments against a local school have been fierce but flawed; their main support is the conviction that only Athens could have produced a leading and lasting style. The evidence, however, speaks against this Athenocentric perspective, and ancient sources remind us of the poverty, perhaps following drought or defeat, of Athens in the early archaic period. Given the coincidence of an irregular record in archaeological evidence and hints from history of some economic trouble, an attempt to balance these factors is appropriate to the purpose and methods of archaeology.

My research on Protoattic pottery was initiated and sponsored at the American School of Classical Studies at Athens, during two years as a Regular and Associate Member (1978–80). Financial support during research was provided by the American School of Classical Studies in the form of an Arthur W. Parsons Fellowship, by Harvard University through the Norton and Sheldon Funds, and by the Archaeological Institute of America with an Olivia James Fellowship.

Museum facilities, illustrations, and permission to publish were generously granted by Dietrich von Bothmer, Wolf-Dieter Heilmeyer, Ursula Knigge, Elisabeth Rohde, and

Emily Vermeule. For the privilege of examining new or unpublished material and discussing it, I am grateful to Wolf-Dieter Heilmeyer, Martha Ohly, Maro Tsoni-Kirkou, and Elena Walter-Karydi. Research and revision saw the benefit of generous counsel from many scholars, especially Sara Immerwahr and my adviser at Harvard, Emily T. Vermeule, but also Darrell Amyx, Ernst Badian, Judith Binder, Barbara Bohen, Evelyn Harrison, Henry Immerwahr, Donald Kagan, Semni Karouzou, Mary Moore, Lynne Reno, Nancy Skon, Evelyn Smithson, and Eugene Vanderpool. Finally, this revision of a doctoral dissertation would never have become a publication without the editorial skills of Sharon Slodki and Becky Saletan and the support of Jerome J. Pollitt, Edward Tripp, and the Department of Classics at Yale University.

CHAPTER 1

INTRODUCTION

1. THE PROTOATTIC PHENOMENON

Greek art emerged from darkness and in Athens, where an organic evolution in vase painting can be traced from the end of the Mycenaean age to the late eighth century. Flashes of Oriental inspiration lit this steady progress; imported luxuries and the raw materials for reproducing them fed the Greek appetite for the exotic. The development of a superior technique in ceramics, of a sophisticated system of abstract decoration, and the final flowering of a figural painting in the late eighth century remain the achievement of native Greek talent. Outside of the potter's craft, sculpture and jewelry made their modest debut in the graves of wealthy Athenian ladies of the ninth and eighth centuries; bronze horses reflect the status of owning a stable in an early Athenian family; iron weapons accompanied a warrior to his solitary grave. Even the newly coined alphabet found its earliest, poetic use on a prize jug for an Athenian dancer.

By the late eighth century, all these promises of future brilliance in art and literature were manifest in Athens. They were to be fulfilled in the wealth of archaic Athens, home of the finest vase painting in the sixth century, monumental buildings and native sculpture in limestone, and a love of narrative expressed not only in art but in a new form, drama. In the century that separates Geometric and archaic Athens, one expects antecedents: hekatompedon temples with tiles (a ceramic invention for which Athenian craftsmen should have been gifted), experimental sculpture transforming the early ivories into monuments, magnificent bronzes to rival those that crowded Panhellenic sanctuaries in the seventh century. Curiously, all these are rare, and it is once again pottery alone, as in the earlier and longer Dark Age, which sustains the promise of great art.

The modern name for seventh-century Athenian pottery—Protoattic—emphasizes what is to come, as if it is to be appreciated only as an antecedent. Its earliest phase is faithful to Geometric, and this loyalty survives through much of the century as a Subgeometric movement. Its latest expression is already black figure, when individual artists

1

emerge and personality dominates the next two hundred years of Greek vase painting. In the middle of the seventh century, when some of the most important changes in Greek art take place, Attic pottery is peculiar. Quantity alone is disappointing, after the prolific output of Geometric pottery and its popularity abroad. The masterpieces of the period, in a new outline style enlivened with black and white contrasts, were appreciated only on Aigina. Yet this Black and White style inaugurates the Western traditions of line and color and the enthusiasm for narrative equally universal and long-lived. Alone, the vases gathered in this monograph claim a place in Western art; against the historical background of early Athens, they become monuments of history as well as art.

2. THE EMERGENCE OF PROTOATTIC

For the past hundred years, scholarship has struggled with the discontinuity in early Attic vase painting. When Böhlau isolated the "early Attic" style in 1887, he approached it as a problem in evolution: how to fill the gap between the Dipylon and François vases, then (as now) landmarks in the early pottery of Athens.[1] Other Orientalizing schools had been recognized, thanks to a greater abundance of material from the Cyclades, Corinth, and East Greece;[2] the absence of convincing links between Geometric and black figure pottery had even led scholars like Furtwängler to dissociate the Dipylon style entirely from Athens.[3] Böhlau's essay, "a remarkable paper that was not superseded for fifty years," was the first to reconstruct a reasonable Attic series between the eighth- and sixth-century landmarks.[4]

Böhlau's system was limited to vases in collections, chiefly that of the Archaeological Society of Athens, and dominated by vases from Phaleron or in the so-called Phaleron style of the early seventh century. His greatest contribution was illustrating the transition to an Orientalizing style in this early period, enriching the familiar but disappointing repertoire of the Phaleron wares with the large vases: the Analatos hydria, the Thebes krater, and the Hymettos amphora in Berlin. Together these defined the

---

1. Böhlau, *JdI* 2 (1887), begins: "In der Geschichte der attischen Vasenmalerei klafft eine Lücke . . ."; cf. A. E. J. Holwerda, *JdI* 5 (1890): 266. The best synthesis of vase-painting scholarship is R. M. Cook, *Greek Painted Pottery*, chap. 15 (pp. 297–321 on the Orientalizing period).

2. For example, A. Conze's *Melische Thongefässe* (Leipzig, 1862) for Cycladic pottery; for Protocorinthian, Furtwängler's observation in a lecture, *Die Bronzefunde aus Olympia* (Berlin, 1879), had established its identity; discoveries on Rhodes in 1859 (Cook, *Greek Painted Pottery*, 309–10) introduced East Greek pottery.

3. Furtwängler, "Zwei Thongefässe aus Athen," *AthMitt* 6 (1881): 109–12, in discussing the Dipylon oinochoe as a non-Attic import with an Attic inscription; cf. R. Young, *Late Geometric Graves*, p. 229, who calls it an Attic vase with a foreign inscription.

4. The quotation is Cook's praise (*Greek Painted Pottery*, 316) of Böhlau's article. Böhlau's sequence consisted of three large vases and more than twenty minor ones, including thirteen Phaleron oinochoae and eleven other miscellaneous ones, of which two (Böhlau, *JdI* 2 [1887], nos. 10, 11, pp. 53–54, figs. 15–16) are Euboean.

Early Protoattic period, but Böhlau's results could not help him explain the evolution toward black figure.[5] Only further discoveries, Böhlau concluded, would contribute more substance to his series, which did not yet fill "the gap" but could only predict its qualities.

Since Böhlau's article, additions to his corpus of early archaic Attic pottery have indeed accumulated through both excavations and acquisitions. The next isolated masterpiece was the Nettos amphora, found in fragments in fill among later graves at the Dipylon cemetery.[6] This amphora, however, by the painter of the Harpies bowl known to Böhlau (above), belonged to the earliest black figure and did little for "the gap." The next discovery from Athens was an amphora from Kynosarges illuminating the mid-century period missing for Böhlau. At the time, this polychrome amphora in a developed Orientalizing style was the "earliest yet published of the series which follow the Hymettos amphora and the Analatos hydria," but it was also the only one, as yet, of such a series.[7] Other pieces already in collections attracted attention for their potential contribution to the typology.[8] New acquisitions, such as the New York Nessos amphora (Pl. 15), may even have reflected a growing taste for this unexplored phase in the early history of Athenian pottery.[9]

With the appearance of these single discoveries and acquisitions, the growing series was arranged into rough "groups," but more as clusters of isolated works than as coherent workshops or phases.[10]

5. He could only suggest the next candidates in the Attic sequence, ironically two well-known vases from Aigina: the krater rim with the ΑΛ dipinto (illustrated in Benndorf's *Griechische und Sizilische Vasenbilder* [Berlin, 1868], pl. 54:1) and the Nettos Painter's Harpies Bowl (*CVA Berlin 1*, pls. 46–47).

6. *Deltion* 2 (1890): 4–5, 30–31; first illustrated by Staïs and Wolters in *Antike Denkmäler* I (1891), pl. 57, in a Gilliéron drawing, pp. 46–48. The Dipylon cemetery, however, produced so few Protoattic examples that the excavators decided that Geometric vases must have been reused during the seventh and sixth centuries: Brückner and Pernice, *AthMitt* 18 (1893): 135.

7. Smith, *JHS* 22 (1902): 41, pls. 2–4. The Kynosarges amphora was published as "Proto-Attic," the English equivalent of "Früh-Attisch" coined on the analogy of Protocorinthian, first introduced here to designate the period between—inevitably—the Dipylon style and the François vase (p. 29):

> The term Proto-Attic, which is our equivalent to the German "Früh-Attisch" and is formed on the analogy of
> Protocorinthian, is of course only a loose definition, intended to apply exclusively to a small class of Attic
> vases which fall between the periods represented on the one hand by the Dipylon, and on the other by the
> vases of the stereo-typed Attic black-figure style.

8. Thus vases in the royal Bavarian collection in Munich were singled out for publication, probably through Furtwängler's interest in the subject of Protoattic: Hackl, *JdI* 22 (1907): 78–105, 141–43. They were hailed with the formulaic lament (p. 97): "ein wichtiges Beiglied mehr . . . in der spärlichen Reihe, die von der Phalerongattung zum eigentlichen s. f. attischen Stil überleitet."

9. The amphora fragments purchased by the Metropolitan in 1912 were "said to be from Smyrna" but recognized by Gisela Richter as "Early Attic," a revival of the German term in preference to "Proto-Attic": "Early Attic Vase," *BMMA* 7 (1912): 68–71; *JHS* 32 (1912).

10. Thus Hackl's four groups were adopted by Richter in her study inspired by the Metropolitan amphora: Hackl, *JdI* 22 (1907): 98–99; Richter, *JHS* 32 (1912): 383–84.

Most new vases, whether excavated or acquired, belonged to the earliest or latest periods of the seventh century, hence interest followed this concentration of evidence. The most important pottery illustrating an independent Orientalizing phase midway between the Geometric and black figure styles did not come from Athens, nor was it immediately publicized. Through the Greek Archaeological Society, excavations on the island of Aigina, fifteen miles south of Athens in the Saronic Gulf, began in 1894 under Valentin Stais at the temple site known as "Kolonna" dominating the harbor of the ancient and modern town.[11] The first pottery to be published from these excavations was the contents of a built bothros filled with early archaic votive debris and sealed in the earliest temple construction.[12] Most of the discarded pottery was Protocorinthian: pyxides, oinochoae, and more than one hundred kotylae. Other imports included Rhodian bird bowls, Argive Late Geometric offering trays, and faience, but, surprisingly, no recognizable Attic pottery later than the Geometric period. The last vase presented in the publication, clearly the most unusual piece, was the Ram Jug (Pl. 10). It did not fit readily into any of the classes (Mycenaean, Corinthian, and Geometric) recognized in the deposit, nor could its Eastern shape, Homeric subject, and then unique technique and fabric be reconciled with any known pottery. The figural style was described as "kindlich" and "naiv," but it was admitted that "ein Stil ist in ihr dennoch erkennen."[13] After considering resemblances to Rhodian, Corinthian, Argive, and Attic pottery, Ludwig Pallat decided that the jug had to be local. Under the circumstances, Pallat could hardly have interpreted otherwise, for only later did the background of the Ram Jug reveal itself. Its closest parallels emerged from the necropolis in the town of Aigina, though not under formal conditions of excavation.

In this first campaign, Stais investigated the town of Aigina and "many places in the island" besides the Kolonna sanctuary.[14] Naturally he was interested in the unusual rock-cut tombs within the modern (and ancient) town, which had attracted architects, epigraphers, and tomb robbers for all too many unsupervised years.[15] In the most recent study of these tombs, at least one seventh-century tomb was reported, and the description of the findspot of the Harpies bowl in the nineteenth century suggests it came from such

11. V. Stais, *Praktika* (1894): 17–20; *ArkhEph* (1895): 235–63.

12. Stais, *Praktika* (1894): 17–18; (1895): 235ff., 240–41. Located some fifty meters east of the temple, the bothros contained scarabs, terracotta plaques of Daedalic fertility goddesses, ash, charcoal, and bones, as well as the pottery published by Ludwig Pallat: *AthMitt* 22 (1897): 265–333.

13. Pallat, *AthMitt* 22 (1897): 329.

14. Stais, *Praktika* (1894): 17.

15. When Ludwig Ross visited the island, the first capital of the modern Greek state, in 1832, he reported that more than one thousand graves had been opened and plundered: Ross, *Archäologische Aufsätze* 1 (Leipzig, 1855), "Gräber auf Aegina," pp. 45–48. He made the first systematic survey of these "catacombs," dug like wells into the soft bedrock. The most elaborate ones had a vertical or stepped shaft, one or more chambers, stone sarcophagi, molded and painted decoration, and inscriptions. The earliest ones are Mycenaean, but most are archaic, classical, and Hellenistic.

a rock-cut tomb.[16] Modern salvage has recovered a few intact tombs, but most of them are now buried by summer homes and pistachio orchards.[17] Numerous archaic antiquities whose provenance is Aigina probably came from these rock-cut tombs, such as the intact Cycladic jug in the British Museum and some faience objects.[18] Stais himself commented on the quantity of chance and secret finds which had emerged from the island's scanty soil and regretted that there had been no systematic investigation before his time. He reports no major finds himself, however, except for a single unplundered classical tomb from the Iriotou property.[19]

Meanwhile, a large collection of Protoattic, Protocorinthian, and local sherds was discovered and left the island under unknown circumstances. The fragments reached the European market sometime before 1916, were mended in Florence, displayed in Halle, and became the property of the Berlin Antiquarium in 1936.[20] The only notice of these vases, before the appearance of a *CVA* fascicle of the Berlin collection, was an article by Georg Karo on the Menelas stand (Pl. 7), written while the entire group was on loan in the Robertinum of Halle in 1928.[21]

What interested Karo most in his examination of the vase, and perhaps inspired its preliminary publication, was the painted inscription labeling one of the warriors

ΜΕΝΕΛΑΣ , transforming a formulaic heroic scene into a specific mythological one.

Neither letters (non-Attic lambda) nor dialect (Doric) agreed with the style of the vase, which Karo identified as Attic; he solved the inconsistency with Hiller von Gaertringen's

16. Welter, *AA* 53 (1938): 496–517, for the early archaic finds (see n. 25 below for complete bibliography on Welter's investigations). For the findspot of the Harpies bowl, see Furtwängler, *AZ* 40 (1882): 198, n. 2: "mit zahlreichen anderen archaischen Scherben meist korinthischer Gattung in einem alten Brunnen gefunden worden. Es waren also wohl Reste geweihter Gefässe in einem Heiligthum."

17. Recent salvage work by the Greek Archaeological Service reported in *Deltion* 19:B (1964): 74–79 (an unrobbed chamber tomb of the sixth century, reused for two to three generations with sarcophagus burials; incised and painted inscriptions in the natural rock wall); *Deltion* 20: B (1965): 124 (five classical tombs); *Deltion* 21: B (1966): 100–103 (seven classical tombs); *Deltion* 25: B (1970): 131 (archaic tomb with four chambers, reused and robbed); *Deltion* 27: B (1972): 180 (robbed chamber tomb).

18. Griffin jug: Loeschke, *AthMitt* 22 (1897). Faience objects: U. Köhler, "Gefässe aus Aegina," *AthMitt* 4 (1879): 366–68; add Webb, *Archaic Greek Faience*, nos. 398, 412, 456, 800, 863, 888, 923, as faience figurines and vessels from Aigina which reached private collections in Europe. Ross, *Archäologische Aufsätze*, 46, laments: "Die Ausbeute der äginaischen Graber an gemalten Gefässen, Thonfiguren, einigem Goldschmuck usw. war, bis auf einige unerhebliche Stücke, über all Welt zerstreut worden." The prodigious wealth of these tombs was used as a false provenance for the famous Aigina treasure, Middle Bronze Age gold jewelry sold to the British Museum through an Aiginetan collector in the late nineteenth century: R. Higgins, *The Aigina Treasure: An Archaeological Mystery* (London, 1979), an update of his article in *BSA* 52 (1957): 42–57.

19. Stais, *Praktika* (1894): 20, on the unplundered tomb (it contained a bronze mirror and two vases); (1895): 235 on the provenance of the Aigina treasure. See below on the Iriotou property in the ancient necropolis (nn. 27–28).

20. Karo, "Menelas," 10; *CVA Berlin 1*, p. 5. A conical stand fragment still in Florence was once reported (Beazley, *Development*, 105, n. 27; Dunbabin, *Gnomon* 25 [1953]: 247, citing Shefton; Kübler, *Kerameikos VI, 2*, 205, n. 41) but is now lost.

21. Karo, "Menelas," 10–14.

suggestion of an Ionian painter.[22] Nevertheless, Karo did not question the Attic manufacture of the Menelas stand and in publishing it made reference to the entire collection **6** of fragments from Aigina, comparing style and date with those of the Ram Jug deposit. He also suggested that both groups of pottery represented burials—presumably because of the rich selection of material and the grave-like pit in which the Ram Jug was found.[23]

In his article, Karo anticipated Richard Eilmann's publication of all the Protoattic vases from Aigina in *CVA Berlin 1, Antiquarium 1 (Deutschland 2)* in 1938. Forty-six catalogued vases were presented in this publication, but over one hundred inventoried fragments represent vases with the same provenance. The Protocorinthian and local sherds from the same context were only mentioned, and are now under study for a companion *CVA* fascicle.[24]

None of this pottery is complete, nor is its exact origin known. But later investigations on Aigina produced Orientalizing pottery related to, and in some cases belonging to, the pottery in Berlin, establishing a valuable context. Under Gabriel Welter the sanctuary and town were investigated between 1926 and 1938; the results were partially published with a brief report on the necropolis, an early one destroyed by the construction of the classical city wall.[25] In the comprehensive publication of the early pottery from Aigina, exact provenances for many sherds were established from pencil marks on the backs of the sherds.[26] From this information, the contents of two sondages by Welter in the early necropolis of the town can be partially reassembled.

The abbreviation "Pyrg. 29" (or "Py. 29") on some of the sherds indicates a

---

22. Ibid., 13.

23. Ibid., 10. Other scholars have suggested, conversely, that both Ram Jug deposit and Berlin hoard are from a sanctuary: Schefold, *Myth and Legend in Early Greek Art*, 43; presumably both Karo and Schefold have conflated the circumstances of the two contexts, for it seems evident that the Ram Jug deposit represents discarded votives from a sanctuary, while the Berlin pottery comes from the necropolis of Aigina (see below).

24. R. Eilmann and K. Gebauer, *CVA Berlin 1*, 5–6. Forty-six vases are presented (A 1–A 46) but comprise a total of forty-eight vases, since A 67 (pl. 1:4) and A 27 (pl. 16:2) are illustrated with fragments of other vessels. In his review J. M. Cook, *JHS* 59 (1939): 151, noticed this discrepancy and referred to "some 48 more or less fragmentary vases"; noted also by Rodney Young, *AJA* 44 (1939): 715. Only two Protocorinthian pieces have seen an informal publication in a guide to the Berlin Museum: U. Gehrig, A. Greifenhagen, and N. Kunisch, *Staatliche Museen zu Berlin: Führer durch die Antikenabteilung* (Berlin, 1968), nos. Ü 7 and Ü 8, pp. 57–58, pl. 40.

25. Reports of Welter's work on Aigina:

Gnomon 1 (1925): 46–49; *AA* 40 (1925): 5 (Kolonna).

AA 43 (1928): 611 (sondage in city: Late Geometric sarcophagus burial, Protogeometric, Geometric, and Protocorinthian pottery).

Gnomon 5 (1929): 415 (classical tumulus); *AA* 45 (1930): 128 (graves destroyed by city wall: Subgeometric stone sarcophagus; pottery reported includes Subgeometric, Protocorinthian, Corinthian, and Protoattic).

AA 46 (1931): 274–78 (necropolis: painted chamber tomb with inscriptions).

AA 53 (1938): 496–517 (chamber tombs, including an unplundered one of the early archaic period with poros sarcophagi; also reported is a "grosse frühattische Grabamphora").

26. Kraiker, *Aigina*; reviewed by J. M. Cook, *AJA* 56 (1952): 220–21; Dunbabin, *Gnomon* 25 (1953): 246–47.

sounding which took place in 1929 in an area of the modern town known as "Pyrgos" (possibly the medieval tower now painted pink and hence known as "Kokkinospyrgos.") A similar sounding produced the sherds now labeled "Ir. 29" (misunderstood by Cook as "Fr. 29"), presumably a reference to the Iriotou property first investigated by Stais in 1894.[27] These two soundings produced early Orientalizing pottery ranging from Early to Late Protocorinthian in date, including East Greek bird bowls and Protoattic as well as Protocorinthian pottery.[28] Among the Protoattic examples are fragments whose painters and in some cases vessels are now in Berlin:

1. A fragment with a palmette tendril (no. 586 from the "Ir. 29" trench) belongs to an ovoid krater in Berlin (Pl. 21, *left*), as noted by Kraiker, *Aigina*, p. 90 (below, 3.5).
2. A rim fragment published, but not illustrated, as no. 553 by Kraiker, *Aigina*, p. 85, also from the "Ir. 29" sounding, probably belongs to the upper rim of the Menelas stand (DAI photo, "Akropolis Vasen 205"; below, 3.1).
3. An early seventh-century conical stand fragment from Aigina, again from the "Ir. 29" sounding, matches fragment A 69 in Berlin (below, 3.5).

Similar associations link Aigina and Berlin through pieces by the same painters, although not from the same vessels:

4. Fragments of a stand with draped figures by the Polyphemus Painter, close enough to belong to the Menelas stand itself (were there room to restore them), came from the "Pyrg. 29" site (Pl. 4: 555, 556; below, 3.1).
5. An ovoid krater by the Polyphemus Painter has recently been restored from fragments from the "Pyrg. 29" site (Pl. 4: 544, 581, 583, 587; below, 3.1).
6. A fragment by the Woman Painter visible on DAI photo, "Aigina Vasen 464" (Pl. 11, unnumbered fragment), was not published by Kraiker but closely resembles Berlin A 34 (Pl. 9).

27. Kraiker, *Aigina*, 21–22, explains some of these associations; Stais, *Praktika* (1894): 20, on the Iriotou property; Cook, *BSA* 35 (1934/35): 215, 218, for his misunderstood labels; Humfry Payne followed a different system of references in his citations of Protocorinthian pottery from Aigina, in *Necrocorinthia*, p. 12, n. 4, p. 14, where such pieces as "F 122, G 20, F 60, F 25, F 54, F 56" have no counterpart labels on extant material in the Aigina Museum.

28. The "Pyrg. 29" sherds published by Kraiker:

Rhodian: Kraiker, *Aigina*, no. 103 (includes eight bowls).

Protocorinthian: nos. 319, 321, 345, 346, 444, 461.

Early Protoattic: no. 541.

Middle Protoattic: nos. 544, 581, 583, 587 (ovoid krater by the Polyphemus Painter: Pl. 4); nos. 555, 556 (by the Polyphemus Painter: Pl. 4); nos. 591, 596, 598.

Sherds from "Ir. 29":

Rhodian: no. 105.

Protocorinthian (early): nos. 201, 235, 236, 241.

Early Protoattic: no. 540 (by the Analatos Painter); nos. 546, 550.

Middle Protoattic: no. 553 (by the Polyphemus Painter); nos. 574, 586 (belongs to Berlin A 31, Pl. 21, *left*); no. 597.

"Boeotian" (?): no. 64 (belongs to Berlin A 69).

Outside of the major painters, a number of minor Middle Protoattic kraters, represented by fragments in Aigina, belong to the same class of grave marker found in great quantity and now in the Berlin collection (below, 3.5).

These connections suggest that Welter's soundings took place at sites previously plundered, where he found additional fragments of vases, and new vases, similar to those now in Berlin. Further connections may emerge from the publication of the Protocorinthian pottery in Berlin from the same context on Aigina, and may enrich the reconstruction of the early necropolis on Aigina.

Elsewhere on Aigina, Stais conducted a brief investigation of the Aphaia sanctuary (then known as the sanctuary of Athena); later, Furtwängler directed excavations at the sanctuary of Aphaia and identified it correctly.[29] No Middle Protoattic material emerged from these excavations, nor have the recent investigations by another German team, also from Munich, brought any significant Attic pottery of the mid-seventh century to light.[30] However, Furtwängler also explored other parts of the island, including the town of Aigina, its chief sanctuary, and necropolis.[31] He found at least two important Protoattic vases, which were known to Hackl and mentioned in the publication of the Munich vases cited above (Pl. 11: 554, 584, 585; above, n. 8).[32] One of these vases is also by the Ram Jug Painter, and was attributed from photographs by Eilmann in the 1930s.[33] The vases themselves were lost for thirty years, to be rediscovered in Aigina after the Second World War and published in illustrations for the first time.[34] Recently, fresh investigations at Kolonna have revealed quantities of early material (in late fill), predominantly Geometric and Protocorinthian but also a modest quantity of Protoattic fragments.[35] The most important recent finds are new fragments of the Ram Jug itself (now joined: Pl. 10) and a new piece of the bowl found by Furtwängler (Pl. 11: 584, 585), establishing its provenance from Kolonna.

Independent acquisitions of material from Aigina also included Protoattic pottery. A specific provenance from Aigina is available for an ovoid krater purchased by the

29. Stais, *Praktika* (1894): 20, found the eastern peribolos wall and fragments of the pediments; Furtwängler, *Aphaia*, i–ix, on the history of the excavations.

30. D. Ohly and E.-L. Schwandner, "Aigina, Aphaia-Tempel I," *JdI* 85 (1970): 48–71; Ohly and Schwandner, "Aigina, Aphaia-Tempel II," *JdI* 86 (1971): 505–38 (especially 520–26 on archaic finds, including joins with Furtwängler material, from terrace fill); Williams, *AA* 97 (1982): 55–68. In June 1980 I was able to check the Orientalizing material from the recent excavations, through the kindness of Martha Ohly, and noted the conspicuous absence of Middle Protoattic material.

31. Furtwängler, *Aphaia*, viii–ix, on investigations at the "Aphrodite" temple.

32. Hackl, *JdI* 32 (1907): 98.

33. *CVA Berlin 1*, 7, under "Maler der Widder-Kanne," no. 5.

34. J. M. Cook, "Archaeology in Greece, 1945–1947," *Archaeological Reports* (1945–47):112, pl. 7b; Kraiker, *Aigina*, nos. 554, 584, 585, pp. 86, 90, pl. 42.

35. H. Walter, *Deltion* 25 (1970): 136–37; *Deltion* 26 (1971): 61–62; *Deltion* 27 (1972): 183–84; Lazaridis, *Deltion* 28 (1973): 77; Walter, "Alt-Ägina 1979/80," *AAA* 13 (1980): 85–90. Elena Walter-Karydi kindly showed me the new material from Kolonna in 1980 and 1982; she estimates that there is at least three times as much Protocorinthian as Protoattic pottery.

Munich Antikensammlung in 1908 and painted by the Polyphemus Painter, known from other works from Aigina (Pl. 3).[36] Presumably such a vase would hold a special interest for an institution involved in excavations on Aigina.

Modern salvage work may also contribute new finds. For example, two Middle Protoattic bowls with animals and ornaments in a wild version of the Black and White style were on display in the old Aigina Museum, although nothing is known about their provenance beyond the labeled indication that they are from tombs in the modern town.[37]

Outside Aigina, examples of these larger vessels by the same painters have not been found in the same concentration, even in Athens. The pottery from the Acropolis, excavated in the 1870s and 1880s, was published between 1909 and 1925, with an estimate that more than one hundred thousand sherds had been recovered.[38] Only forty sherds were presented as "Early Attic and related," with reference to forty minor un-catalogued Orientalizing sherds; these numbers do not include Late Protoattic pottery, of which fourteen pieces were published. Other seventh-century sherds were equally scarce: only fifteen Protocorinthian sherds were published, of which most are not from Corinth but Attic imitations. Even if these statistics are not the most accurate reflection of what was recovered and recognized, they still emphasize the alarming modesty of the seventh century in Athens, as observed in a closed context.

Only fourteen examples from the Acropolis belong to the Black and White style, of which six pieces can be associated with painters represented on Aigina.[39] An addition to the Acropolis pottery is the finest Protoattic figured piece from the site, a fragment by the Ram Jug Painter found in modern renovations of the Acropolis Museum (Pl. 11, face with bird).[40]

Richer sources for this Middle Protoattic pottery were the main cemetery and the city center of Athens, where excavations began in the 1930s. The Kerameikos cemetery, outside the Sacred Gate on both banks of the Eridanos stream, produced a number of undisturbed seventh-century graves.[41] Compared with the Aigina hoard, however, the

36. J. Sieveking, *MJb* 3 (1908): 60; *MJb* 4 (1909): 203, fig. 17; *AA* 25 (1910): 56–57, fig. 9; *CVA München 3*, pl. 131:2; 133:2; below, 3.1.

37. Despite the efforts of Iphigeneia Deikoulakou, Ephor of the Second Archaeological District of Attica (which includes Aigina), it has not been possible to locate a published or oral report of the finds.

38. Graef and Langlotz, *Vasen von der Akropolis;* statistics in P. Wolters's introduction, p. xxxi; discussion of Geometric pottery in text, p. 23, Protoattic on pp. 34–40, Protocorinthian on pp. 41–43. Over half the Acropolis sherds are black figure and one sixth, red figure; among the older finds there are several thousand Geometric sherds, of which fewer than one hundred were published.

39. Graef and Langlotz, *Vasen von der Akropolis*, nos. 347–48, 357, 361, 364–69, 371, 374–75, 377 show added white; nos. 347, 357, 370–71, 374, 377 are by painters under discussion in this monograph (see below 3.1–2; Pl. 11).

40. J. M. Cook, "Archaeology in Greece, 1951," *JHS* 72 (1952): 93, pl. VI 4b. The fragment was one of many buried in the foundations of the old museum, material unknown to Graef and Langlotz.

41. The richest area in the seventh century was the hill of the Agia Triada church, explored from 1932 to 1939; less spectacular finds came from the north bank of the Eridanos in 1940 and 1943 (for the history of excavations, see Kübler, *Kerameikos VI, 1*, pp. 1–7).

quantity of Black and White style vessels by the painters popular on Aigina and the number of Middle Protoattic burials in general are low in the Kerameikos.[42] Only one grave in the Kerameikos series can be associated with a vase comparable to those found on Aigina, a large krater by a follower of the Ram Jug Painter; but it was not found in situ, only reassembled from fragments found in at least three later graves intersecting the mound to which the krater presumably belonged (Pl. 14; below, 3.3). Other fragments of related style turned up as frustratingly small surface finds in the Kerameikos, but only half a dozen at the most recall the style of the vases from Aigina.[43]

In the Athenian Agora, burials decreased in the seventh century, presumably as the public demands of the growing city transformed the area.[44] Yet the mixture of well groups, destroyed burials, and surface levels provides a wider range of deposits and wares than the selective grave sequences of the Kerameikos.[45] Like the Kerameikos, however, the Agora never produced a homogeneous body of Middle Protoattic material worthy of comparison with the collection from Aigina. A singleton is the closed vessel by the Polyphemus Painter (Pl. 5, *below;* see below, 3.1), a surface find above the archaic cemetery near the Areopagus where the amphora must have served as a grave marker before later disturbance.[46]

Outside of these two major excavations in Athens, salvage work in response to modern construction has recovered occasional contributions to the Middle Protoattic period. Expansion of the road south of the Acropolis uncovered the Nymphe sanctuary, with thousands of vases dedicated to the "Bride" goddess.[47] From the northward extension of the Kerameikos cemetery a single Middle Protoattic amphora with sphinxes, in an eccentric style related to the Aigina vases, was recovered in Greek salvage excavations.[48]

Consistently, seventh-century material is missing, or at best poor in comparison

42. Kübler, *Kerameikos VI, 1,* Appendix 45 gives a chart of the seventh-century burials, with chronology on pp. 105–23. Only two graves (offering channels α and β) represent the early seventh century with pottery burials on the south bank, plus Grave LXII (62) on the north bank. Others without offerings (nos. II, III, V) are dated by context to the first half of the century.

43. Kübler, *Kerameikos VI, 2,* pl. 109, nos. 104, 107–08, 120; p. 525, fig, 61, nos. 209–10, 212.

44. Brann, *Agora VIII,* 1, 106–113, summarizes the topography of the Agora, including wells, graves, and deposits published by Burr, *Hesperia* 2 (1933); Young, *Hesperia* 7 (1938) and *Late Geometric Graves;* and Brann, *Hesperia* 30 (1961).

45. Such contexts proved both more useful to chronology and rich in ceramic evidence such as cooking ware, a potter's workshop, and plastic and polychrome creations: Brann, *Agora VIII,* 3–4, 29, 54–56 (cooking ware); 27, 103, 110–11 (potter's debris); Burr, *Hesperia* 2 (1933): 621–22, no. 330, fig. 88 (griffin's head).

46. Young, *Hesperia* 20 (1951); 86, pl. 37, c J.

47. J. Travlos, *Pictorial Dictionary of Ancient Athens* (New York, 1971), 361–64, figs. 464–68, with summary of earlier reports; M. Brouskari, *The Acropolis Museum,* (Athens: National Bank of Greece, 1974), 84–94. Although none of the vessels from the sanctuary, still unpublished, seems to date before the middle of the seventh century, the excavations also recovered pottery from what must have been a cemetery in that area, including fragments in the Black and White style. I am grateful to Maro Tsoni-Kirkou of the Greek Archaeological Service for showing me photographs of this material and discussing it with me.

48. *Deltion* 17 (1961/62): 22–23, pl. 25; see below, 3.6.4.

to the quantity of Geometric or archaic pottery, wherever random or systematic exploration has taken place in Athens, or indeed Attica. Even where Protoattic pottery does emerge, it is more often of the early or late periods, rarely from the middle of the century.[49] Outside of Athens, southern and eastern Attica have produced no Middle Protoattic pottery which can be classified with that from Aigina.[50] West of Athens, however, the cemetery at Eleusis produced a spectacular Middle Protoattic amphora with mythological scenes, in many aspects the finest example by the most prolific painter represented on Aigina (the Polyphemus Painter, named after this amphora: below, 3.1; Pl. 6). It is also the only example of this workshop which was actually found in situ, although under the following circumstances, providing little information as to its date or intended use.[51]

The West Cemetery at Eleusis produced 417 tombs in modern excavations, of which 267 date to the historical period. As noted in Attica, the early archaic period is low in evidence, with only twenty burials from the seventh and sixth centuries, chiefly inhumations and predominantly child burials. Most of these burials were in pithoi or undecorated amphorae; the exception is the splendid Middle Protoattic amphora by the Polyphemus Painter. The lower half of the amphora was sawed off to introduce the child's body, which was placed with the head pointing toward the foot of the amphora. The vessel was then clamped back together with lead, in the manner of ancient repairs, and placed on its side in the grave, the main decorated side down. The shallow depth of the burial (some 0.20 m below the modern surface) exposed it to later ploughing, which destroyed much of the side under the handle where Perseus was represented. Although the large size and emphatic decoration on a single side of the amphora suggest it was intended to be a grave marker, the original function of this vessel was sacrificed to local custom. It has been suggested that the top-heavy shape on a narrow foot was unsuited to stand independently above a grave, or that the vessel was reused; but the more straightforward explanation, that it was "misused," accounts for the adaption of the vessel to local burial customs.[52]

The location, in both time and place, of the grave which contained this amphora

49. In the Olympieion area, for example, debris from an early cemetery disturbed by the Themistoclean city wall (like the archaic necropolis on Aigina) included Early (the Analatos Painter) and Late (the Nettos Painter) but no Middle Protoattic pottery: Brann, *Hesperia* 28 (1959): 251–52, pl. 44 (the sherds were discovered by Travlos in 1956).

50. Even the rich cemetery at Vari sheds more light on the Late Protoattic period; the few examples publicized from Vari for the Middle Protoattic period belong to a more modest Athenian class: *Deltion* 18: B (1963): 115f.; *Deltion* 20: B (1965): 112–117; Humphreys, "Family Tombs and Tomb Cult in Ancient Athens: Tradition or Traditionalism?" *JHS* 100 (1980):108–10 on Vari, plus some useful reminders of how difficult the study of archaic Attica remains, given the lack of publication of important sites (98, 106, 108, 110).

51. Mylonas, *O protoattikos amphoreus tes Eleusinos*, 1–9, on the discovery; *To dutikon nekrotapheion tes Eleusinos*, vol. 1, pp. 91–92, with pl. 6., pls. 222–25.

52. W. Schuchhardt, "Amphore von Eleusis," *Antike Welt* 4 (1973): 32, argues for instability of shape, but the pointed amphora is typical of the period (see Mylonas, *O protoattikos amphoreus*, 12, fig. 10, for a conspectus of contemporary amphorae).

is worth observation. The burial is surrounded by poor, prehistoric (mainly Middle Helladic) graves, into which other seventh-century burials intruded. Two of these graves, for example, represent "recycled" material: a Late Geometric and an early seventh-century burial both contain Middle Bronze Age vessels, suggesting earlier graves were disturbed in the early archaic period and the older vessels reused.[53] The Middle Protoattic amphora burial itself contained a Late Geometric handmade lekythos; another seventh-century plain amphora burial is dated by Protocorinthian imports, although the amphora itself is Geometric.[54] Such combinations of outdated or "misused" vessels and plain urns make the splendid Middle Protoattic amphora a freak in its context. Unlike the large quantity of Middle Protoattic pottery on Aigina, there are only a few surface sherds of the period from Eleusis, despite a decent sample of Early and Late Protoattic.[55]

Outside of Attica and Aigina only a single site has produced Middle Protoattic pottery: the sanctuary of Hera near Argos. A conical stand was discovered at the same time as the Ram Jug and classified as "local" for many of the same reasons (Pl. 17; below, 3.4).[56]

Further expansion of the present corpus of these large, lavish Middle Protoattic funerary markers seems unlikely.[57] The largest collection will always be that from Aigina, which filled Böhlau's "gap" in both number and quality as no other evidence has. Yet scholarship has dissolved this concentration in the evidence, as emerges in a brief review of the modern classification of Protoattic pottery.

3. MODERN SCHOLARSHIP

The 1930s were prolific in both Protoattic archaeology and scholarship, as introduced above. In 1935, when over ninety publications on Protoattic pottery could be cited,

53. J. C. Overbeck, "Some Re-Cycled Vases in the West Cemetery at Eleusis," *AJA* 84 (1980): 89–90; cf. other peculiar configurations in Attic cemeteries of the period (Humphreys, *JHS* 100 [1980]: 105–10) which suggest a change in the population using these burial grounds.

54. For the handmade lekythos found inside the Polyphemus amphora, see Mylonas, *To dutikon nekrotapheion*, pl. 225a (cf. Brann, *Agora VIII*, 58, no. 232, pl. 13); on other seventh-century graves at Eleusis with older offerings, Mylonas, *To dutikon nekrotapheion*, 115, pl. 243.

55. For the Middle Protoattic sherds from Eleusis see J. M. Cook, *BSA* 35 (1934/35): 193, pl. 51b; p. 200, n. 3; however, none can be attributed to the painters represented on Aigina. These sherds were recovered in the old excavations at Eleusis: Stais *ArkhEph* (1898): 76–122; Philios, *ArkhEph* (1889): 171–94; Skias *ArkhEph* (1912): 31–39.

56. Waldstein, *The Argive Heraeum*, vol. 2, pp. 161–64, pl. 67.

57. There is a tantalizing reference in François Salviat, *Guide de Thasos* (Paris: École Française d'Athènes, 1968), 156: "On mentionnera un vase proto-attique de style 'noir et blanc,'" presumably a vase on display in the museum. No such vase is to be found in the Thasos Museum, nor have my efforts to track it down, with the help of the French School of Athens, been rewarded with any other record of this vase. Presumably Salviat was describing another similar Orientalizing vase.

John Cook produced what is still the fundamental classification of Protoattic pottery, in an article in the annual of the British School at Athens.[58] Since the wealth of material emerging from Athens and Aigina was only partially available for his compilation, his interest followed the concentration of material in the Early Protoattic period.[59] In terms of the Middle Protoattic pottery under discussion in this study, Cook was the first to identify the pottery from Aigina and its relatives on the mainland as a stylistic group and to apply the traditional methodology of vase-painting scholarship to the evidence.

In Cook's chronological arrangement, the most "Oriental" vases, in both style and technique, fall naturally in the middle of the seventh century. Cook characterized the phase dominated by experiments with outline, incision, and added white paint as the "Black and White Style."[60] More properly, this style was a technique with heterogeneous applications and a variety of stylistic manifestations.[61] In a later refinement of his Protoattic classification, Cook isolated an important phase of added red between the Black and White style and true black figure.[62]

Since Cook, scholarship on Protoattic pottery has been limited to the publication of new examples, with appropriate attributions. Cook himself concentrated on individual hands to explain the transition from Early to Middle Protoattic, and attributed what he saw as "a very different spirit" in the Black and White style to "a change from one personality to the other."[63] The appeal of personality in this period and style, marked by strikingly individual as well as innovative painters, has continued to dominate Protoattic publications succeeding the work of Cook.

Such was the next publication, Richard Eilmann and Kurt Gebauer's 1938 study of the pottery in Berlin,[64] and its reviews. Their discussion of the individual pieces in the *CVA* volume was limited to the restoration of the original shapes and scenes from

58. J. M. Cook, *BSA* 35 (1934/35).

59. Cook devoted twice as many pages to Early Protoattic as to the Black and White style, and pursued this interest thereafter: *BSA* 42 (1947). This critical period, the transition from Geometric to Orientalizing, had also been the focus of Böhlau's pioneer article (above, nn. 1–5) and continues to absorb scholarly interest: Brokaw, *AthMitt* 78 (1963); Burke, *AJA* 78 (1974); King, *AJA* 80 (1976).

60. J. M. Cook, *BSA* 35 (1934/35): 165–66, on his chronological scale, 187–95 on the Black and White style.

61. Cook, *BSA* 35 (1934/35): 187–88, on the use of white; see also Beazley, *Development*, chap. 1, for a discussion of the technical evolution toward black figure.

62. J. M. Cook, "Protoattici vasi" (p. 500 on the Middle phase). This refinement was made possible through an abundance of new material from the Kerameikos, Agora, and Vari excavations, documenting the transition to black figure: S. Karouzou, *Angeia tou Anagyrountos*.

63. Cook, *BSA* 35 (1934/35): 200. The chief personality for Cook was the painter of the Ram Jug, a vase to which he tried to relate the other known Black and White style pieces. Having exhausted the career of the Ram Jug Painter, Cook also reached the end of the Black and White style, which he concluded must have ceased with the demise of its chief artist (p. 195).

64. *CVA Berlin 1 (Deutschland 2)*, Munich, 1938.

the fragments. Of chronology little was said other than to place the entire group in Berlin in the first half of the seventh century.[65] Of the artists there was more to say: eight painters were identified in a list of attributions relating selected Berlin vases to each other and to other vases from Aigina and Attica. Leading the list of artists was the painter of the Ram Jug, with nine attributed vases and five others suggested as "possible late works."[66] The other painters identified in the *CVA Berlin 1* volume (pp. 7–8) were new discoveries: the Horse Painter, the Woman Painter, the Checkerboard Painter, the Painter of the Wild Amphoras, the Protome Painter, and the Painter of the Flowery Ornaments.[67] With the exception of the first two painters, the Berlin material did not suggest a high number of accomplished prolific hands, despite the quantity of homogeneous fragments from a common context. What the fragments did document was regularity in shape— twenty-five ovoid kraters, eight amphorae, and three conical stands—and similarity in decoration—large scenes of animals and myth, generous ornaments—all executed in various applications of the Black and White style. These qualities, analyzed below in chapter 2, identify a workshop, and the provenance of the sherds locates it on Aigina.

The next landmark in Protoattic scholarship involved a krater originally found in Athens in the nineteenth century; it was lost between 1895 and its rediscovery by Semni Karouzou after the Second World War.[68] The krater was known, in the years when it was lost, from the Gilliéron drawing, so that both Cook and Eilmann could discuss it in relation to the Ram Jug Painter.[69] Karouzou's lengthy article on the Pernice krater included a new series of attributions to the Ram Jug Painter, totaling fifteen works.[70]

Two years later the spectacular Middle Protoattic amphora was found at Eleusis, to be published by its discoverer, George Mylonas, in 1957 (Pl. 6; above, n. 51).[71] His monograph analyzes every detail of the amphora, including the artist, whom he named the Polyphemus Painter although the artist absorbed works of the Horse Painter. In isolating this painter, Mylonas also reexamines the personality of the Ram Jug Painter, to whom he concedes a reduced oeuvre (only five vases are attributed); thus the work of Mylonas introduced the complex relationships among painters in the Middle Protoattic period.

65. *CVA Berlin 1*, p. 5; in his review, Young, *AJA* 44 (1939): 714, points out three fragments with added red which could date after the middle of the century.

66. *CVA Berlin 1*, p. 7, "Maler der Widder-Kanne." Most of Cook's suggested attributions, although unknown to the two authors, were duplicated by them; a few works unknown to Cook were added.

67. The main response to the Protoattic pottery in Berlin questioned these painters, beginning with the reviews of the *CVA* volume: Cook, *JHS* 59 (1939): 151–52; R. Young *AJA* 43 (1939): 715.

68. Pernice, *AthMitt* 20 (1895); S. Karouzou, *ArkhEph* 1952, 149–66.

69. Cook, *BSA* 35 (1934/35): 193, fig. 9; *CVA Berlin 1*, p. 7, "Maler der Widder-Kanne," no. 1.

70. Karouzou, *ArkhEph* 1952, p. 166. Her attributions were not a simple adoption and expansion of previously suggested works (she omitted five proposed by Cook or Eilmann and added others of her own selection, without sufficient discussion of these choices).

71. Mylonas, *O protoattikos amphoreus*; below, 3.1, for a discussion of the amphora.

The most recent article on an individual vase and its painter dates from 1971, when Emily Vermeule and Suzanne Chapman published a fragmentary krater on loan to the Boston Museum of Fine Arts (Pl. 16).[72] Despite the poor condition of the krater, its style is unmistakable and could be identified as the work of the Middle Protoattic painter represented in another American collection, in the New York Nessos amphora (Pl. 15). Beyond these two pieces, the painter's work is scarce, with only fragments from the Athenian Agora to supplement the two fine vases in America.

15

Beyond studies of individual pieces and painters, explorations of phases and workshops emerged from the two important collections excavated in the Athenian Agora and the Kerameikos. Single pieces from the Athenian Agora had been cited by Cook, Eilmann and Gebauer, Karouzou, and Mylonas, as they were known from preliminary publication or personal access. Several individual deposits were thoroughly published in *Hesperia*, beginning with Dorothy Burr's monograph on a discarded votive deposit excavated in 1932.[73] The early publication of the Agora wells by Rodney Young and Eva Brann represented the first stratigraphic scholarship on Protoattic pottery.[74] The final publication of the eighth- and seventh-century pottery from the Agora by Eva Brann in 1962 admitted a sensible latitude of up to twenty-five years around proposed dates, without serious challenge to Cook's chronology.[75] In fact, the Agora provided a welcome confirmation of the stylistic sequence proposed by Cook. New synchronisms, however, were not abundant, especially for the Middle Protoattic period and the Black and White style. Instead, the Agora contributed many new fragments associated by Brann with old and new personalities.[76]

New evidence from the Kerameikos cemetery was likewise published in preliminary reports, allowing a few vases to be cited in contemporary publications.[77] An essay in 1950 by Karl Kübler, excavator and publisher of the Geometric and archaic Kerameikos, introduced a controversial approach to the subject.[78] His chronology measured

72. Vermeule and Chapman, *AJA* 75 (1971); below, 3.4.

73. Burr, *Hesperia* 2 (1933). Few Middle Protoattic sherds of large funerary vessels figured among the terracotta shields, figurines, and small polychrome ware of the votive deposit, but elsewhere in the same fill there were such examples, including a sherd later associated with the painter of the New York Nessos amphora (Pl. 15; below, 3.4.).

74. Young, *Hesperia* 7 (1938); *Late Geometric Graves*; *Hesperia* 20 (1951); and Brann, *Hesperia* 30 (1961).

75. Brann, *Agora VIII*, 4–8, on chronology, following Dunbabin's "give or take a quarter century."

76. Her exploration of painters and workshops practising the Black and White technique made a "portrait gallery" from potsherds; for reviewers like Cook and Coldstream, Brann overattributed in combining too many pieces under the rubric of, for example, the Ram Jug Painter: Cook, *Gnomon* 34 (1962): 822–23; Coldstream, *JHS* 82 (1962): 217.

77. For example, a piece from *Opferrinne* 2 (Karl Kübler, "Ausgrabungen im Kerameikos 1933/34," *AA* 49 [1934]: 211, figs. 9, 10, and 11) is cited by Cook, *BSA* 35 (1934/35): 189, 193, 201; another vase from the same offering channel (*AA* 49 [1934]: 217, fig. 13) is attributed by Cook, p. 192, and in *CVA Berlin 1*, p. 7, no. 5, to the Ram Jug Painter.

78. Kübler, *Altattische Malerei*; reviewed by J. M. Cook, *Gnomon* 22 (1951): 213, and Amyx, *AJA* 57 (1953): 294–95.

units smaller than a decade, yet he stretched the framework established by Cook to reach earlier and later points in the eighth and sixth centuries, respectively.[79] His attributions, on the other hand, were few, to the disappointment of scholars who regretted his neglect of the rich new material.[80] Instead, Kübler's associations suggested less specific groupings by workshop; one of them inspired the following response from Cook: "The attribution of [25–26] . . . to a provincial Attic workshop raises the more general question of Aeginetan participation in the production of Attic vases."[81]

Kübler himself did not explicitly name Aigina as the province responsible, but the "wild" vase he cited as possible evidence for such an industry was from Aigina, one of those in Berlin attributed to the Checkerboard Painter (Pl. 20). Thus it was Cook who first combined Kübler's stylistic judgment with the evidence for local fabric (the unpublished krateriskoi in Berlin) and local letters (the dipinto on the Menelas stand) to suggest the role of Aigina.

In its final publication twenty years later, the Kerameikos of Athens did not provide the expected testing ground for Protoattic chronology. Synchronisms with Protocorinthian pottery are few, and a peculiar formula to gauge time between intersecting burials was applied to the sequence of graves, independent of their contents.[82] In terms of artists, Kübler pursued his system of broad groups rather than individual personalities, an important step for the study of Orientalizing pottery. The variety of ceramic traditions in this period calls for a more comprehensive analysis than the identification of painters alone, and Kübler's categories first isolated the Aigina workshop.

To his exhaustive analysis of details in shape and decoration Kübler appended a summary of three stylistic groups, arranged by motifs (chiefly ornaments). The first two, subdivisions of a mainstream Attic tradition, are represented by the elaborate ornaments of the Kynosarges amphora and its relatives in the Kerameikos. The second group, a provincial branch, is a mixture of Kerameikos and other Attic vases in a more conservative ornament style, the work of "less creative painters" and "non-Athenian workshops."[83] This "provincial" class is limited to the first half of the seventh century and apparently dies out with the more homogeneous development toward black figure. Many miscellaneous pieces, such as vases which could be Boeotian imitations, fall into this

79. Kübler, *Altattische Malerei*, 6–7, 21ff. (criticized by Cook, *Gnomon* 22 [1951]: 213).

80. Cook, *Gnomon* 22 (1951): 213; U. Knigge and E. Walter-Karydi, *Gnomon* 46 (1974): 207.

81. Cook, *Gnomon* 22 (1951): 213.

82. Kübler, *Kerameikos VI, 2*. Protocorinthian pottery: Kübler, *Kerameikos VI, 1*, 124–57. Even the two rich offering channels contain only a plain pyxis, a battered aryballos, and a single oinochoe (Kübler, *Kerameikos VI, 1*, pls. 57, 58, 67). Cf. Cook, *BSA* 35(1934/35): 200–01; Dunbabin and Robertson, *BSA* 48 (1953): 176; Brann, *Agora VIII*, 4 (aryballos by the Aetos Painter). Kübler, *Kerameikos VI, 1*, 104–23, "Zeitbestimmung," was criticized by Knigge in *Gnomon* 46 (1972): 200–02, with the conclusion that "absolute Datierungen mit Hilfe des topographischen Befundes unzuverlässig sind."

83. Kübler, *Kerameikos VI, 2*, 293ff., on the stylistic groups, summarized on pp. 327ff. For the "provincial" group see pp. 304ff., 328, 330, 336–38.

"provincial" classification by Kübler, but it is dominated by vases from Aigina. As in the earlier treatise on Protoattic painting, Kübler does not name Aigina as the home of this provincial style and in fact explicitly denies that evidence such as Aiginetan dipinti demonstrates an origin on Aigina.[84]

Kübler's wider groupings isolated diagnostic categories and recognized the divergence of trends in Middle Protoattic painting (compare Brann's description of "what seem almost intentional disparities of style").[85] The Aigina pottery, however, would not fit comfortably into a single category; Kübler comments on the astonishing mixture of finest Athenian wares, provincial workshops, and "zum Teil auch wohl aiginetische Nachahmungen" included in the material from the island.[86]

Other scholars have commented on the Protoattic pottery from Aigina in terms of a local contribution to its manufacture. One of the first to suspect this was the epigrapher Lillian Jeffery, who attributed both letter forms and dialect on the Menelas stand to Aigina, with the conclusion that the artist was from Aigina.[87] Cook himself, in his original article, mentioned the high incidence of Protoattic on Aigina without comment, before responding to Jeffery's article and Kübler's "provincial" classification with a consideration of the role of Aigina (above, n. 81). John Boardman, in publishing a Protoattic plaque fragment at the Kolonna sanctuary, considered a local provenance but was discouraged from such a conclusion by the "admitted" (by whom?) technical intransigence of local clay and the affinity of the example he found to Attic fabric and style.[88] However, in a footnote, he admitted the possibility that clay, and even potters and painters, could have been imported to Aigina.[89] Another modern solution inverted this possibility, by suggesting that natives of Aigina participated in off-island ceramic workshops:

> Yet we may well ask whether Aeginetans did not have some part in the manufacture of the pottery made in various centers for export to the island, particularly the nearer centers such as Athens and Corinth. If we assume that Aeginetans were employed in the shop in Attica that made the Menelaos stand, it would sufficiently account for both the Aeginetan inscription and for the fact that so many products of this shop have been found in Aegina.[90]

It was Eva Brann who defended the most sensible solution, a local workshop in the Black and White style, when confronted with the paucity of evidence from the Agora: "It is perhaps not pure accident that the style is represented in the Agora only by small scraps, for its products may have been made mostly in a branch workshop on Aigina."[91]

84. Ibid., p. 328, n. 92.
85. Brann, *Agora VIII*, 20.
86. Kübler, *Kerameikos VI, 2*, 328, n. 92; p. 336.
87. Jeffery, *JHS* 69 (1949): 26, fig. 2.
88. Boardman, *BSA* 49 (1954): 185–87.
89. Ibid., p. 186, n. 16.
90. E. Vanderpool, *AJP* 74 (1953): 322.
91. Brann, *Agora VIII*, 20.

INTRODUCTION

18 A conflict between evidence and expectations has confused scholars: how to classify and explain the "Attic" pottery found on Aigina? Instinctive recognition of a provincial style in the pottery has been suppressed by a strong conviction that Athens must have produced the finest pottery of the century and that a neighbor such as Aigina could only have been a follower. An evaluation of all aspects of the pottery found on Aigina and of the associated pottery from Attica, as presented in the next chapters, demonstrates the case for a local workshop and its historical background.

CHAPTER 2

THE WORKSHOP FROM AIGINA

Context alone suggests that a special class of Black and White style pottery was popular in the necropolis of Aigina, to the exclusion of other Middle Protoattic pottery. In addition, shape, style, and outside influence both distinguish the group from contemporary Protoattic work in Athens and indicate a single source. A workshop of at least a dozen craftsmen displays a mixture of talents, curiosity for the new and exotic, admiration for (or fidelity to) each other's work, and the audacity necessary for great art. Such qualities may have been endemic to the Orientalizing response of the seventh century, but they are striking in this workshop, exposed to more currents than those in neighboring states with an established native tradition. The vase painters themselves, the subject of chapter 3, express all this most vividly, but the foundations of their craft initiate the distinction.

1. DISTRIBUTION

On the basis of distribution alone, the workshop associated with Aigina could have been produced under local conditions and for local purposes. Its vases were found in great concentration on the island, with a few exports: one to the Kerameikos, half a dozen to the Agora and the Acropolis, and two singletons to Eleusis and Argos.

In principle, the distribution factor alone can be overruled as evidence for provenance: newly discovered artifacts are often assumed to be local until proven imported.[1] In the face of this pattern, it may appear simplistic to consider pottery found primarily at one spot as the product of that locale. In the case of Aigina, however, distinctions in shape, style, and letter forms corroborate a local provenance.

1. R. M. Cook, *JdI* 74 (1959); *JHS* 99 (1979): 152–55, attacks the facile interpretation of history and trade from distribution maps. Type sites still dominate terminology, e.g., Sesklo and Dimini wares, Pyrgos chalices, Kamares ware, Megarian bowls, despite changes in distribution.

In terms of distribution, Aigina is still the exclusive home of this Middle Protoattic pottery, unlike other misnamed classes (e.g., "Naukratite" ware) which soon turned up in quantity over a wider area, undermining the role of the original findspot. Even after a century of new examples elsewhere, the Middle Protoattic pottery found on Aigina cannot represent a regular supply from Athens but rather a single group of vessels manufactured under exclusive conditions. Such large, awkward vases are hardly convenient for shipment, even so short a distance as from Athens to Aigina. Moreover, the quality of the painting, ranging from a master to his wilder followers, is too uneven to represent a selection suitable for export; yet the range occurs within a single workshop and excludes other Athenian craftsmen. One might argue that Aigina had no need for smaller Attic shapes such as mugs and pyxides, for the islanders preferred Protocorinthian equivalents; but this would fail to explain the absence of more substantial sizes, such as the Kerameikos kotyle kraters, to mark graves on Aigina. It is important to evaluate the Aigina vases without facile comparisons with other exported classes, such as Chiote, Chalcidian, and Nikosthenic workshops. During the Middle Protoattic period, no pottery was "exported" from Athens, for special historical conditions prevailed (below, chapter 4).

2. FABRIC

Since the discovery of the Ram Jug, its fabric has been questioned as often as its style (below, 3.2). Elsewhere, among the Aiginetan vases in Berlin, Eilmann and Gebauer distinguished three groups of clay and paint types, and attempted to relate them to chronological and stylistic criteria.[2] Young, in his review of the fascicle, pointed out that three vases in Berlin attributed to the same artist (the Ram Jug Painter) were also assigned to three different fabric groups, suggesting that limited significance could be extracted from visual distinctions in fabric.[3] Moreover, one of the three fabric groups isolated in the 1938 publication consists chiefly of the unpublished krateriskoi—acknowledged local imitations of Attic pottery—yet also includes minor pieces published as Attic. The stylistic confusion between these two groups is examined below (3.5); a reminder of the visual properties of the fabrics involved may help.

To the eye, the Protoattic vases from Aigina, with two exceptions (Pls. 10, 22), exhibit the range in color from pale to deep shades of pinkish buff, the silvery mica sparkles, and the well-fired surface of Attic clay.[4] During the seventh century, the color and texture of Attic pottery show weaknesses not visible in Geometric or black figure examples: the fabric is softer, with a tendency to flake, and large vases suffer from

2. *CVA Berlin 1*, pp. 5–6.
3. Young, *AJA* 44 (1939): 714.
4. Brann, *Agora VIII*, 29, for a description of Attic fabric.

irregular firing, with patches of different color ranging from red to black.[5] Whatever the reasons for the apparent decline in the manufacturing standards of Attic pottery, the vases from Aigina are no exception to this range in fired color and surface, and no distinction can be made between Protoattic from Athens and the Black and White style workshop found on Aigina. With two exceptions, all Aiginetan vases are made of Attic clay, and one must assume that clay was imported by the island to supply the proposed local workshop. The distance between the island and the mainland was no greater challenge to a boat loaded with clay in bags or jars than to one with a cargo of pottery. Boardman has suggested that clay was transported as far as from Chios to Naukratis, as ballast in empty grain ships.[6] For Aigina, the distance to a clay source was less formidable than from the coast of Asia Minor to Egypt, and Boardman admits this: "The problem of the clay is not insurmountable; clay could be imported. But, if the local fine ware industry in the eighth and seventh centuries relied on clay from Attica it looks as though it imported its potters and painters also, and their products remain Attic unless the influence of local styles can be detected in their work."[7]

The research presented in this monograph suggests that there is, indeed, evidence for such a local style, in a significant number of features distinct from contemporary Attic tradition. Thus the model of which Boardman was an unconscious architect—a group of artists residing on Aigina, producing pottery of Attic fabric primarily for local use—would best suit the assembled evidence, which points to Aigina.

Although such a resident workshop preferred Attic clay, it is important to mention here the role of a fabric local to Aigina. At least two vases from Aigina—the Ram Jug and the amphora decorated in a hybrid Attic-Corinthian style—were made of a clay neither Attic nor Corinthian (Pls. 10, 22; below, 3.2, 3.5); yet both artists also made other works in Attic clay. Without a local workshop, one would have to assume that clay from Aigina was imported to Athens, then the finished product returned to the island as an "import." It is far more plausible to imagine craftsmen on Aigina working primarily in Attic clay, with an occasional piece in the inferior local fabric.

A major objection raised against the idea of local ceramic manufacture has been the assumption that Aigina never had a fine ware industry of her own.[8] Yet scientific as well as stylistic analysis has confirmed the origin on Aigina of several wares, notably

5. Burr, *Hesperia* 2 (1933): 570–71, 628, was the first to comment on the inferior quality of Protoattic (a decline which had even persuaded H. Dragendorff, *Thera II, Theraische Gräber* [Berlin, 1903], 188–89, that seventh-century Attic vases were not of the same origin as the Dipylon style).

6. Boardman, "Chian and Naukratite," *BSA* 51 (1956): 55–62; *The Greeks Overseas*, 123–24. This explanation would account for the identical clay and style of the "Chian" pottery at Naukratis and that from Chios.

7. Boardman, *BSA* 49 (1954): 185, n. 16; above, 1.3. The crossing to Aigina cost two obols in classical times: Plato, *Gorgias*, 511.D.

8. Typical pronouncements: Friis-Johansen, *Les Vases sikyoniens* (Paris: E. Champion, 1923), p. 170: "Il semble que cette île n'ait jamais eu de production ceramique originale de quelque importance"; cf. Vanderpool, *AJP* 74 (1953): 822; Dunbabin, *Gnomon* 25 (1953): 244; Boardman, *BSA* 49 (1954): 186; cf. above, 1.3.

22

Middle Helladic matt-painted pottery but also a group of Hellenistic terracottas.[9] Other classes of pottery found on Aigina were once thought to have been made there, such as Protocorinthian and Thapsos wares, by reason of their high concentration on the island.[10] Although these major classes were made elsewhere, there is no reason to assume that a high quantity of fine imports necessarily discourages local enterprise. Important criteria in addition to distribution support Aiginetan ceramic industry. The most prominent is stylistic (chapter 3), not only a Middle Protoattic workshop with local connections but also miscellaneous products, including terracotta figurines, of the Geometric and Orientalizing periods which do not represent known workshops.[11] Equally persuasive is evidence of products in local fabric in modern as well as ancient (Pls. 10, 22) times, despite claims that Aigina has no good local clay except a porous fabric suitable only for water jars.[12] To be sure, the modern islanders specialize in the manufacture of such *kanatákia*, which keep their contents cool by evaporation through the porous walls; the jars are sold in quantity to nonisland Greeks and can be purchased only on Aigina. In addition, the same potters who turn out the water jars also produce smaller handmade cups and pitchers of pale buff clay, semifine in fabric (with a grainy feel). A modern survey of potters in the Mediterranean, conducted by an archaeologist and a ceramic specialist, discovered that all of Aigina's craftsmen get their clay from the island.[13] A recent mineralogical study of Aigina clays and pottery confirms two types of clay in modern use, "a very clean greenish buff" which corresponds to the fabrics resembling Corinthian (compare the unpublished Aiginetan krateriskoi: below, 3.5) and "a somewhat coarser red," presumably the source for the local Neolithic pottery and the classical cooking wares in which Aigina specialized.[14]

9. The Aiginetan provenance of much Middle Helladic pottery has been confirmed through gamma ray spectroscopy analysis by R. E. Jones of the Fitch Laboratory of the British School at Athens; Hellenistic terracottas: D. Fillières, G. Harbottle, and E. Sayre, "Neutron-Activation Study of Figurines, Pottery, and Workshop Materials from the Athenian Agora, Greece," *JFA* 10 (1983): 55–69.

10. Aigina was suggested as the home of Protocorinthian ware by Graef (*AA* 8 [1893]: 17), Thiersch (Furtwängler, *Aphaia*, 448), and Welter (*AA* 52 [1937]: 25); as the home of Thapsos ware by Weinberg (*AJA* 45 [1941]: 30–44). Even Payne distinguished "an Aeginetan group on grounds of fabric" among the Protocorinthian finds in the Aigina Museum (Payne and Dunbabin *Perachora II*, p. 1, n. 3; unfortunately, his notes on this study are no longer to be found in the British School library).

11. Significant are not only those sherds now recognized as local Geometric on Aigina (Kraiker, *Aigina*, nos. 107–14) but others assigned to "Unbekannte Werkstätten" (Kraiker, *Aigina*, no. 106) and the "Argive" sherds (Kraiker, 66–76) now rejected by Courbin (*La Céramique géométrique de l'Argolide*, 552) and still unassigned to another locale. On the terracottas, see the Daedalic plaques from Aphaia and Kolonna (below, n. 38), and the seventh-century terracottas in the Aigina Museum (Higgins, *Greek Terracottas*, 57; Mertens-Horn, *JdI* 93 [1978]: 48, fig. 13).

12. Vanderpool, *AJP* 74 (1953): 322.

13. Hampe and Winter, *Bei Töpfern und Zieglern in Süditalien, Sizilien, und Griechenland*, 137–38, including the reports of Ludwig Ross in 1837 on the itinerant potters of Siphnos in the nineteenth century (p. 141); cf. Karl Gustav Fiedler, *Reise durch . . . Griechenland* (1840), 1:273–75; 2:578.

14. M. Farnsworth, "Greek Pottery: A Mineralogical Study," *AJA* 68 (1964): 223–24; cf. Welter, *AA* 52 (1937): 17–26. In my own interviews of modern potters, I confirmed the results of Hampe and Winter's survey: both green and red clay are used, often mixed, in modern workshops.

In addition to a thriving modern industry, ancient literary sources defend Aigina's reputation as a center for pottery. This reputation survived in the city's nickname, Χυτρόπωλις, or "Pot Seller"; other references among lexicographers include a special epithet for Aiginetan pots (distinct from the designation for citizens of Aigina) applied to a κέραμος (pot or tile) as an example of a product of Aigina, as if such an industry were common on the island, or at least not impossible.[15] The testimony of Herodotus should also be included: in his account of the war which resulted in a prohibition of Attic pottery on Aigina (below, 4.3), he refers to the local χυτρίδες which were used instead (5.88), a causal reference implying that the island made and used its own pottery.

Various explanations have been devised in scholarship to explain how a city without modern recognition as a manufacturer of pottery came to be associated with pottery in antiquity. Most commonly, it is maintained that the island's reputation was for trading and selling pottery, not for making pots; a similar argument explains the number of slaves associated with Aigina as only exchanged through her market, not resident on the island.[16] This transfer of epithet certainly explains the term Αἰγινητικά as a reference to trinkets circulated by merchants from Aigina; most of these objects were probably Oriental or foreign and not made on Aigina, such as jewelry, ivory, faience, shells, or seals, and the role of Aigina in the traffic of minor arts will be defended in chapter 4. However, pottery was clearly made on Aigina at different periods in antiquity, according to the evidence of style, fabric, and literature, and it seems perverse to maintain the contrary.

3. SHAPES

The individual shapes popular in Aigina during the Middle Protoattic period do not overlap with contemporary ones from Athens; instead, the Aigina vases indicate conservative potters, who chose vessels traditional as grave markers in the Late Geometric and Early Protoattic periods. Little development was exercised on these shapes, but then little evidence of change could be observed among fragments of large vessels from a short-lived workshop.[17] Yet broad tendencies can be identified, beginning with the preference for three shapes: the neck-handled amphora, the ovoid krater, and the dinos with stand.

The neck amphora appears in the oeuvres of the Polyphemus Painter, the Ram

15. Χυτρόπωλις: *ComAttFrag*, ed. Kock, *comica adespota* 669; on citizens and ceramics of Aigina, see Stephanus of Byzantium, s.v. *gaza*, where Αἰγινῆται are compared to Αἰγιναῖοι.

16. The arguments are reviewed in a dissertation by Figueira, "Aegina and Athens," 101–04, with bibliography; on slaves and Aigina, see below, 4.1.

17. Davison, *Geometric Workshops*, 102–03, noted the difficulty of drawing consistent chronological and stylistic conclusions from shapes around 700 B.C.; Burr, *Hesperia* 2 (1933): 629–31, noted "degeneration," "weak and unimaginative profiles," and even suggested that a lack of metal vases in this period reduced inspiration.

Jug Painter, and the New York Nessos Painter, as well as in those of minor artists (Pls. 1, 5, 6, 12, 15, 22).[18] The shape's popularity on Aigina contrasts sharply to its absence in Athens, as noted by Brann: "There are few amphorae of the first half of the 7th century in the Agora; the scraps . . . show a counter tendency to huge format which is also consonant with a counter school in painting (e.g. *JHS.*, XXXII, 1912, p. XI, the New York Nessos amphora)."[19]

While it is true that the lack of amphorae in the early seventh-century Agora can be explained partly by the nature of the context, where one would not expect large numbers of grave markers (above, 1.2), it is also striking that none are found in the Kerameikos.[20] Examples of the period are either from Aigina or by painters chiefly represented on Aigina, which Brann recognized in the phrase "a counter school in painting." These amphorae are of exaggerated size, compared with the slimmer vessels of the Early Protoattic period, and suggest "a revival of the use of monumental funeral vases."[21] The shapes certainly recall an older Geometric tradition in pottery, if not in funeral customs; at the same time they represent an eccentric style in decoration. Kübler, like Brann, noted this congruency in his third "provincial" group of seventh-century vases, whose "wild style" was not limited to debased shapes or to be dismissed as a minor phenomenon. Instead, the style appears on large, even leading shapes, the only ones worthy of export.[22] Thus both scholars observed a particular style appearing on particular shapes but pursued the distinction no further. This coincidence is significant: it applies exclusively to the vases from Aigina and, in fact, neatly summarizes two aspects of the workshop.

The ovoid krater evolved from the Geometric standed krater to become "the most distinctive shape of the 7th century."[23] Characteristic of the krater called "egg-shaped" is its tall foot, sometimes enough to be a separate stand and often decorated with open-worked cutouts or fenestration, in contrast to the ribbing standard for the Geometric version.[24] The handles are either doubled loops, set vertically on horizontal roots, or double bull's-head horns.[25] The preserved range of ovoid kraters is insufficient for a typological study of profile changes.[26] The shape is rare in Athens; the Agora, for example, produced only two examples for this period, both freaks within the Attic

18. Mylonas, *O protoattikos amphoreus*, 12, fig. 10; Brann, *Agora VIII*, 30.

19. Brann, *Agora VIII*, 30.

20. Kübler, *Kerameikos VI, 2*, 151–52.

21. Hurwit, *AJA* 81 (1977): 24. On the trend toward slimmer shapes in the Early Protoattic period, see J. M. Cook, *BSA* 35 (1934/35): 166, 169–70; Brann, *Agora VIII*, 2; contra Davison, *Geometric Workshops*, 102–03.

22. Kübler, *Kerameikos VI, 2*, 304.

23. Brann, *Agora VIII*, 41.

24. For Geometric examples with ribbed stand see Brann, *Agora VIII*, 42, nos. 92, 93.

25. For the upright basket handles, see the Checkerboard Painter's krater (Berlin A 22, Pl. 20); for bucranium handles, see the Oresteia krater (Pl. 13) and the New York Nessos Painter's krater (Pl. 16).

26. "No particular shape development is observable" (Brann, *Agora VIII*, 43, no. 95).

tradition.[27] "The largest collection of this shape is in *CVA Berlin 1*":[28] in fact, more than half of the forty-eight vases published in that fascicle are ovoid kraters. That official number is considerably lower than the quantity suggested by appropriate sherds; illustrated on a single plate of the *CVA* publication are seven rims, eleven stand and body fragments, and eighteen from the lower body of such kraters.[29] Other fragments from Aigina (including one by the Oresteia Painter himself) are likely to belong to such vases.[30] The shape was popular among leading painters (Pls. 3–4, 9, 13, 16, 19–21) as well as in miniature imitations, according to the unpublished krateriskoi (below, 3.5).

The history of the ovoid krater is also relevant to the workshop. It disappears abruptly with the Black and White style, an additional link between shape and style that defines the workshop.[31]

The third shape favored in this workshop is a combination of two vessels, sometimes manufactured as a composite vase: a deep bowl on a conical stand, imitating contemporary Oriental cauldrons on stands of metal. The bowl, when it imitates a bronze dinos faithfully, has a continuous curve to its bottom; the one in Berlin by the Ram Jug Painter (Pl. 12) even has imitation ring handles and a rim resembling those of hammered bronze.[32] A special feature of the latest bowl from this workshop (Pl. 8) is a spout; this spouted type may have been more popular than extant evidence suggests.[33] However, none of the bowls from Aigina or by related painters was decorated with protomes, as was the custom in the contemporary Athenian Kerameikos. It seems this Aiginetan workshop preferred painted decoration, even reproducing in two dimensions the plastic protomes on cauldrons without adding plastic attachments to the vases themselves.[34]

The stand which often supported the Orientalizing cauldron shape was created by

---

27. Brann, *Agora VIII*, no. 95, pp. 42–43, pl. 5 has unusual light-on-dark decoration; no. 549, pp. 93–94, pl. 34 with facing ducks: "this extraordinary piece has no real parallels."

28. Ibid., 42–43 (no. 95).

29. *CVA Berlin 1*, pl. 39, nos. 12–18 (rims), A 82–A 93 (joint of stand to body), A 61–A 81 (body). For an attempt to restore and classify these fragments, see below, 3.5.

30. Kraiker, *Aigina*, no. 582, p. 90, pl. 42 (below, 3.3, n. 102).

31. Ibid., p. 42: "this egg-shaped krater is a precursor in shape of the classical lebes gamikos . . . , but the krater itself disappears in the last quarter of the 7th century B.C." However, there may be some stragglers (e.g., from Vari: *Deltion* 18 [1963]: pls. 50–51).

32. Below, 3.2. For a bronze prototype of the sandwiched rim, cf. an example from Leontinoi with rams'-head attachments (U. Gehrig et al., *Berlin: Führer*, p. 111, pl. 10, "Misc. 8600"). See Kübler, *Kerameikos VI, 2*, 164, n. 74, on the relationship between bronze originals and terracotta imitations. The fragmentary condition of most examples makes it difficult to ascertain whether a deep open shape had a continuous curve or not: e.g., the Ram Jug Painter's other bowl, from Kolonna (Pl. 11: 584, 585), or fragments of a bowl by the Polyphemus Painter (Pl. 8: below, 3.1, n. 44) could be dinoi.

33. D. Callipolitis-Feytmans, *Les Louteria attiques*, on spouted bowls. The new fragment of the bowl by the Ram Jug Painter from Kolonna, for example (below, 3.2), has a scar which might belong to a spout or handle.

34. For the plastic extravagances of the Athenian Kerameikos, see the contents of a single offering channel, Kübler, *Kerameikos VI, 2*, pls. 32–58. For an Aiginetan representation of a protome cauldron, see the upper rim of the stand by the Polyphemus Painter, Pl. 8.

the Aigina workshop at least six times (Pls. 7, 8, 11, 17, 18, 22), including important fragments from the Acropolis (Pl. 11). Only one (A 41, Pl. 8; now lost) preserved its complete profile with upper bowl, pared down to hold a dinos; rim fragments from the other three examples suggest the same shape, with a deep, slightly flaring bowl as the crowning element. Similar combinations were attempted on a smaller scale: an example in Berlin consists of a shallow bowl joined to a cylindrical base by a torus molding (A 46, Pl. 22). This version was occasionally popular in the Kerameikos of Athens, but the style of painting on the only composite stand from Aigina clearly points to a provincial (Aiginetan) painter (below, 3.5). The association between stand and bowl is reinforced by the evidence from the rim of A 41, by the Polyphemus Painter: the edge was worn by the bowl it supported, and in the frieze around the rim women carry cauldrons with protomes, painted white to imitate metal (Pl. 8).

Stands and bowls from Aigina claim a history typical of the workshop: early antecedents but little later history. The stand revives a Late Geometric type, whose history was recently expanded by a new example in Munich with the profile (conical base, torus molding, and deep bowl) that became standard in the seventh century.[35] Stand and bowl then disappear in Athens during the Middle Protoattic period except in the Aigina workshop; later the dinos-and-stand combination is revived by the first generation of black figure painters.[36]

As potters, the Aigina vase painters were less interested in new shapes than in new subjects—with the exception of the Ram Jug. Unlike contemporary potters of the Athenian Kerameikos, who maintained traditional scenes on new shapes, they reproduced new motifs from Corinth and the East, but on familiar shapes, more substantial in size and more generous for decoration.[37]

4. TECHNIQUE

The Middle Protoattic period lies between two styles of vase painting based on silhouettes and was open to the influence of new techniques in sculpture and metallurgy. Between the reigns of the Geometric and black figure systems, experiments met in the Black and White style.[38]

35. Late Geometric example: Munich 8936 (acquired in 1966), published in *MJb* 18 (1967): 241–45, figs. 1–3. Cf. Protocorinthian parallel from Ithaca: Robertson, *BSA* 43 (1948): no. 225, pp. 47–48, figs. 32–33, pl. 15.
36. Beginning with the Gorgon Painter's name dinos and stand in Paris (Boardman, *Athenian Black Figured Vases*, fig. 11); cf. A. Brownlee, "Attic Black-Figured *Dinoi*" (Ph.D. diss., Harvard University, 1981).
37. An exception to the Attic pattern is the group under Protocorinthian influence from *Opferrinne* β, Kübler, *Kerameikos VI, 2*, pls. 22–26, with exotic animals in proto–black figure; p. 195 discusses the lack of Attic interest in East Greek shapes, outside of the Ram Jug.
38. Beazley, *Development*, 1–12; Boardman, *Athenian Black Figured Vases*, 9, 14; *The Greeks Overseas*, 14.

The foundations of the Black and White technique were laid in Early Protoattic or even earlier, in the Late Geometric period. Painting in dark glaze on reserved clay, in panels and friezes which defined decorative zones, had been an Attic tradition for centuries. Figures were introduced almost casually into the strict system of decoration, then developed into an actual figural style in the mid-eighth century, probably in the hands of a single artist—the Dipylon Master. Silhouettes, abbreviations for the human body, grew outline heads; shields and skirts became outlines open to interior detail, and the new Oriental motifs encouraged curvilinear use of the brush. This gradual exploitation of an open rather than a closed figure—reservation—was "the most steady feature in the development of technique."[39]

White paint was introduced to highlight armor, lend texture to wool and linen skirts, and enliven ornaments, beginning in the Late Geometric period.[40] Early attempts were executed in a solution of slip the color of the clay; later a true white of a different composition than the clay (and hence prone to flake off) was developed, although a few stragglers still painted "white" in slip.[41] The potential of added white paint, coinciding with the new areas opened up by the reservation of dark paint from outlined shapes, created the opportunity for "free" painting. Areas of solid dark, solid white, and natural clay—essentially a three-color palette, not just black and white—could be combined in differentiated shapes, with interior details overlaid in contrasting color.

The Black and White style thus developed naturally from a coincidence of technical progressions within the medium of vase painting. It is important to recognize this internal origin for the novelties of the Middle Protoattic period, often attributed to external influences. Even the large scale for the figural scenes was initiated on large Geometric shapes like the newly published stand in Munich (above, n. 35). The "monumentality" and "painterly" qualities attributed to Middle Protoattic painting thus represent the result of a gradual evolution, not a sudden admiration for monumental painting. The qualities of these vase paintings suggest "true paintings" to the Western eye in that they are suitable for framing—compositions with narrative content and original design independent of their function as decoration on pottery. This impression has been confused with an actual inspiration from monumental paintings, evidence for which is disputed.[42]

39. Cook, *BSA* 35 (1934/35): 171.

40. Ibid., pp. 167–68, 187–89; Brann, *Agora VIII*, nos. 416, 417, p. 78, pl. 25, for Early Protoattic added white; Kübler, *Kerameikos VI, 2*, 144, n. 2, on eighth-century examples of added white.

41. For an example of added slip, see the Subgeometric Hymettos amphora: *CVA Berlin 1*, pls. 43–44; but even the ovoid krater from Aigina (*CVA Berlin 1*, A 33, pl. 21) has added slip which fired pink: below, 3.5.

42. The Thermon metopes, at present the earliest dated evidence for "monumental" Greek painting, are not only later than Middle Protoattic vases but, as terracotta panels, participate in the tradition of vase painting (Robertson, *Greek Painting*, 50). Fragments of painted plaster panels on the early archaic temple of Poseidon at Isthmia have been dated in the early seventh century (O. Broneer, *Isthmia I: The Temple of Poseidon* [Chicago, 1971], 55), but the roof tiles have later parallels (cf. Aigina: E.-L. Schwandner, "Der ältere Aphaia Tempel auf Aegina," 120, in *Neue Forschungen in griechischen Heiligtümern* [Tübingen, 1976]).

The technical and stylistic phenomena celebrated in the Black and White vases can and should be explained within their own medium.[43]

28   The Black and White vases from Aigina do not show evidence for a third color, applied red paint, which heralds the next phase of vase painting—black figure. None of the painters isolated among the Aigina vases used red, although attributions of the past have ascribed vases with red touches to artists like the Ram Jug Painter.[44] Despite evidence for added red bands at the beginning of the Early Protoattic period, and an Athenian Middle Protoattic workshop specializing in plastic works with polychrome decoration, the painters of Aigina were indifferent to red or simply did not work long enough to experiment with this color.[45] Many of their vases, however, fired reddish-brown under oxidizing conditions which cannot have been intentional, as there is little control of misfired red which appears inconsistently over a single vase.[46]

In contrast, incision saw a variety of experiments in the hands of painters producing for Aigina. This technique already appears in earlier generations of craftsmen, as a new method probably inspired by metalworking.[47] During the succeeding Middle Protoattic period, incision is variously used by different painters, or even at different stages of an individual career. Thus the Ram Jug Painter begins to substitute incision for white paint late in his career, with less ease than when painting the same details (below, 3.2). On a single vase, he uses the techniques of paint and incision in alternation, as on the amphora with Peleus and Cheiron (Pl. 12). The Polyphemus Painter, on the other hand, shows a more comfortable command of an engraving tool by the middle of his career (as on the Eleusis amphora: Pl. 6).[48] By the end of his career (Pl. 8) he has almost entirely

43. Judgments like the following are simply unfair to the evidence: "These Protoattic vase paintings point to the existence of true large-figure plaque and wall paintings. They consciously avoid the black-figure style because they aim at true painting" (Boardman, Fuchs, Dörig, and Hirmer, *The Art and Architecture of Ancient Greece* [London, 1967]. Only Jeffery appreciated the struggle with size: "Thus many early Protoattic drawings are basically small-scale concepts, arbitrarily blown up to disproportionate and straggling size by hands as yet unskilled in drawing big human or animal figures" (*Archaic Greece*, 85).

44. See the kotyle krater from the Kerameikos with swans in added red (but no incision: Pl. 27), attributed by Brann, *Agora VIII*, 92 (no. 541), to the Ram Jug Painter.

45. The Early Protoattic stand in Mainz with added red bands has been attributed to the Analatos Painter (Hampe, *Ein frühattischer Grabfund*, pls. 10–11, stand A); the plastic and polychrome works from the Kerameikos, Kübler, *Kerameikos VI, 2*, pls. 32–58, pp. 146–49, 200, 292, 328–29 (influence of monumental painting).

46. Vases from Aigina in Berlin which misfired red: *CVA Berlin 1*, A 27, A 33 (Pl. 21), A 43 (Pl. 12), pls. 10–11; from the Agora, Burr, *Hesperia* 2 (1933): 628, on uneven glaze and intentional color; Brann, *Agora VIII*, pl. 28, nos. 463, 472; pp. 27, 30–31. Both vases by the New York Nessos Painter, for example, vary from red to chestnut to dark brown even across small areas; but it is incorrect to interpret this misfiring as a deliberate polychrome effect with chronological implications, as has been suggested: Vermeule and Chapman, *AJA* 75 (1971): 285, 289 (cf. below, 3.4).

47. Cook, *BSA* 35 (1934/35): 171. The Analatos Painter already shows sure control with engraved lines on a team of horses, where he separates the two animals and articulates the mane into strands with clean strokes: *CVA Louvre 18*, pls. 31–34.

48. Mylonas, *O protoattikos amphoreus*, 128, for references to incised lines (*encharaktoi grammai*); note judicious incision on the Eleusis amphora, to define areas of overlap and anatomical details, as compared to the painter's earlier piece, the Horses krater in Berlin (Pl. 2).

replaced painted lines with incised ones. The New York Nessos Painter uses "much white" and "much incision" on his name vase, in a mixture which Beazley called "semi-black-figure" prior to the establishment of "a settled technique and a settled style."[49] Ultimately it is this third technique of the Black and White style, incision, which overrules reservation and white paint. Thereafter, black figure artists used incision as a tool of draftsmanship, to outline a silhouette, emphasize a painted line, or articulate a painted form, with the added color of red paint. Although vases by such early black figure artists are found on Aigina, none are by the painters isolated in this monograph. Cook's pronouncement on the lower limit of the workshop still holds true: "At this point the career of the Ram Jug Painter seems to have come to an end and the 'Black and White' style to have gone out of fashion."[50]

5. ORNAMENTS

As with shape, the Early Protoattic tradition is particularly persistent in the choice of ornaments. The Analatos hydria, as a prominent example, anticipates many features adopted in Middle Protoattic workshops.[51] Its reverse side is devoted to elaborate floral ornament: this emphasis of a major, narrative side at the expense of a minor, ornamental side becomes exaggerated in the Middle Protoattic period, as the hasty work on the backs of the Eleusis and New York Nessos amphorae demonstrates. Small motifs such as birds appear under the handles of vases from the Analatos workshop; this area becomes the focus of extraneous decoration on Middle Protoattic vessels (Pls. 2–6, 13–16). Most Middle Protoattic filling ornaments can be traced to the Analatos and Mesogeia workshops: this legacy includes the outline cable and dotted cable strand, stuffed palmette, dotted trefoil, stacked zigzag, multiple lozenge, and pendent dotted triangle.[52] Decorative extensions such as dotted scales were already applied to wings in the early seventh century; in the Middle Protoattic workshop period, scales spread to cuirasses, drapery, and lions' manes (Pls. 6–7, 11, 13, 18).[53] In any study of ornament, it becomes clear how little any single motif can help pinpoint an attribution or posit a direct line of

49. Beazley, *Development*, 7, 12.

50. Cook, *BSA* 35 (1934/35): 195. Cf. below, 3.1 on the Woman Painter (Painter of Berlin A 34: Pl. 9), Beazley's earliest black figure painter (*ABV*, 5; *Paralipomena*, 1); Kübler, *Kerameikos VI, 2*, 329.

51. Cook, *BSA* 35 (1934/35): pl. 38b (Hurwit, *AJA* 81 [1977]: 25 overemphasizes the novelties of the Eleusis amphora).

52. On ornaments and their use in Early Protoattic workshops, see Cook, *BSA* 35 (1934/35): 172–73; Davison, *Geometric Workshops*, 13–20; Brann, *Agora VIII*, 24, 79, no. 422, on the pomegranate ornament and the Mesogeia connection to Middle Protoattic.

53. For Early Protoattic scales on wings, see Cook, *BSA* 35 (1934/35), pl. 40 (the Analatos Painter), pl. 45 (the Mesogeia Painter); Brann, *Agora VIII*, no. 419, pl. 26.

succession.[54] But the total repertoire of ornaments on a vase, their arrangement, and execution can often help identify a master (as for Pl. 1), and even a debased version of a selection can indicate a group of followers like the Wild Style (Pls. 15–20).

6. GREEK AND ORIENTAL NARRATIVE

Much attention has been attracted to Middle Protoattic pottery because of its rich narrative subjects. Earlier vase painting suggested epic subjects without names—a man fighting a centaur, a shipwreck, a duel over a fallen warrior, a hero's funeral—but specific mythological episodes appear of a sudden, in unprecedented detail, in this Middle Protoattic workshop. Repeated illustrations have celebrated these scenes: the blinding of Polyphemus (Pl. 6), the escape of Odysseus from the giant's cave (Pl. 10), Perseus fleeing the Gorgons (Pl. 6), Herakles and Nessos (Pl. 15), and the ambiguous scene on the Oresteia (?) krater (Pl. 13).[55] Episodes outside the Homeric poems, from lost works such as the *Kypria*—the childhood of Achilles (Pl. 12), the sacrifice of Iphigeneia (Pl. 16), an assembly led by Menelaos (Pl. 7)—enrich philology with evidence for an active oral tradition.[56] Heroes popular in the archaic period (Herakles, Perseus) make their debut on these vases; the many hoplite scenes (Pls. 7–8, 11, 17, 18) reflect interest in contemporary developments in history and warfare, next to the affection for the heroic past.[57]

Corinthian vase painters played a prominent role in introducing such scenes and probably inspired their adoption by the painters of Athens and Aigina. Lists of early mythological representations in Greek art cannot prove whether Athens or Corinth was a leader in introducing specific myths, or the general fashion, to vase painting. The man-and-centaur motif, for instance, appears in the Corinthian world on an ivory seal and an oinochoe, and on several vases by Middle Protoattic painters (Pls. 15, 19). The adventures of Perseus are illustrated in two separate episodes by different schools of vase painting: the hero armed with sword advances to decapitate Medusa on a Middle

54. Brann's attempt to make the Ram Jug Painter a successor of the Analatos Painter, and the Polyphemus Painter a pupil of the Mesogeia Painter, simplifies a complicated network (Brann, *Agora VIII*, 24). A major problem is the ambiguous relationship between the Analatos Painter and the Mesogeia Painter; see J. M. Cook's criticism of Brann's characterizations in *Gnomon* 34 (1962): 822.

55. Both general studies of early Greek narrative (by Schefold, Fittschen, von Steuben, Johansen, Dunbabin [1957]) and compilations of a specific subject (by Fellmann, Kemp-Lindemann, Schiffler) feature the Eleusis amphora, the Ram Jug, the New York Nessos amphora, and the Oresteia krater as prominent examples; cf. general works on Greek art (Beazley and Ashmole, Boardman et al., Richter, Robertson).

56. Friis-Johansen, *The Iliad in Early Greek Art* (Copenhagen, 1967), 38–39, on the prominence of non-Homeric epic scenes in early archaic art.

57. Lorimer, *BSA* 42 (1947): 88–90, discusses early representations of hoplites, e.g., Berlin A 41; most recently, Salmon, *JHS* 97 (1977).

Protocorinthian kotyle (Pl. 24; not visible), while the Polyphemus Painter depicts Perseus in flight, after the deed is done (Pl. 6).[58] Other subjects appear almost simultaneously on early archaic vases from different locales, such as the Judgment of Paris and the Polyphemus adventure.[59] Some scenes appear in a cluster only on Corinthian or Attic vases, but not both, probably through an accident of preservation. The house of Atreus themes are exclusive to Protoattic vases (Pls. 7, 13, 16); Bellerophon, a hero with strong Corinthian associations, appears on a Middle Protocorinthian kotyle from Aigina (Pl. 23) but not on Attic vases until a generation later.[60]

No conclusion from a comparative study of such scenes can confirm a consistent direction of influence in early narrative painting. Nor can one presume mutual access to monumental models such as paintings, as has been suggested (above, 2.4). However, a consistent pattern does emerge within the history of Attic narrative painting: in the seventh century, mythological scenes are concentrated (in time and place) on the Middle Protoattic pottery from Aigina.[61] In contrast, the Kerameikos produced few vases before the late seventh century with such narrative episodes; instead, stock themes of the Geometric tradition—mourning women at a bier, chariots, and warriors—decorate equally traditional Geometric shapes.[62] Even anonymous centaurs, common in earlier Protoattic and without specific narrative significance, do not appear on vases from the Kerameikos, except by the Oresteia Painter (Pl. 14), a member of the eccentric workshop from Aigina.

It could be argued, of course, that mythological themes were appropriate only to large funerary markers; the smaller, elegant shapes intended for Athenian offering channels did not afford a suitable field for elaborate narrative. However, large funeral vessels also marked graves in the seventh-century Kerameikos without inspiring any narrative themes; the popular kotyle kraters (below, 3.6.3) presented formulaic motifs such as lions, birds, and chariots. The painters of the mythological vases from Aigina, on the other hand, are closer to the Corinthian tradition, where different forces were at work in both history and art. In Corinth, where pottery was an export item during the seventh century, small shapes were gaily decorated, presumably to advertise their contents. Although many such vases found their way into graves as offerings, they were originally

58. Von Steuben, *Frühgriechische Sagendarstellungen*, 14–16, on the Perseus myth in Attic and Corinthian painting.

59. Cf. the Chigi vase and a krater rim from Aigina (below, 2.7).

60. On Bellerophon, see von Steuben, *Frühgriechische Sagendarstellungen*, 13–14; Dunbabin, "Bellerophon and Chimaera," in *Studies . . . Robinson* 2:1176–84.

61. Thus they appear as isolated experiments, and active interchange in subject matter, as well as in technique, between Attic and Corinthian schools begins only with the Nettos Painter, in the Late Protoattic period: von Steuben, *Frühgriechische Sagendarstellungen*, 71, on this pattern; Dunbabin, *BSA* 45 (1950): 193–201, on the interaction of Attic and Corinthian artists in the Late Protoattic period.

62. Kübler, *Kerameikos VI, 2*, 196ff., on the paucity of mythological scenes from the Kerameikos, where he tries to explain funerary subjects by the burial function of vessels but cannot explain the nonfunerary subjects of the Middle Protoattic grave markers outside the Kerameikos.

32   produced for a variety of purposes, unlike the exclusively funerary vessels of the Kerameikos. Mass production of Corinthian pottery also sponsored the decoration of vases
for a wide clientele, non-Greek as well as native; thus motifs of exotic origin (sphinxes,
centaurs) and encounters between men and monsters, derived from Oriental minor arts,
were appropriate to Greek Orientalizing pottery with a wide circulation. The role of
Corinth in publicizing narrative as vase decoration must have been influenced by these
conditions of manufacture, while the workshops of Athens were limited to producing
vessels for local and funerary use. At the end of the seventh century, Athens adopted
Corinthian techniques, Corinthian priorities in manufacture for export, and mythological
subjects as common themes for vase decoration. The Nettos Painter thus represents these
simultaneous changes in the Attic industry: he is not only the first black figure craftsman
but also the first post-Geometric Attic artist whose works are exported, and the earliest
archaic Attic painter whose iconography participates in a coherent tradition.[63]

Before his activity, only the Middle Protoattic vases found chiefly on Aigina are
exceptions to the Attic pattern of specialized funerary production, probably through closer
acquaintance with Corinthian pottery. The quantity and variety of Protocorinthian pottery
found on Aigina are far greater than those from Athens; in fact, Aigina was once thought
to be the home of Protocorinthian manufacture.[64] This coincidence—generous examples
of Protocorinthian pottery plus a concentration of Protoattic vases which reflect Protocorinthian motifs, from the same island—supports the evidence for local "Protoattic"
manufacture on the island under Protocorinthian inspiration.

Protocorinthian influence manifests itself in flora, fauna, and figural style, as well as
in mythological subjects. Exotic animals and monsters on the Middle Protoattic vases, such
as sphinxes, centaurs, lions, and boars, compare to Protocorinthian versions, which they
reflect more vividly than they do their Attic counterparts. Minor creatures—owl, grasshopper, rooster, and scorpion—enliven unrelated figural friezes in a manner more appropriate
to the Protocorinthian and Corinthian tradition than to Attic vase painting of the period.[65]
The ingenious Gorgons of the Eleusis amphora and the fishy monsters by the New York
Nessos Painter may have been influenced by Protocorinthian art, just as techniques of
composition (use of the border) were borrowed (Pls. 6, 8, 25). Even the figural style of the
Ram Jug Painter, the Polyphemus Painter, and the New York Nessos Painter recalls
Protocorinthian faces: the Ajax Painter (Pl. 23) can be compared to the Ram Jug Painter
(Pl. 12), while an unpublished oinochoe from Aigina in Berlin is not unlike the faces by the
Polyphemus Painter and the New York Nessos Painter (below, 3.1, 3.4, n. 54).

63. The Nettos Painter: Cook, *BSA* 35 (1934/35): 204; Beazley, *Hesperia* 13 (1944); cf. *ABV*, 4–7; *Paralip.*,
1–6; Kübler, *Kerameikos VI*, 2, 329 (von Steuben, *Frühgriechische Sagendarstellungen*, 71).

64. Payne, *Necrocorinthia*, 2, 39, n. 1; Payne and Dunbabin, *Perachora II*, 1, summarize past disputes over
provenance; above, 2.1, 2.2, n. 10.

65. For a general discussion of the Corinthian bestiary, see Payne, *Necrocorinthia*, 67ff., on "Natural History";
exotica have been tabulated in surveys (e.g., by Schiffler); on boars and lions, birds and insects, see below 3.1–4.

The enlarged versions of Protocorinthian motifs, transformed to suit the size of Protoattic vessels, obscure this influence through a change in scale. The traditional contrast in scholarship between a "miniaturist" Corinthian and a "monumental" Attic tradition has exaggerated an artificial distinction. Behind the different expressions lie similar motifs, circulated through minor arts rather than by the example of monumental, panel, or "free" painting.

If Protocorinthian influence can be observed in elements of narrative and style on these Middle Protoattic vases, many images have no Greek precedents but are exotic and Oriental in origin. The monsters under the handle of the Oresteia krater (Pl. 13) are relatives of the hairy apes on gilt silver bowls from Phoenicia; the squatting goblin on the stand in Berlin (Pl. 18), more like a monkey on another Aigina vase (Pl. 22, *right*), is as old as Elamite cylinder seals and was popular in Luristan bronzes.[66] Likewise, the three-headed sea monsters by the New York Nessos Painter (Pl. 16) recall creatures popular in the Near East, such as the mountain monster on the gold bowl from Hasanlu.[67] Such luxury items may have introduced visual formulas like the mounted archer shooting backward as he rides, if the figure by the Ram Jug Painter (Pl. 11: 584) is compared with corresponding figures on Oriental metal bowls. Even the stacked friezes on a krater with hoplites from Aigina (Pl. 21, right) compare to the Phoenician design on a silver cauldron (below, 3.5). These Oriental prototypes are typical of the portable luxury arts circulated in the Greek world in the early Iron Age. In chapter 4, the role of Aigina in such early trade will be presented to account for the exposure of artists on Aigina to motifs from the Near East.

Thus analyzed, the painted decoration on the Middle Protoattic vases from Aigina incorporates the Attic tradition into new Protocorinthian narrative subjects and transforms new Oriental motifs into Greek decoration. The result differs from contemporary Athenian pottery by distinctions which preclude identical workshop conditions.

7. EPIGRAPHY

The few examples of letters on these Middle Protoattic vases have played a major role in scholarship (above, 1.3). The first vase to receive attention was the conical stand with the label "Menelas" in letter forms dismissed as Ionian, later identified as Aiginetan (Pl. 7). The mere occurrence of a dipinto was then unusual for the seventh century; the closest contemporary parallels known to Karo were, and still are, later than the Menelas

66. E. Porada, *The Art of Ancient Iran* (New York, 1965), p. 38, fig. 13; p. 48, fig. 23; p. 78, fig. 49; p. 88, fig. 60 (n. 23). For a similar Orientalizing monkey, see a Laconian III kylix from Sparta, R. M. Dawkins, *The Sanctuary of Artemis Orthia at Sparta* (London, 1929), pls. 9, 10, p. 88.

67. Porada, *Ancient Iran*, pp. 96–102, pl. 23, figs. 63–64, for a summary of its discovery and interpretation, including Hurrian mythology.

stand and probably non-Attic: a krater rim from Aigina and a Late Protoattic dipinto in letters corrected from non-Attic to Attic dialect.[68]

34   In the context of early Greek writing, such evidence has a limited value. The recent discovery of a bronze bowl with a Phoenician inscription in a tenth-century tomb on Crete has given a new and surprisingly early date for the first appearance of the Semitic alphabet in Greece. The earliest Greek alphabet, the most important of all Orientalizing inventions, is still that on the Dipylon oinochoe with its incised verse inscription, dating two hundred years later.[69] Informal graffiti—owners' names scratched on cups, names of deities on votives—are the primary source of epigraphic evidence from early archaic Athens.[70] In the absence of overseas trade, literary figures, and commercial activity in Athens during the seventh century, this near illiteracy should not be surprising (below, 4.2). Contemporary dipinti from other schools of vase painting usually explain subject matter when it is helpful to give proper names to figures; therefore it is appropriate to find few such labels in Athens and many on Corinthian and Aiginetan pottery, where narrative was popular. Those extant for seventh-century Athens are relatively late.[71] The few significant dipinti are associated with Aigina, in either context, letter forms, or style. The earliest Greek dipinto, in fact, was found at the Kolonna sanctuary on Aigina.[72] Few diagnostic letters are preserved; the four-bar sigma is more common to Aigina, the letter interpreted as an Attic pi could equally represent a gamma from Aigina. The next two significant "Attic" dipinti are on polychrome fragments which suggest a date after the middle of the seventh century, if not in the Late Protoattic period.[73]

However, the fragmentary state of these early inscriptions and the poor evidence, in general, of early archaic writing preclude any sound conclusions on the identity of

68. The krater rim from Aigina shows a bearded face next to two letters (ΑΛ) restored as ΑΛΕΞΑΝΔΡΟΣ in Aiginetan script: Rumpf, *Malerei und Zeichnung*, pp. 25, 31 (explained as the work of Aiginetan artists in Athens). Cf. Beazley, "Some Inscriptions on Vases III," *AJA* 39 (1935): 475, for an Attic restoration as ΑΓΑΜΕΜΝΟΝ. On the original inscription of the Nettos amphora in non-Attic letters, see A. Boegehold, "The Nessos Amphora—A Note on the Inscription," *AJA* 66 (1962): 405–06.

69. Maurice Sznycer, "L'Inscription phénicienne de Tekke, près de Cnossos," *Kadmos* 18 (1979): 89–93 (ca. 900 B.C.); cf. Frank Cross, "An Archaic Phoenician Inscription from Crete," *BASOR* 238 (1980): 15–17 (ca. 1000 B.C.). Dipylon oinochoe: Athens, National Museum 192: Jeffery, *Local Scripts*, pl. 1:1, p. 68; Boardman, *The Greeks Overseas*, 83, fig. 91.

70. See the Hymettos graffiti: Blegen, *AJA* 38 (1934); Langdon, *A Sanctuary of Zeus*, pp. 9 ff., on early dedications and Attic graffiti, with comments in the review by C. King, *AJA* 82 (1978): 60.

71. Typical are two cups from the Agora with owners' names: Brann, *Agora VIII*, no. 132 (= no. 511), pl. 8; the cup of Tharios (Young, *Hesperia*, suppl. 2, 1939, B 55).

72. Boardman, *BSA* 49 (1954): 185–87. The inscription on the fragmentary votive plaque is incomplete but was probably in hexameter; J. M. Cook's restoration completes the line in verse: *Gnomon* 34 (1962): 823.

73. The "Antenor" sherd from the Acropolis (Graef and Langlotz, *Vasen von der Akropolis*, no. 368) has been attributed to the Ram Jug Painter, but this attribution is rejected here (below, 3.6.3; the yellow-brown paint on the sherd represents a fashion postdating the Black and White style, although in the fashion of the painters in the Middle Protoattic workshop under discussion and perhaps by a successor); for the ΑΛ krater from Aigina, see above, n. 68.

painters. A comparison of Aigina with Attica is complicated by the similarity of their early alphabets; given an inscription of this period, it would be difficult to attribute it to either locale, nor does a general study of the early scripts indicate whether Athens or Aigina learned the alphabet first.[74] Historical reasons (examined below in chapter 4) suggest that Aigina had greater use for the alphabet than Attica in the seventh century, such that even the evidence of graffiti on Attic transport amphorae could be relevant to Aigina, not Athens. A single non-Attic inscription, from a period when epichoric forms are flexible, is not sufficient to reattribute an entire class of pottery. Moreover, in Athens literary sources, foreign artist-names, and non-Attic signatures emphasize the participation of resident aliens in a busy ceramic industry.[75] In terms of the Middle Protoattic pottery from Aigina, epigraphy alone cannot explain the origin of the pottery. The dipinto by the Polyphemus Painter is still unique and has perhaps been overrated. However, the other associations with Aigina reinforce and are reinforced by the implications of local writing.

8. CHRONOLOGY

Protoattic pottery is still largely an inventory of museum pieces and excavated finds without sufficient context, whose arrangement has to be relative and stylistic. "There is in Protoattic nothing that points to absolute dating" was Cook's lament, and it is still true.[76] Reliable criteria are borrowed from Protocorinthian synchronisms, of which few are stratigraphic and most are analogies in stylistic development. For the Black and White style, useful stratified synchronisms were and still are limited to a battered Middle Protocorinthian aryballos in a mid-seventh century offering channel of the Kerameikos.[77] This slender link through stratigraphic context is less useful than the general stylistic coincidence of Middle Protoattic and Middle Protocorinthian vase painting. As Cook first expressed it, "The 'Black and White' style should cover approximately the same period as the Protocorinthian Archaic Style B; besides a general resemblance in the figure-scenes there are occasional close parallels in the ornament."[78] In this study, a more precise synchronism for the Middle Protoattic Black and White style is provided by two means: recent revisions in Protocorinthian chronology and specific correlations between subjects and style on the vases associated with Aigina and Middle Protocorinthian artists.

74. Jeffery, *Local Scripts*, 109–10.

75. Dunbabin, *BSA* 45 (1950); Brann, *Hesperia* 30 (1961): 313–14; A. Boegehold, *AJA* 66 (1962): 405–07; Boardman, *Athenian Black Figured Vases*, 12.

76. Cook, *BSA* 35 (1934/35): 200.

77. First reported in Kübler, *AA* 49 (1934): 205, fig. 3, and dated around 650 B.C. (date raised by Cook, *BSA* 35 [1934/35]: 201, and Kübler, *Kerameikos VI, 1*, 132).

78. Cook, *BSA* 35 (1934/35): 202; Brann, *Agora VIII*, 4–8.

36
Controversies over the relative and absolute chronology of Protocorinthian pottery are far from settled; the latest discussions place Middle Protocorinthian II (the equivalent of what Cook called Archaic Style B) between 670 and 650 B.C., with the inception of Late Protocorinthian around 650 B.C.[79] The work of the Black and White style painters in this monograph shows specific agreements with the work of painters of the phase from Middle Protocorinthian II to Late Protocorinthian: the Hound Painter, the Bellerophon Painter, the Sacrifice Painter, and the MacMillan Painter (Pls. 23, 24).[80] The earliest work by the Polyphemus Painter (Pl. 1) already reflects a Protocorinthian motif, the flying eagle; his latest work, along with the late Hoplites bowl by the Ram Jug Painter (Pl. 11), reveals an acquaintance with the Chigi vase (Pl. 24; below, 3.1–2). Such Protocorinthian anchors are still the only ones available for the Black and White style workshop from Aigina, but they also help provide a locale, since many such Protocorinthian parallels were more readily available on Aigina than in Attica.

The internal chronology of the Middle Protoattic workshop is refined through the new definition of the Wild Style (below, 3.4). The life of the workshop, in general, has been abbreviated; it is difficult to see the career of the Polyphemus Painter beginning before around 670–660 B.C. or lasting after 640 B.C. The result is a briefer and more brilliant, but more isolated, workshop than has previously been understood.

79. Protocorinthian chronology: R. M. Cook, *Greek Painted Pottery*, 338; cf. *EAA*, 1965 ed., vol. 4, p. 507; Ducat, *BCH* 86 (1962): 180; R. M. Cook, *BSA* 64 (1969): 13–15.
80. Dunbabin and Robertson, *BSA* 48 (1953): 176.

CHAPTER 3

MIDDLE PROTOATTIC ARTISTS

1. THE POLYPHEMUS PAINTER

The most important and prolific artist, as well as the one most closely associated with Aigina, suffered from circumstances of archaeology and later from confusion in scholarship. His emergence as a distinct personality was delayed until he could be separated from the Ram Jug Painter. His first vase to reach modern attention was the Menelas stand, publicized in 1928 and attributed to the Ram Jug Painter by Cook in 1935.[1] In the last fifty years new discoveries and fresh studies, particularly by Mylonas (1957) and Brann (1962), have expanded his oeuvre, but the range of his career has still been underestimated.

His career begins inauspiciously enough in the second quarter of the seventh century with a banded neck amphora now in the Metropolitan Museum, published here for the first time (Pl. 1).[2] Shape and decoration (banded body with figures on the neck only) belong to an important class of Late Geometric and Early Protoattic grave markers, perhaps the milieu for the painter's early training.[3] The decoration on the neck, however, points to the Protocorinthian influence which sets this artist apart from Athenian painters: the flying birds (familiarly called "eagles" in scholarship) were popular as shield devices, filling ornaments, and in friezes throughout archaic art.[4] In Protoattic painting the motif is relatively rare; in fact, the only prominent example is by the same painter on the

1. Karo, "Menelas" (above, 1.2); Cook, *BSA* (1934/35): 189–93; *CVA Berlin 1*, A 42, pls. 31–33, pp. 24–25; Kübler, *Altattische Malerei*, 17, fig. 48; Beazley, *Development*, pp. 7–8; Mylonas, *O protoattikos amphoreus*, 108ff.; Brann, *Agora VIII*, 94–95, pl. 35.

2. Metropolitan Museum of Art 1949.101.17 a–q; Brann, *Agora VIII*, 91, no. 528. I am grateful to Dietrich von Bothmer for the privilege of publishing the vase here for the first time.

3. Delivorrias, *Deltion* 20:A (1965), for an example and discussion of the class.

4. Payne, *Necrocorinthia*, 76, n. 9; Payne and Dunbabin, *Perachora II*, no. 254, p. 43 (with parallels); A 33, p. 416 (one of fifteen ivory seals with birds); Kübler, *Kerameikos VI, 2*, p. 44, n. 75, p. 62.

Eleusis amphora, where a large bird under the right handle is headed for collision with Perseus.[5]

38   The ornaments are conventional to Early Protoattic painting: some, like the concentric triangle, disappear from the painter's repertoire in his later work; many others function later as the painter's signature—cable strand, stacked zigzag, multiple lozenge. In this early work, the arrangement of ornaments is more significant than individual motifs: a pronounced slant to the right is consistent in this artist's placement of decoration.

The technique in which the Metropolitan eagles are rendered is already characteristic of the painterly brushwork evident on the Eleusis amphora's human figures and bird. Free strokes applied for dark silhouettes leave careless streaks but also produce an attractive impressionistic effect. Deliberate experiment in black and white painting also appears on the bird. Three different means of indicating eyes were applied to the three preserved birds: an applied white ring, a reserved round with dot, and a reserved head with dotted ring. The second technique may have been the most satisfactory: the painter applied an identical type of eye to the rooster on a later work (Pl. 5, *above*). In this early and isolated work, the future master of the Black and White style juxtaposes the techniques available to an Orientalizing artist, as if in a deliberate experiment.

The next vase which can be attributed is a standard kotyle krater from Aigina now in Berlin, once associated with a "Pferde-Maler."[6] This krater is a standed version of a shape popular in the Kerameikos but unique among the Aigina vases.[7] It also agrees in subject and style with the group of kraters from the Kerameikos. The scenes on the krater and on its lid are identical: Early Protoattic grazing horses with reserved heads and ladder manes, crowded among ornaments which also reflect the early fashion (compare the lozenge star, meander square, stuffed rosette, and especially the trefoil under the handle with the Kerameikos kraters: Pl. 27; below, 3.6.3). In technique, however, the Polyphemus Painter already distances himself from the Athenian krater painters, by introducing incision and white-filled outlines to traditional subjects. These novelties show signs of their recent acquisition on the Berlin krater: the black and white rosette between the legs of the left horse had to be repainted (Pl. 2), for an earlier black outline shows under the white paint (compare the same problem on the sphinx by the Oresteia Painter: below, 3.3). Incision was also applied here with the skill of a novice: the horses' hind-

5. Mylonas, *O protoattikos amphoreus*, pl. 4 (the vase is badly damaged here); Brann, *Agora VIII*, 91, no. 528, compared the two amphorae without recognizing the same painter.

6. *CVA Berlin 1*, A 35, pls. 25–26, p. 7; Mylonas, *O protoattikos amphoreus*, pl. 16, pp. 107, 112–13. The attribution escaped the first publishers of the Berlin collection, who must have been misled by the difference between the horses on the Menelas stand and those on the kotyle krater. However, both the grazing horse with outline mane and the horse with upright head and loop mane could appear in the same repertoire, as early as the Analatos Painter (below, n. 85).

7. At least 73 examples once marked graves in the Kerameikos, according to surface finds from the excavations: Kübler, *Kerameikos VI, 2*, 156–59, 515–40 (below, 3.6.3).

quarters are separated by a misjudged line, the shoulders are represented by a most undeltoid loop, and the tail is a tangle of incised lines.

This krater marks an early stage of a developed black and white animal style. Its connection to mature works by the same painter (Pls. 7, 8) escaped the notice of earlier scholars.[8] Two ovoid kraters from Aigina and two amphorae from the Athenian Agora represent this animal style, a transition to the mature work of the Polyphemus Painter.

One krater from Aigina has been in Munich since 1907 (Pl. 3).[9] The vase was originally restored with a ring foot under the ovoid body, but this foot has recently been removed as a false restoration; it is likely that the krater originally stood on a tall foot, like other ovoid kraters from the same workshop (Pls. 19, 20).

Both sides show a lion attacking a deer, in an elegant animal style with sure strokes of incision articulating paws and muscles. The lion's tail curls up and intersects his back just as on the Eleusis amphora (Pl. 6). Elaborate ornament dominates the area under the handles, with a continuous spiraling and sprouting tendril terminating in palmettes; the same ornament appears in a reduced version on the groundline between the animals. This combination of a distinctive animal style and luxurious ornament characterizes a fragment with a centaur from the Aigina necropolis, now restored as another ovoid krater (Pl. 4).[10] New fragments (found in storage) added to the centaur in the recent restoration give him a branch with a dangling deer, suggesting the figure of Cheiron rather than Nessos, as once suggested by Cook. Thus the story of Cheiron and his foster son, Achilles, appeared at least twice on vases from the Aigina necropolis by two leading painters, the Ram Jug Painter (Pl. 12) and the Polyphemus Painter. The myth may have had special significance for natives of Aigina, home of Peleus; in the version by the Polyphemus Painter it shows Protocorinthian influence, for the hairy type of centaur is a Protocorinthian specialty (Pl. 23).[11] What Peleus and Achilles looked like—or whether they even existed on this krater by the Polyphemus Painter—cannot be ascertained from the extant fragments; the restoration provides only the figure of a

8. Even Mylonas, who was able to associate two other Berlin vases with the newly discovered Eleusis amphora, made the kotyle krater a late work and turned the "Pferde-Maler" into the Polyphemus Painter (*O protoattikos amphoreus*, 110).

9. See above, chap. 1, n. 36, for the acquisition of the vase; fully published in *CVA München 3*, pl. 131:2 and 133:2; attributed in *CVA Berlin 1*, p. 7, under the "Pferde-Maler"; dated ca. 660 B.C. by Fr. Brein in *Der Hirsch in der griechischen Frühzeit* (Vienna, 1969), 204.

10. Kraiker, *Aigina*, no. 583, p. 90, pl. 43 (a "Pyrg. 29" sherd from the necropolis sounding: above, chap. 1, n. 28), now restored with fragments from the same context (Kraiker, nos. 544, 581, 587) by Elena Walter-Karydi and on display in the new Aigina museum. J. M. Cook (*BSA* 35 [1934/35]: 192, n. 7) had dated the centaur fragment to the same period as the Munich krater, without attributing it.

11. Hairy centaurs fighting Herakles on the aryballos by the MacMillan Painter (Pl. 23) and the Sacrifice Painter (on a fragment from Perachora: Payne and Dunbabin, *Perachora II*, no. 285, p. 47, pl. 16). The earliest hairy Corinthian Cheiron extant dates from the Early Corinthian period (Kemp-Lindemann, *Darstellungen des Achilleus*, p. 10, VI. 331 C 1). Cf. an earlier Argive Cheiron: R. Hampe and E. Simon, *The Birth of Greek Art* (London: Thames and Hudson, 1980), fig. 96.

40 headless centaur near the left handle with a black and white cable below the rim, and two zones of ornaments—black and white tongues, black spiral rays—below the figural scene. Several fragments, especially on the centaur's newly discovered tail and on the zones of bands, show crude incision where painted bands were separated, in contrast to the elegant incised lines on the body of the centaur.

Animals, technique, and ornaments on the Cheiron krater demonstrate close kinship not only with the companion krater in Munich but with other examples from the Agora. The finest candidate is part of a closed vessel—presumably an amphora—from the archaic cemetery near the Areopagus (Pl. 5, *below*).[12] The main scene circling the amphora body was a frieze of grazing horses with reserved ladder manes, the same motif painted more crudely on the Horses krater in Berlin by the painter at a younger age (Pl. 2). Between the hind legs of one of the horses on the Agora amphora is a creative floral ornament of tendrils and palmettes, an unmistakable touch of the Polyphemus Painter's style. This ornament, together with the black and white rosette in the field, closely resembles the same motifs on the Cheiron krater (Pl. 4). Another fragment from the Agora is less distinctive but seems a safe attribution to this painter.[13] The head and long ears of a mule with bared teeth are still visible (with difficulty, given the condition of the sherd); in the field are several ornaments which help identify the painter (dotted cable strand, stacked zigzag, and a pendent spiral ray). A third animal fragment from the Agora which suggests the Polyphemus Painter is from the neck of an amphora and preserves a white cock in thickish outline, filled with white (Pl. 5, *above*).[14] The motif anticipates the frieze of feeding cocks on the Flowery Ornaments stand (Pl. 8), the technique is repeated for the figure of Odysseus on the Eleusis amphora (Pl. 6), and the ornaments in the field are also appropriate to the painter (four-dot eight-point rosette, trefoil).[15]

These four vases comprise the early to middle phase of the painter's career, characterized by an extravagant floral style in ornaments, a developing skill in incision, and a dominant taste for black and white contrasts (in ornaments such as the cable band, leaves, and rays). Were more preserved on the Cheiron krater, one might be able to

---

12. Brann, *Agora VIII*, no. 558, pp. 94–95, pl. 35 (above, chap. 1, n. 46).

13. Ibid., no. 562, p. 95, pl. 35.

14. Ibid., no. 560, p. 95, pl. 35; Mylonas, *O protoattikos amphoreus*, 110–11, fig. 39a. The black and white rays just visible in the shoulder zone match those on the shoulder of the horses amphora, but the fragments do not belong to the same vase.

15. Less diagnostic are two fragments from the votive deposit published by Burr, both with horses, which were attributed to the Pferde-Maler in the *CVA* publication: *CVA Berlin 1*, p. 7, no. 3, by the Pferde-Maler (= Burr, *Hesperia* 2 (1933), no. 157, p. 582, fig. 41); Mylonas, *O protoattikos amphoreus*, 110; Brann, *Agora VIII*, no. 561, p. 95, pl. 35. *CVA Berlin 1*, p. 7, no. 4 (= Burr [1933], no. 147); Mylonas, pp. 110–11; Brann, no. 559, p. 95, pl. 35. See Rodney Young's objections in his review of the *CVA* volume (*AJA* 43 [1939]: 715): "there is little reason to put together the Agora fragments Burr 147 and 157, nor to attribute them to the 'Pferdemaler.'"

appreciate the earliest human features by the Polyphemus Painter, in anticipation of the next phase of his painting.

That next phase introduces mythological narrative in scenes with human figures, where flora and fauna become subsidiary in secondary zones or as abbreviated filling ornaments. In this stage one can almost pinpoint the transition from exotic Orientalizing to Greek-inspired narrative art. New shapes also herald this phase: conical stand and bowl are added to the earlier kraters and amphorae. The two masterpieces—the Eleusis amphora and the Menelas stand—are hard to separate in time and should perhaps be considered contemporary.

The stand is a classic example of the shape best preserved in the latest work by the same painter (Pl. 8), with imitations by two followers (Pls. 11, 18). The conical base is divided into a tall figural frieze under a shorter one; a torus molding connects this base to the bowl-shaped top. The stand is broken above the torus molding but was not pared down for reuse as originally suggested.[16] The upper bowl should be imagined in analogy to its companion stand in Berlin (Pl. 8), according to the evidence of two rim fragments. A nonjoining sherd in Berlin was published in association with the stand; its subject, a lion's head, matches a rim sherd still in Aigina.[17] The association of this fragment with the Berlin stand establishes a good context for the stand—from the necropolis of Aigina—and also adds a lion to the painter's repertoire.

The lion belongs to one of the two poorly preserved animal fights around the upper bowl of the stand, where theme and technique establish important links to other painters. The lions' heads were outlined and filled with white in contrast to their black bodies, a convention practised by the Ram Jug Painter (Pl. 12), the New York Nessos Painter (Pl. 15), and their followers (Pls. 18–21). On the Menelas stand, one deer is outlined and painted white, the other is solid black with white dots; both types are imitated by the wilder followers (Pls. 19–21).

Antecedents of these polychrome animal fights should be located on a kotyle krater with lions from the Kerameikos (Pl. 27).[18] The comparison of Attic and Aiginetan vases noted above, in the description of the Horses krater (Pl. 2), repeats itself. Motif (animal fight) and ornaments (including white dots on animals) are common to Kerameikos kraters

16. Karo, "Menelas," 10, corrected in *CVA Berlin 1*, p. 24.

17. Compare *CVA Berlin 1*, pl. 31:3, and Kraiker, *Aigina*, p. 85, no. 553 (not illustrated but on record on a DAI photo, "Aigina Vasen 205"). Cook, *BSA* 35 (1934/35): 194, attributed this fragment to the painter of the Burgon krater (his reference to the sherd by the number "Fr. 29" must be "Ir. 29": see above, chap. 1, n. 27). The ornament on the sherd from Aigina is also found above the head of Odysseus on the painter's name vase (Pl. 6), as well as on the Agora amphora neck (Pl. 5, *above*); the lion wears a mane of tongue-shaped scales identical to the corsets of the Gorgons, also on the Polyphemus amphora (Pl. 6).

18. The earliest animal fight in Attic vase painting has been identified on this krater, from evidence added since its publication in 1970 (Kübler, *Kerameikos VI, 2*, pl. 85) for Knigge, *Gnomon* (1974): 203, reports a new fragment adding a bull to the two lions.

and Aigina stand.[19] Yet in technique the two artists represent different preferences in the Black and White style: the krater shows painted (white) details for muscles and **42** markings, the Berlin stand reproduces the same features through incision.

The next frieze on the Aigina stand departs in a similar manner from the Attic tradition. On the torus molding is a row of crouching sphinxes with black bodies, reserved wings with overlapping "roof-tile" feathers in outlined white, and goggle eyes fixed in their reserved faces. Both species and pose are old-fashioned and derive from Early Protoattic sphinxes in the Mesogeia workshop.[20] However, these Middle Protoattic descendants suggest the influence of Protocorinthian sphinxes, in contrast to the sphinxes of the Pernice krater and its tradition.[21]

Below the torus molding, the upper band of the stand is decorated with a frieze of horsemen, curious legless riders leaning back to whip their mounts. The style retains much that is Attic, such as the misjudged incision to separate the hindquarters, the hair knot, and the dotted chitons.[22] The riders and their horses, however, are closest to Protocorinthian cavalry scenes; the walleyed horses with riders who spur them on are seen best on a series of kotylae from Aigina (Pl. 25).[23]

The lowest zone on the stand occupies more than half of the preserved piece and is decorated with a ceremonial procession of draped men with spears. The five bearded figures are dressed in white chitons with dark, dotted scales, under dark himations, dotted white. Their feet, exposed below, are black and bootlike but presumably unshod. Faces and right arms, extended forward to grasp a white-bladed spear, are white above a reserved neck. The dark hair of these figures is bound with a white fillet and falls divided, in the manner of the sphinxes' hair on the frieze above them. No two profiles are alike, with imaginative variation on such details as ears, but there is no internal

19. Compare the diamond with attached dotted triangles (Kübler, *Kerameikos VI: 2*, inv. 99, pl. 85) to the same motif on the animal fight frieze of the Berlin stand (Pl. 7); the tails of the two lions on the Kerameikos krater (Pl. 27) were dotted in contrasting colors, like the variegated patterns for the deer on the stand. The ornaments on this stand have been closely analyzed: Mylonas, *O protoattikos amphoreus*, 34–42, fig. 17. Next to those which recall the Kerameikos kraters (multiple lozenge, meander cross, stacked zigzag, and spiral ray), others developed from the Analatos tradition (stuffed rosette, for example: see above, 2.3, for the relationship between Early and Middle Protoattic ornaments).

20. Cook, *BSA* 35 (1934/35): 188, pl. 51c, attributed to the painter of the Berlin stand (p. 190).

21. Karouzou, *ArkhEph* 1952, pls. 5–6; on the Pernice krater, see below, 6.2. The ancestors of the Pernice krater sphinxes appear in the Analatos workshop: *CVA Louvre 18*, pl. 33: 1–2; Hampe, *Ein Frühattischer Grabfund*, pls. 10–11. For Protocorinthian sphinxes, see Kübler, *Kerameikos VI, 2*, 92, 249, 385.

22. For Attic parallels, see the Vlastos krater (Cook, *BSA* 35 [1934/35], pl. 51c) and the chariot race from the Acropolis (Graef and Langlotz, *Vasen von der Akropolis*; Pl. 11; above, chap. 2, n. 73).

23. Kraiker, *Aigina*, nos. 191–93, p. 42, pls. 12–13, published as Early Protocorinthian but more likely Middle Protocorinthian (Dunbabin, *Gnomon* 25 (1953): 246; Kübler, *Kerameikos VI, 2*, 205, n. 41). Compare also the same motif on the Berlin aryballos by the Ajax Painter (Pl. 23): Payne, *Protokorinthische Vasenmalerei*, pl. 11; Dunbabin and Robertson, *BSA* 48 (1953): 176, n. 3, who attribute Kraiker no. 191 to the early Ajax Painter.

distinction among the figures.[24] Instead, the leader is identified by a dipinto in the field before him naming him "Menelas," crowned by the elaborate stuffed rosette which could almost be the painter's signature.

Much excitement has been caused by this dipinto, which is clearly not in Attic letters or dialect.[25] In the context of other borrowed elements, the foreign dipinto adds itself to the stylistic factors which speak for a separate workshop and Protocorinthian influence. For the addition of letters to vase decoration appears with the earliest mythological scenes where familiar figures are identified, and the Aigina painters seem to pick up both narrative and labels from Corinth (see above, 2.6–7). On this stand, whose other subjects (animals, sphinxes, and riders) are standard for the middle of the seventh century, the addition of letters introduces a Homeric context to a generic heroic scene. Menelas and his warriors could be assembling for the Trojan expedition, although their costume suggests a council or ceremony, not a departure to war. If the gathering of the Greeks at Aulis is meant, this scene would share in the House of Atreus themes suggested on other vases of the same workshop (e.g., the sacrifice of Iphigeneia on the krater in Boston: Pl. 16).[26] Extra fragments, also from the Aigina necropolis, look as if they belong to a similar stand: one shows a draped man holding a spear, and the edge of a dotted cable strand in the field (Pl. 4: 555).[27] As mentioned above (1.2), there is no room on the Menelas stand to restore an additional draped figure, and one assumes a second stand with a similar subject. The other fragment, from the Menelas or putative other stand, bears the painter's characteristic black and white rosette (Pl. 4: 556).[28]

The artist responsible for the Menelas stand was not identified until the discovery of the Eleusis amphora, the second major monument of his mature career (Pl. 6).[29] It has become a familiar landmark in the history of early Greek art yet is rich enough to provide ever fresh delight and information on the artist and his workshop.

The amphora is by far the largest (1.42 m in height) and most complete example known of the Black and White style, if not the finest (Mylonas did not hesitate to call

24. That the strokes on the sleeve of Menelas are meant to identify him, as suggested in the *CVA* publication, seems doubtful: *CVA Berlin 1*, p. 25; the Gorgons by the same painter (Pl. 6) show the same variation in sleeves.

25. Since Jeffery identified the inscription and the artist as Aiginetan, various attempts have been made to reconcile the foreign letters with the "Attic" style (above, 2.7).

26. Vermeule, *AJA* 75 (1971): 292, n. 24, suggested this thematic link, although the ambiguous subject of the Oresteia krater (below, 3.3) no longer qualifies.

27. Kraiker, *Aigina*, no. 555, p. 86, pl. 43; also associated with the painter of the Menelas stand by Cook, *BSA* 35 (1934/35): 193.

28. Kraiker, *Aigina*, no. 556, p. 86, pl. 42.

29. Discovery, analysis and attribution in Mylonas, *O protoattikos amphoreus*; its narrative content has been exhausted in scholarship (e.g., Fellmann, *Die antiken Darstellungen*, 11–13, on the myth of Polyphemus; in surveys of Greek art, see Boardman, Dörig, Fuchs, Hirmer, *Art and Architecture of Ancient Greece*, 150, pls. 75, V; Robertson, *Greek Painting*, 40–46).

it "one of the best, if not *the* best, found thus far on Greek soil").[30] Its traditional function as a grave marker was neglected in favor of inhumation (above, 1.2); despite this brutal treatment, its major narrative zones survive.

44

Both neck and body are decorated with narrative episodes from specific myths, in keeping with the sudden obsession for mythology in Middle Protoattic painting (above, 2.6). The story of Perseus, though undoubtedly codified in Corinth, appears earliest on the belly of this amphora, but under Peloponnesian influence.[31] Crucial evidence for such influence is the running Gorgon with cauldron head and snake protomes on its shoulders.[32] This type of full-figure Gorgon with large, squarish head split by a horizontal mouth, and protomes on head and shoulders, is not simply an imaginary conflation of Oriental vessels and monsters by the artist. This Gorgon is an early Peloponnesian type, found on an ivory disc seal from the Argive Heraion in a similar guise, as two running females with toothy grins and "wings."[33] The correspondence between motifs on the large Black and White style vases and in contemporary minor arts, including pottery, from the northeast Peloponnese is familiar. The laced boots of Perseus, for example, must be Protocorinthian too; at least, Herakles wears them on the aryballos by the MacMillan painter (Pl. 23), where the hero's bow is similar to the archer by the Ram Jug Painter (Pl. 11). Yet the iconography of the goddess Athena is directly inspired by epic poetry, where she appears unarmed but equipped with her ῥάβδος to aid heroes (*Odyssey* 16: 172, 456). The Polyphemus Painter was not only literate in that he knew his letters (Pl. 7) but was also conversant enough with epic poetry to transform a poetic formula into an original image.

The neck scene on the Eleusis amphora reveals another connection to the Corinthian world. In the blinding of Polyphemus, the three heroes brandish a stake which doubles as the upper border of the scene until it separates from the black frame to pass through the hands of Odysseus and into the eye of the giant (Pl. 6). This device is characteristic of early mythological scenes on vases; most striking is a Protocorinthian parallel from Aigina, the name kotyle of the Bellerophon Painter (Pl. 25).[34] Here Bel-

---

30. Mylonas, *O protoattikos amphoreus*, 125.

31. Von Steuben, *Frühgriechische Sagendarstellungen*, 14–15, on the myth of Perseus.

32. Mylonas, *O protoattikos amphoreus* (pp. 61–79, pls. 10–15), Fittschen (*Untersuchungen*, 153), and Kübler (*Kerameikos VI, 2*, p. 260, n. 389) call the protomes "lions"; but J. Floren (*Studien zur Typologie des Gorgoneion* [Münster/Westphalia, 1977], p. 37, n. 65) points out that the forked tongues indicate snakes.

33. Waldstein, *The Argive Heraeum*, 2:351, no. 4; R. Hampe, *Frühe griechische Sagenbilder* (Athens, 1936), p. 65, fig. 26, and G. Riccioni, *RivIstArc* 9 (1960): 152, fig. 35 (dated to 700–675 B.C.; they may be later but are still seventh-century).

34. Kraiker, *Aigina*, no. 253, pp. 48–49, pl. 18; Dunbabin and Robertson, *BSA* 48 (1953): 177, for the attribution (Middle Protocorinthian II, ca. 650 B.C.); Hurwit, *AJA* 81 (1977): 25, n. 122:

> Again, such a similar use of open form argues for a close community of interest among Athenian and Corinthian narrative artists of the seventh century; despite stylistic differences, Protoattic artists and Protocorinthian shared in the development of expressive formal modes.

lerophon grasps a similar "weapon," in the form of the border, to attack the Chimaera. One cannot exclude the possibility that these Protocorinthian and Protoattic examples are simply contemporary and independent solutions to an identical problem in design, as both date around the middle of the seventh century (above, 2.7). Certainly the Polyphemus Painter embraces the device with enthusiasm, extending it to his hoplites' on his later stand (Pl. 8).

The third scene on the Eleusis amphora is the boar-and-lion confrontation on the shoulder, the only figures without mythological content (Pl. 6). The boar should be compared with the one with the same projecting bristles by the Ram Jug Painter on the Acropolis stand (Pl. 11: 357). In linking the two painters, this motif also points to the same Protocorinthian model, such as the kotyle by the Bellerophon Painter from Aigina.[35] On the Eleusis amphora, the hog's back ridge has been extended into a continuous contour of bristles, unlike the single row by the Ram Jug Painter (Pl. 11: 357b).

The lion facing the boar does not resemble the other lion by the same painter, on the rim of the Menelas stand (above, n. 17). This lion is more elaborate, with stylized features which reflect specific connections. The dotted muzzle and detailed teeth and tongue are similar to those of lions on the Burgon krater and by the Ram Jug Painter (Pl. 12), while the wavy lines for the mane resemble the convention for woolly fleece on the Ram Jug (Pl. 10). The tail on the Eleusis amphora, however, raised above the back and overlapping the shoulder with an incised contour, is an attitude peculiar for a lion but not for this painter: compare the lions on the Munich krater (Pl. 3) with the long and elegant carriage of the tail on the Ram Jug Painter's lions (Pl. 12). The animal most likely to hold its tail in this manner is a boar in its Middle Protocorinthian guise, such as the one from Aigina noted above (n. 35). To find a boar's tail on a lion is not so unexpected in a workshop where horses' heads and manes appear on rams (Pl. 10) and lions (Pl. 12), and again shows admiration for the Protocorinthian tradition.

Ornaments on the Eleusis amphora represent a rich legacy: Early Protoattic (the pomegranate), Middle Protocorinthian (cross-hatching borrowed from shield interiors), and Oriental (highlights such as the rosettes on human thighs).[36] Within the fields of two vases, the painter interchanges and adapts them comfortably. Cross-hatching, for example, covers the handles of Protocorinthian aryballoi but also decorates the jaws of the Gorgons on the Eleusis amphora and the pomegranate ornaments in the field, as well as on the open-worked handles. The diluted glaze ripples of the lion's mane reappear on the triangular "nose" of the Gorgons; the scales which decorate lion's mane and sphinxes' wings on the Menelas stand (Pl. 7) are converted to dress the torsos of the Gorgons on the Eleusis amphora (Pl. 6).

35. Kraiker, *Aigina*, no. 273, pl. 22, pp. 51–52; new fragments reported by Dunbabin, *Gnomon* (1953): 246.

36. Fellmann, *JdI* 93 (1978).

This flexibility in ornamental devices is matched by an ease in a range of techniques. Thigh ornaments and ankles, and fringes and toes, are incised, whereas they are painted on the Menelas stand: this distinction suggests a distance in date between the two vases, according to the evolution from painted to incised technique observed throughout the workshop (above, 2.4). However, the painter still retained a range of brush strokes: delicate dashes and dots but sweeping impressionistic outlines (for the bodies), careless swoops over the ornamental back of the vase but minute patience for finicky ornaments.[37]

The latest stage in the career of the Polyphemus Painter anticipates the last phase of Protoattic and was once identified as the Painter of the Flowery Ornaments. This personality was isolated in the publication of the Berlin collection and is represented by a conical stand and its cauldron, both in Berlin (Pl. 8).[38] The stand was the most complete example known (it was lost in the Second World War) for the workshop and serves as a model for reconstructing the other fragmentary ones (Pls. 7, 11, 17, 18). The very lowest band of the stand, above the ring foot, bears a frieze of swans with raised wings, a decorative motif that appears after the middle of the seventh century.[39] The wings on these birds have painted white feathers, one of the few instances of applied white on this stand (the "white" shields and greaves are reserved; only the cauldrons are painted white). The swans and their white feathers recall those on the kotyle kraters from the Kerameikos (Pl. 27), as if in this late phase the Polyphemus Painter were in touch with Athenian conventions.

The lower stand is dominated by a procession of nine warriors similar to those on the Menelas stand, here dressed in even more colorful robes and surrounded by the elaborate ornaments that gave the painter his name. Each garment is different: as well as an alternation of black and white himations, each chiton underneath is "embroidered" in a different pattern (spirals, hooks, scales, ladders, or rays). A single figure, unfortunately not preserved above the waist, wears a short chiton under a shorter himation and prances with lifted heels; he holds no spear and must have played flutes to keep the flat-footed warriors in step. This figure matches the flautist on the new fragment by the Ram Jug Painter (below, 3.2) and either is a parallel quotation from Protocorinthian hoplite scenes or was copied by one Aiginetan from another. The draped figure marching behind the flautist holds no spear, and it has been proposed that he was a lyre player.[40]

---

37. In evaluating this brushwork, one should be careful not to confuse the irregular preservation of added white with a deliberate *chiaroscuro* on the part of the painter. Nor can one attribute these new techniques to the influence of the monumental medium, as refuted above (2.4); they should be appreciated within the medium of vase painting, and as a skill of the painter responsible.

38. *CVA Berlin 1*, A 41 (cauldron), pls. 30, 34:2, pp. 7, 23–24.

39. Kübler, *Kerameikos VI, 2*, 236.

40. Ibid., pl. 30, *right*, p. 24 (compare Apollo on the Oresteia krater, Pl. 13, for a lyre player from the same workshop).

The next frieze above the warriors shows hoplites in battle: black silhouettes with white shields, greaves, and helmets, black weapons and helmet plumes. The shield exteriors are as colorful as the robes below, with a variety of devices (black and white rosettes, whirligigs, and plain white shields). Where the shield interior of a warrior in profile is exposed, only "half" a shield is visible in "front" of his body. This attempt to show a shield in profile must derive from a Protocorinthian convention, in keeping with the inspiration behind these scenes of musicians and hoplites.[41]

On the warriors, the distinction between helmet and face is still simplified: the effect suggests a helmet-shaped face with lips, nose, and beard barely projecting and the eye painted on the helmet. The general impression of these hoplites is a more sophisticated conception of an armed and active figure than the hoplites by the Ram Jug Painter (Pl. 11), and a more experienced manipulation of colors and planes.

The torus molding separating stand from bowl is decorated with a frieze of black, incised roosters, an immediate association in motif to the white cock by the younger Polyphemus Painter (Pl. 5). Like the single white bird, one of these fowl has lowered his head to feed; two others are pecking at a scorpion, giving the decorative frieze a liveliness found in nature, like the bird tugging at a worm in the hoplites frieze below the torus.[42]

The upper bowl of the Flowery Ornaments stand is decorated with a procession of twelve women bearing protome cauldrons, painted white to represent the gleam of metal, balanced on their heads. The location of these figures on the stand, just below the rim, suggests a conscious allusion to the clay (or metal?) cauldron supported on the stand, directly above their heads. The women wear plainer dress—simple white chitons under dark mantles—than the warriors in the procession below, distinguishing them as more humble figures, perhaps serving women. Their mouths are open, perhaps in a song of praise for the warriors (unless they lament their captivity?). The total effect of this stand is explicitly epic, with men marching to war, a battle scene, and a crowning frieze of the prizes in war—women and cauldrons.

The animated fauna on this stand—dancing flautist, pecking roosters, flapping birds—perform in a jungle of flora both more elaborate and more crowded than on the painter's earlier work. The rosette painted in front of a warrior's face is as big as the shield in the frieze above him; the device is anticipated in the painter's earlier work

41. Compare the Chigi vase (Pl. 24) for hoplites marching to the flute; for profile shields, see the MacMillan Painter's name vase (aryballos in London: Matz, *Geschichte der griechischen Kunst*, pl. 151a).

42. Independent insect life has a special place on the vases of this workshop; compare the grasshopper (?) climbing the border on the Oresteia krater (Pl. 13) and an enigmatic fragment with a cricket perched on an ornament, from the Acropolis: Graef and Langlotz, *Vasen von der Akropolis*, no. 361, p. 37 (drawing). Cook, *BSA* 35 (1934/35): 187, n. 2, appreciated the grasshopper but did not know its then unpublished relative on the Oresteia krater, unlike Beazley (*Development*, p. 9). At Corinth, such insects are more popular in the sixth century (e.g., on the Amphiaraos krater: Pfuhl, *Malerei und Zeichnung*, fig. 179).

(Pl. 7) but becomes prominent in his later career. Ground ornaments between the draped figures have grown into veritable bushes; again, one can claim antecedents (Pls. 3, 6, 7), but the field of ornaments is by far more crowded on this later stand, leaving little open space. The human figures, however, keep to a more modest style than on earlier vases: ears are a single reverse S-curve, the palmette spray on foreheads is more discreet, there are no superfluous tattoos on thighs and buttocks, and no triple bracelets and necklaces. The contrast to earlier extravagances in figural painting suggests an advance in time; this phase of the Polyphemus Painter's work represents a more developed phase of Middle Protoattic painting, when conventions of figure style are reduced to a more sober canon. In technique, too, the painter has learned from his earlier experiments. He has limited the use of white to its Geometric function, for highlights on metal cauldrons (but not on armor); on the birds, added white reflects the influence of a less eccentric group of painters in the Kerameikos. His use of incision is limited to the frieze of roosters, as if this technique, too, is less important a device than the painted line.

The conical stand in Berlin may have supported the dinos also from the Aigina necropolis (Pl. 8).[43] The vessel had a spout and is restored with a flat base, but it may have had a continuous round bottom like the dinos by the Ram Jug Painter.[44] The shoulder of the bowl is encircled by a figural frieze of foot soldiers and chariots running under the spout; how much of the bowl was devoted to this subject cannot be determined from the remaining fragments. The hoplites are akin to those on the conical stand, with flat-topped helmets over tiny noses, and shields with the same devices. The single horse preserved is a mature version of those by the Ram Jug Painter (Pl. 11) and the Polyphemus Painter (Pls. 2, 7), with a well-placed eye and a neat, incised mane. The charioteer's face is a throwback to the goggle-eyed type of the early seventh century; his dotted chiton and activity recall miniature chariot scenes from Athens (Pl. 11: 368).[45]

Finally, even the Acropolis of Athens produced sherds which can be associated with the Polyphemus Painter. In particular, a fragment with drapery (a chiton covered with scales) and the edge of a meander square in the field suggests a conical stand similar to the one with Menelas and his warriors.[46] Three other fragments suggest his

---

43. *CVA Berlin 1*, A 44, pl. 36:1, pp. 7, 24; Kübler, *Kerameikos VI, 2*, 300.

44. *CVA Berlin 1*, where the nonjoining sherd with a flat base is questioned, even though it is illustrated on the same plate with the other fragments of the bowl; cf. above, 2.3.

45. Cook observed this resemblance when the new fragments from the Agora were published, introducing a variety of styles that could not be reduced to the single personality of the Ram Jug Painter: J. M. Cook, *Gnomon* 34 (1962): 822 (also Cook, "Protoattici vasi," p. 501, where he connects vases from the Kerameikos offering channel to the Berlin stands A 40, A 41). Although shape (spouted bowl) and style are close, the chief distinction is size: the Berlin bowl is at least twice the diameter of the Agora bowl and this corresponds to a discrepancy in style.

46. Graef and Langlotz, *Vasen von der Akropolis*, p. 38, no. 377 (not illustrated: see DAI photo, "Akropolis Vasen 12").

mature phase, two with profiles like the warriors on the Flowery Ornaments stand, one with a lion and the characteristic starburst ornament.[47]

This completes the oeuvre of the Polyphemus Painter, whose work is concentrated on Aigina, like the vases assembled as the work of the Ram Jug Painter (below, 3.2). His personality has been defined with some difficulty in the history of scholarship.[48] His latest phase, where he approaches the synthesis between Attic and Corinthian fulfilled by the Nettos Painter, was incorrectly identified as a separate painter, "der Maler der blumigen Ornamente," and now can be linked with early black figure artists whose work is also found on Aigina. For the closest successor to the newly defined Polyphemus Painter is the Woman Painter, renamed by Beazley the Painter of Berlin A 34 after an ovoid krater from Aigina (Pl. 9).[49] Its figural scene, a procession of women, represents an even more formal version of the warriors by the mature Polyphemus Painter (Pl. 8), although the faces are too poorly preserved for a stylistic comparison. Novelties which date the Woman krater to a new phase of Attic vase painting are the color red, used with black and white to dress the women in polychrome garments sprinkled with white rosettes, and the nonradiate form of the dot rosette, which marks the Late Protocorinthian phase of vase painting.[50] Contemporary with the Woman Painter is the fragment of a collar-necked krater from Aigina with a dipinto, known since the nineteenth century.[51] If the restoration as "Alexandros" in Aiginetan letters is correct, the krater would represent Late Protoattic painting on Aigina, still under the influence of the Chigi vase with its Judgment of Paris scene. But a workshop the size of the Middle Protoattic group around the Polyphemus Painter cannot be identified after his demise.

The newly expanded oeuvre of the Polyphemus Painter deserves a fresh portrait. As a potter, he prefers and perhaps makes popular the three shapes standard for the workshop: krater, amphora, and conical stand. As a painter of such shapes with an ample field, he is generous with his brush, a quality which suggests free painting but

47. Ibid., nos. 347a, b, p. 35, pl. 13 (profiles); DAI, "Akropolis Vasen 14" (lion); Cook, *BSA* 35 (1934/35): 194, n. 2.

48. Confusion arose when Mylonas renamed the Horse Painter, who was retained as a separate artist by Mylonas and as a younger phase of the Polyphemus Painter by Brann. Mylonas, *O protoattikos amphoreus*, 110, rejected the Munich krater, which he preferred to see as the work of a lesser follower (on the basis of the *periergos* lion?); Brann, *Agora VIII*, 24, 95, apparently misunderstood, for she cites this Mylonas rejection as evidence that the Horse Painter is the Polyphemus Painter in his youth.

49. *CVA Berlin 1*, p. 7, "Frauen-Maler"; Beazley, *ABV*, 5, *Paral.*, 1. A fragment of this krater is still in Aigina, omitted in Kraiker's publication but recorded on DAI photo, "Aigina Vasen 464," Pl. 11, unnumbered fragment.

50. Payne, *Necrocorinthia*, pls. 11, 12.

51. Cook, *BSA* 35 (1934/35): 196, pl. 54f.; above, 1.2, n. 5; 2.7, n. 68. The fabric of this piece (on exhibit in the National Museum of Athens) is a bright red, covered with a white slip, and looks neither Attic nor Aiginetan (Cycladic, perhaps?). Attributed to the Woman Painter by Beazley, *ABV*, 5.

does not make him an artist accustomed to a monumental scale, as has been suggested.[52]
Nor do his subjects necessarily reflect a model in the form of a wall-painting; it has even
50 been suggested that the non-Attic dipinto on the Menelas stand was copied, with the
scene, from a Doric monumental painting.[53] It is far more likely that the Polyphemus
Painter picked up this taste for labeling figures from Corinthian vase paintings; that is
where he also learned other motifs (eagles, boars, Gorgons, hoplites, horsemen, musicians) and techniques such as heavily incised feline paws, a curly tail, and the use of
a border as a prop. Even his figural style can be compared with some of the finest
Protocorinthian work, in particular with an unpublished Middle Protocorinthian oinochoe
from Aigina.[54] Under the handle of this oinochoe (missing neck, handle, and foot) is the
head of a bearded male in profile, the earliest protome in Greek art. The size of this
head is a reminder that not all Protocorinthian painting was miniature and that an
important group of Protocorinthian "Big Style" vases belies the traditional dichotomy
between Attic and Corinthian styles in the Orientalizing periods.[55] A comparison of this
profile with the faces by the Polyphemus Painter (Pls. 6, 7) suggests that the Protoattic
artist distorted a Protocorinthian original, with a ski-slope nose, elaborate variations on
the ear, and a row of spit curls across the forehead. In addition, the pointed chin of
Athena (Pl. 6) suggests that the painter had to improvise a female profile without a decent
model of an unbearded face, and reinforces the idea of his dependence on Corinthian
models. Once again, the coincidence of many Big Style vases on the same island, and
often in the same necropolis, as Middle Protoattic figural painting suggests that the
milieu for influence between the two classes of pottery was Aigina.

    As well as the resemblance among individual motifs and figural style, the narrative
mode of the Polyphemus Painter shows the most striking affinity to contemporary Protocorinthian painting. The popularity of several kinds of scenes—mythological, epic,
and animal—within the works of a single painter emphasizes the variety of influences
and traditions at work, which cannot be reduced to a single inspiration, such as monumental paintings or recorded poems. Some of his subjects are similar to specific examples in ivory and metal as well as pottery, and reflect an environment rich in Orientalizing imports.

    In terms of ornaments, this leading painter can be recognized by a distinctive

---

52. Brann, *Agora VIII*, 23: "Especially the Polyphemus Painter, who uses the whole pot as a picture area
and paints with much white color, would have come into his own in wall-painting" (she qualifies her comparison in
a footnote, "In fact, however, he was probably unaffected by murals," citing Robertson, *Greek Painting*, 44ff.).

53. Suggested by K. Schefold in his review of Pfuhl's *Malerei und Zeichnung* in *Die Antike* 8 (1942): 76.
Kübler, *Kerameikos VI, 2*, 328, n. 92, objects with his own explanation of the Aiginetan dipinto (below, chap. 4).

54. Berlin Ü 8, from the unpublished Protocorinthian material from Aigina: U. Gehrig et al., *Berlin: Führer*,
p. 58, pl. 40.

55. This oinochoe is a successor to the Early Protocorinthian oinochoae with large motifs (Dunbabin and
Robertson, *BSA* 48 (1953): 174) and belongs to the Big Style vases found at Perachora, Aigina, and Athens (Dunbabin
and Robertson, 172–73, 177; Payne and Dunbabin, *Perachora II*, p. 65; Kraiker, *Aigina*, pls. 12–14).

combination of motifs derived from the Early Protoattic tradition. The reverse side of the Analatos hydria anticipates many of his extravagances and even the use of a minor area exclusively for ornament.[56] Other motifs—the pomegranate ornament in particular— can be related to the Mesogeia Painter, on the strength of which Brann called the Polyphemus Painter a pupil of the Mesogeia Painter.[57] Given the resemblance between the sphinxes on the Menelas stand and the Vlastos krater sphinxes (above, n. 20), such an association might find additional support. However, other motifs prominent in his early work and thus closer to his apprenticeship point to Athenian painters of kotyle kraters, banded amphorae, and even Protocorinthian eagles (Pl. 1). Thus even the young Polyphemus Painter pays attention to a number of traditions and refuses to be classified as a pupil of a single workshop.

If these elements contribute to the origins of the Polyphemus Painter's style in the second quarter of the seventh century, his later development exposed him to the technique of incision and to an interest in mythological subjects. He also gathered a circle of followers, whose numbers suggest that he controlled a shop or at least was the most influential painter of a productive group. Finally, through his mature phase, the influence of the Polyphemus Painter spread into Late Protoattic painting, without establishing a generation of successors. If the Polyphemus Painter represents the origin of a style independent of Athens, though influenced by the Kerameikos, his workshop, and with it the historical occasion which sponsored it (chapter 4), lasts only a generation.

2. THE RAM JUG PAINTER

The discovery of the Ram Jug introduced the Black and White style to modern scholarship and inspired generations of analysis and attribution. In antiquity the painter's oeuvre was more limited than in modern eyes, and his importance in his own time less than that of the Polyphemus Painter. But his work is no less intriguing, thanks to an idiosyncratic personality.

His name vase (Pl. 10) introduces many of his eccentricities. Affectionately called "Kanne," or "Jug," since its debut, it imitates a Rhodian oinochoe with rotelle handles, not popular in Athens but imitated in Corinth.[58] Technique and style were anomalous at the time of discovery, before associated vases emerged; but the fabric was and still is emphatically non-Attic. Pallat's original description—"ein reiner, fester, im Bruch hell-brauner [Thon]"—indicates those aspects, especially color, that cannot be Attic.[59]

---

56. Cook, *BSA* 35 (1934/35), pl. 38b; cf. above, 2.5.

57. Brann, *Agora VIII*, 24, 79 (no. 422).

58. For a good parallel, see a Protocorinthian imitation exported to Samos, dating to the mid-seventh century: H. Walter, "Korinthische Keramik," *AthMitt* 74 (1959): 60–63, pls. 54, 102–03, 114:2; fig. 1 (not a Naxian vase, as argued by Kübler, *Kerameikos VI, 2*, 179, n. 4).

59. Pallat, *AthMitt* 22 (1897): 325.

By a process of elimination, Pallat concluded that the jug's style and fabric had to be local; in later years it was called Argive, imitation Corinthian, Cycladic, or Cretan by vase-painting scholars including Payne and Beazley.[60] Although most scholars, including Payne and Beazley, eventually accepted the Ram Jug as Attic, reservations about the style have persisted: "The Ram Jug Painter has more kinship with Protocorinthian than other Attic painters."[61]

The scene on the jug—the escape of Odysseus and his companions from the cave of Polyphemus—forms a narrative sequence to the *Odyssey* episode illustrated by the Polyphemus Painter (Pl. 6).[62] Although this is the earliest extant representation of the episode in Greek art, both subject and scheme are not without Corinthian connections. The placement of Odysseus directly opposite the handle is typical of Protocorinthian compositions.[63] The best parallel to the scene on the Ram Jug may have been an unpublished kotyle in Berlin (now lost), also from Aigina.[64] Its description suggests an odd style, probably a local imitation of Protocorinthian (below, 3.5); its classification as a Middle Protocorinthian II illustration of the escape from the cave of Polyphemus would make it a contemporary parallel to the Ram Jug, from the same island. On the Ram Jug, the placement of the scene ignores the convex curve and the handle, as if the painter were the first to apply such a challenging subject to an exotic shape.

The technique and style of the jug, unique at the time of discovery, have been compared to contemporary outline painting such as that on Rhodian and Cycladic vases.[65] Details of anatomy, however, are eccentric to any tradition. The rams are almost equine, with large hooves, long rippling tails, and elongated horses' heads. The heroes wear

---

60. Argive: C. Smith, *JHS* 22 (1902): 34, possibly with the Argive Heraion stand or Aristonothos krater in mind; Corinthian imitation: Pfuhl, *Malerei und Zeichnung*, 109; Cycladic: Payne, *JHS* 46 (1926): 208, n. 5; Cretan: Beazley and Ashmole, *Greek Sculpture and Painting* (Cambridge, 1932), 9. Cook defended an Attic provenance, maintained by Richter and Rumpf, by invoking its similarity in "clay, slip, and varnish" to "Attic sherds in the Aegina Museum and elsewhere": Cook, *BSA* 35 (1934/35): 189 (Richter, *JHS* 32 (1912): 383; Rumpf, *Gnomon* I (1925): 327–28, citing the Pernice krater). Given the associations with Aigina of many such vases, Cook's argument found a home for the Ram Jug but not necessarily an Attic one. Since the other vases by the Ram Jug Painter seem to be of standard Attic fabric, the fact that he worked in several kinds of clay defies a claim for provenance on the basis of fabric alone.

61. Dunbabin, *BSA* 45 (1950): 201; cf. Payne, *Protokorinthische Vasenmalerei*, 32, n. 2; Beazley, *Development*, 9–10.

62. In recent years, new fragments complete the scene without the cave postulated by Pallat to hide half of the missing ram; instead, the ram carrying Odysseus is the largest, the other two are to be restored on a smaller scale: Pallat, *AthMitt* 22 (1897): 326–28; Fellmann, *Die antiken Darstellungen*, 79–81; cf. *Odyssey* 9.425–35.

63. For example, on the oinochoe from Samos compared to the Ram Jug above (n. 58); on aryballoi by the MacMillan and Boston painters (Matz, *Geschichte der griechischen Kunst*, pls. 151a and 152a); cf. Lorimer, *BSA* 42 (1947): 98–104; Kübler, *Kerameikos VI, 2*, 208–12.

64. Dunbabin and Robertson, *BSA* 48 (1953): 173, n. 5; Fellmann, *Die antiken Darstellungen*, 80, n. 81.

65. Pallat, *AthMitt* 22 (1897): 329, cites a Rhodian ram; Payne, *JHS* 46 (1926); 208, n. 25, compared the animals to those on the Cycladic griffin jug from Aigina.

triple bracelets and belts, a circle indicates their anklebones, and they are equipped with two right hands.[66] Faces are perhaps the most distinctive clue to the painter's hand. On both rams and men the eye is large below a generous brow; the upper lid describes a larger curve than the lower, shorter one and ends in a low outside corner, giving the eye a downward tilt. The human profile is dominated by a huge nose above a modest mouth; the chin runs into the jaw and meets the low ear. The closest parallel to this style is Protocorinthian; the faces by the Ajax Painter, in particular (Pl. 23), bear the same tilted eye, large nose, and low ear.

Ornaments on the Ram Jug, all in solid black, are conventional for the period; the particular combination of radiate dot rosette, multiple lozenge, dotted triangle, and spiral ray is characteristic of the painter, when they match critical details of execution and arrangement. The painter applied each ray of a rosette separately, often producing an uneven number of rays, unlike the multiple crosses applied by other painters to form rosettes (e.g., Pls. 2, 8). Within the field, the Ram Jug Painter's ornaments fill but do not crowd; his avoidance of the stacked zigzag, in particular, gives a more open space to the background.

There is no incision on the Ram Jug, as if the painter preferred the brush and white paint for interior details. His brush commanded a range of effects—from rippling hair to solid hooves, from delicate strokes in dilute glaze to firm ones in thick black paint. Where figures overlap, problems inevitable in the Black and White style arose, such as where legs of men and animals intersect below the rams' bellies. In the group left of the handle, for example, human legs appear behind those of the ram; in the other groups, the men seem to hang in front of the rams. (One would expect the heroes' legs to fall between the rams' hind legs.) Where the genitals of the suspended men would be hidden by the rams' bodies, the artist has cut out a section of ram, as if to display the genitals.

Such details reveal a painter with an unmistakable style, whose own combination of familiar shapes, subjects, and techniques appears on a limited number of other works. A total of five vases from Aigina and two fragments from the Athenian Acropolis is accepted in this study; they represent but a fraction of modern attributions. The Ram Jug belongs to the midpoint of a career which flourished near the middle of the seventh century; as with the Polyphemus Painter, technique as well as style provide the key to a chronology of this artist's works.

Like the Polyphemus Painter, the Ram Jug Painter debuts with an early "animal style," characterized by traditional animal friezes, generous ornament, and experimental

66. Compare Daedalic decorations on contemporary statuettes (Boardman, *Greek Sculpture: The Archaic Period* (London, 1978), figs. 54, 57) and on bronze work (the Kaineus relief from Olympia: Mallwitz and Herrmann, ed., *Die Funde aus Olympia* [Athens, 1980], no. 42, pp. 97–98).

54

use of incision. An early stand by him is preserved in fragments, several previously unrecognized, from the Athenian Acropolis (Pl. 11: 357, 370).[67] The best preserved fragment is broken from the torus molding between conical base and flaring bowl; it once bore a running-dog frieze in the Protocorinthian tradition, now visible as a single dog between the tail of the next, on the right, and a cable border, on the left. The animal is a translation of a Protocorinthian incised figure into the Black and White style. The running dogs on the Chigi vase have been compared to these Protoattic dogs, but one might recall examples closer to this workshop—those from Aigina by the Hound Painter.[68] Style and technique represent the painter's early animal style: dark body with white highlights (collar, shoulder), neat reserved head with heart-shaped ear, large eye and angled brow. Ornaments in the field also identify the Ram Jug Painter (radiate dot rosette, spiral ray, dotted triangle, meander square), with more colorful decoration reserved for a separate zone. On the flat band above the torus, solid black and white rosettes alternate, their petals and outline defined in contrasting paint, their shapes separated by vertical rows of broken meanders.[69] The rosettes, Oriental in origin, share similarities with Rhodian and Cypriote versions, and show up later in the work of an admirer (Pl. 18).[70] Two rim fragments, attributed by Cook, probably belong to the same stand: they suggest a frieze of deers and boars circling the upper bowl. The deers are barely preserved and were not illustrated by Graef and Langlotz; a pair of hindquarters and a tail seem to belong to a traditional Attic species.[71] The boar, on the other hand, is more common to Rhodian and Protocorinthian workshops, and appears elsewhere among the Aiginetan painters (Pl. 6). Details of technique (applied white "collar" and eye on the boar) and ornaments are identical to the torus fragments and help associate the pieces. An additional portion may be represented in a mysterious fragment not discussed by Graef and Langlotz but recorded on one of the original German photographs (DAI, "Akropolis Vasen 12"). It shows the neck of a grazing horse with reserved ladder mane, with a white shoulder line resembling other animals by the Ram Jug Painter. The large size and flat

67. Graef and Langlotz, *Vasen von der Akropolis*, nos. 357a, b (grazing deer and boar); 370a (dog and rosettes); uncatalogued fragment with horse's mane visible on DAI photo "Akropolis Vasen 12." Various associations were made by Eilmann and Gebauer (*CVA Berlin 1*, p. 7, no. 14), by Cook (*BSA* 35 [1934/35]: 194, nn. 2–4) and Karouzou (*ArkhEph* 1952, pl. 9:1–2; p. 166, where the fragments are assigned to two different vases: nos. 9, 10).

68. The Chigi vase was suggested by Karouzou, *ArkhEph* 1952, 161; for the Hound Painter see Kraiker, *Aigina*, pl. 17, no. 252; pl. 20, no. 263. On other Protoattic running dogs under Corinthian influence, see Brann, *Agora VIII*, 17, 89 (no. 513), 95 (no. 563); Kübler, *Kerameikos VI, 2*, 238, n. 278. Compare also Naxian and Rhodian dogs: Kardara, *Rhodiake angeiographia*, pp. 38, n. 2, 148–49.

69. One fragment of this frieze was assigned to a different vessel by Graef and Langlotz (*Vasen von der Akropolis*, p. 38, no. 370b) but probably belongs to a different side of the same stand.

70. For Cypriote adaptions of these Oriental rosettes, see Walberg, *RDAC* (1979): 277–80.

71. Graef and Langlotz, *Vasen von der Akropolis*, no. 357a (DAI photo "Akropolis Vasen 12"). See the deer by the Dipylon Master (Coldstream, *Greek Geometric Pottery*, 40, pls. 6–7) or the Analatos Painter (Böhlau, *JdI 2* [1887] pls. 3–4).

shape of the sherd would fit the wide lower cone of the stand; the type of horse is common to the work of related painters (Pls. 2, 5, 13, 15).

A dinos by the Ram Jug Painter matches the conical stand in style (Pl. 12). They may have been produced as a pair, like the set by the Polyphemus Painter (Pl. 8); but the Ram Jug Painter's dinos was found on Aigina, not with the stand on the Acropolis of Athens.[72] The shape imitates a round-bottomed metal cauldron, complete with flat rim of folded "bronze" and false ring handles, molded flat against the shoulder. Appropriate to such an Oriental shape, a frieze of exotic lions marches to the right, spanning the convex field like the rams carrying Odysseus and his men. The proximity to Early Protoattic works, such as the Thebes krater by the Analatos Painter, and the painted white details on the lions (paws, muscles, and manes) place the dinos in the painter's early animal phase. Heart-shaped ears and dotted muzzle, although also related to earlier lions, appear in a group of lions associated with Aigina.[73] Finally, the ornaments on this dinos link it to the Acropolis stand, through the familiar dot rosette, spiral ray, and dotted triangle. Exceptional are the palmette enclosed in a double volute (under a lion's extended paw) and the ornaments dominating the underside of the dinos (elaborate rosette pinwheels with black and white leaves between outline cable chains). These relatively extravagant motifs, separated from the figures, suggest an acquaintance with the luxurious ornament of the Polyphemus Painter and anticipate a converging relationship between the two styles.

The next stage in the career of the Ram Jug Painter, which includes his name vase, introduces epic narrative episodes, perhaps under the direct influence of the Polyphemus Painter. A neck amphora from the Aigina necropolis, now in fragments in Berlin, illustrates a scene from the *Kypria*: Peleus entrusting his infant son, Achilles, to the centaur, Cheiron (Pl. 12).[74] The recent restoration of an amphora by the Polyphemus Painter with a similar scene (Pl. 4), from the same context, suggests the artists worked close to each other. It is particularly appropriate to find the story so popular on Aigina, as the earliest literary version is in Pindar's odes for Aiginetan victors.[75] It suggests that both painters were fond of local traditions as well as of each other's vases.

The Peleus amphora, even in its incomplete state, is the largest vase from the

72. *CVA Berlin 1*, A 43, pl. 34: 1 and 35; attributed on p. 7 (no. 6); Kübler, *Altattische Malerei*, fig. 16, pp. 10–11; Karouzou, *ArkhEph* 1952, fig. 22, pp. 160, 166.

73. Kübler, *Kerameikos VI, 2*, 266ff., isolated a "dritte Reihe" of lions, including those by the Ram Jug, Polyphemus, and Checkerboard painters.

74. *CVA Berlin 1*, A 9, pl. 5; attributed to the Ram Jug Painter, "vielleicht spät," p. 7 (no. 10). For a detailed appreciation, see Beazley, *Development*, 10–12.

75. *Nemean 3*, ll.47–55; *Nemean 4*, ll.60–65; Hesiod fragment 40 (Merkelbach-West), from a scholion to Apollonius of Rhodes. As the son of Aiakos, legendary king and founder of the island's dynasty, Peleus is as important to Aigina through his forebears as in his offspring, Achilles: scholia to *Nemean 5*, l.10; *Olympian 2*, l.78; also Pausanias 1.44.9; 2.29.7.

painter's oeuvre, and the scene is correspondingly magnified, spanning both sides of the vase (as on the Ram Jug and the Hoplites bowl). One side showed Peleus facing right, holding baby Achilles before him on outstretched arm. The face of Peleus is the largest and most developed profile by the Ram Jug Painter: the line of the nose is confident; the mouth is articulated into two distinct lips; the chin is a continuous curve with a proper jaw running up to the well-formed, if still rather low, ear. A true throat begins below the chin, an improvement over the neckless figures elsewhere (Pls. 10, 11). Both father and son wear their hair long, with painted (rather than incised) divisions. Baby Achilles, one of the earliest infants in historical Greek art, is a miniature version of the youthful figures on the Hoplites bowl and wears the same dotted chiton with plain sleeves. His father, Peleus, sports a forehead palmette in the style of the period (cf. Pls. 8, 26).

On the reverse, Cheiron is barely preserved except for the back of his head, his lower arms, and hindquarters. He faces left as if to meet the approaching Peleus and receive Achilles in his outstretched right hand, his dinner suspended over his back on a branch held in his other hand. Details such as hair, fingernails, triple "bracelet," tail, and hindquarters are incised, in contrast to the use of paint for the same details on the first side. But Cheiron's captives are abbreviated versions of other animals by the Ram Jug Painter, with large outlined heads, generous eye, and angled brow; here, white paint was applied to separate hind legs and neck.

In ornaments, too, the Peleus amphora belongs to a phase of increasingly elaborate incision and influence by the Polyphemus Painter. Next to standard motifs (dot rosette, spiral ray, multiple lozenge, dotted triangle), a huge rosette with alternating stuffed and dotted leaves dominates the shoulder zone.[76] Both neck panels are filled by a single floral ornament—a palmette fan nesting in two large leaves, sprouting from a tall cone— with outlined petals and incised leaves and stalk. These embellishments are typical Middle Protoattic enlargements of Early Protoattic motifs from the Analatos workshop (above, 2.5), but on an amphora whose subject is shared by the Polyphemus Painter they also recall the mid-career extravagances of that painter (Pls. 2–5).

The final works of the Ram Jug Painter continue to reflect the Polyphemus Painter, with the increasing influence of Protocorinthian style. A fragmentary dinos from the Kolonna sanctuary on Aigina, the same context which produced the Ram Jug, illustrates this late orientation to Protocorinthian work (Pl. 11: 584, 585).[77] Three fragments (two joining) from a bowl with incurving rim and narrow, everted lip have recently been augmented by a new, unpublished fragment from recent excavations. Below the meander hook band along the rim, a reduced version of the band around the Ram Jug neck, a military procession circles the bowl to the right. At least three hoplites (on the two

---

76. Kübler, *Kerameikos VI, 2*, 124, called such stuffed and dotted leaves "Eastern," although they were established Attic techniques by the seventh century (Knigge, *Gnomon* [1974]: 205).

77. The fragments were found by Furtwängler, noted by Hackl, attributed by Eilmann and Gebauer, but never illustrated or published until after the Second World War (above, 1.2, n. 34).

joining pieces), a mounted archer (the third fragment), and a flautist (the new fragment) make a spirited scene, with an explicit debt to the Protocorinthian tradition of the Chigi vase (Pl. 24). Details of the scene by the Ram Jug Painter make this connection clear.

There are no filling ornaments in the field around the figures, an unusual background for the Ram Jug Painter but perhaps a deliberate imitation of the Chigi vase. The technique in which the figures are executed reveals an attempt to apply Protocorinthian incision to the Black and White style, with mixed results. The three preserved hoplites alternate in black and white: the first from the left is a black silhouette wearing white armor, the second is white with reserved armor, the third one black again. The overlap of warriors, where shields and spears intersect adjacent figures, plus the flaking and fading of paint since the original application, has created some confusion. The painter has complicated his task in his fidelity to several Protocorinthian conventions: he has painted the shields white, although one would expect to see the wickerwork interior of a shield held on the left arm.[78] The exposed shield interior lacks its central armband (πόρπαξ), and the handgrip (ἀντιλαβή) which belongs on the rim of the shield has been moved inside and down.[79] Furthermore, right and left arms of the marching figures have been confused: the right (?) arm of the first warrior seems to pass behind his torso to hold shield and spears—one recalls the two right hands on the heroes of the Ram Jug (Pl. 10).

Among the black and white hoplites one can almost distinguish stages in the evolution of the Black and White style. On the first (black) warrior, the black body was painted over the white shield "behind" it and has now flaked off the unstable ground, leaving an oddly transparent torso. Outside this white shield, his black limbs, painted on clay instead of white paint, have survived better. His white greaves, in turn, were painted using two different techniques: the left one was applied to a black leg and hence has flaked off, the right-hand greave was painted on a reserved leg and is still clearly visible. The second (white) warrior's dark cuirass and greaves did not adhere to the dark silhouette beneath, and the dark rays bordering his shield are barely visible. Finally, the third warrior, black again, seems to have profited from the lessons of the first figure, for his black silhouette was applied directly to the clay, not on the troublesome white paint.

Incision was introduced throughout this experimental piece, where it appears lavish compared with its total absence on the Ram Jug. The technique was used to separate the pair of spears held by each hoplite, to indicate the scales of the cuirasses, and to give an emphatic outline to the painted figures. The artist has outgrown his exclusive use of the brush and seems challenged by Protocorinthian techniques, but he has not discovered a happy compromise.

78. Lorimer, *BSA* 42 (1947): 95, called this confusion between shield interior and exterior "confined to early proto-Corinthian art" before this bowl was published.

79. Lorimer, *BSA* 42 (1947): 76ff.; Snodgrass, *Early Greek Armour*, 61–68, on shields.

The third fragment from this bowl shows a mounted archer, assuming that the long black object on his back represents a quiver.[80] Protocorinthian representations seem to

58   have inspired this archer, when one compares archers such as Herakles in the centauromachy by the MacMillan Painter (Pl. 23).[81] The archer on the bowl, however, faces right to shoot back as he rides a horse moving to the left, an Oriental scheme which must have reached Greece on portable objects from the Levant, or could have reached Aigina via Protocorinthian versions.[82] The archer is a relative of other figures by the Ram Jug Painter: with his dotted chiton with short sleeves, black "cap" of hair with looser waves down the back, divided by painted white lines, and a palmette tendril on his forehead, he is a close relative of Peleus (Pl. 12). His face, along with the miniature version on the newly discovered young flautist, exhibits the characteristic profile: large brow and eye, beaked nose, and low ear. The horse carrying the archer wears an unusual mane, with both outline loops outside the silhouette of his neck, and white loops painted directly on the dark neck. The painted white loops are a Protocorinthian convention popular with the Ram Jug Painter, who even applied them to lions (Pl. 12).[83] These horses help associate the hand of the Ram Jug Painter with a fragment from Aigina with no exact provenance (Pl.11: 577).[84] It belongs to the rim of a bowl, probably similar in shape to the Hoplites bowl, and preserves two overlapping horses from a chariot team, sharing a mane of incised loops. Their outlined heads with large, angled brow indicate the painter (compare especially the rams on the name vase), as do the pendent spiral ray and meander square. With the horse on the Hoplites bowl, they represent the Protocorinthian species of horse with upright neck and short loop mane (rendered in three techniques), popular next to the grazing horse with ladder mane (compare the Acropolis horse; above, n. 67) since the Analatos Painter.[85]

A final fragment from the Acropolis concludes the work of the Ram Jug Painter. It was found in modern construction of the Acropolis Museum rather than in the early

80. Cook, *Archaeological Reports* (1945–47), p. 112, first identified the figure as an archer; Kraiker, *Aigina*, p. 90, no. 584 (rider); Kübler, *Kerameikos VI, 2*, 207, n. 54, reserves judgment on the evidence; Robertson (review of Kraiker, *Aigina*), *JHS* 73 (1953): 185, suggested Troilos. Two diagonal lines from the base of the quiver across the figure's left arm could be part of a bow.

81. Note the hide-wrapped bow held by the Protocorinthian Herakles, which helps identify the object on the Hoplites bowl.

82. For Phoenician prototypes of the "Parthian shot," see the bronze bowl from Olympia (F. Poulsen, *Der Orient und die frühgriechische Kunst* [Berlin, 1912], fgs. 12, 13); for Greek ivory seals with the same motif, see examples from Perachora and Megara (Payne and Dunbabin, *Perachora II*, pl. 175, A 23a, and p. 412, n. 3, NM 11750).

83. The white loops are barely visible now but were noted at the time of publication (Kraiker, *Aigina*, 90, no. 584). For a Protocorinthian example, see the oinochoe in Munich with a horse protome (Munich 8765: D. Ohly and Kl. Vierneisel, *MJB* 16 (1965): 229–30, fig. 1), from a class also found on Aigina (above, n. 54).

84. Kraiker, *Aigina*, p. 89, pl. 42, no. 577; attributed by Brann, *Agora VIII*, p. 92, no. 537 (Robertson, *JHS* 73 [1953]: 185).

85. See the lid in the British Museum where both types of horses appear: Cook, *BSA* 35 (1934/35), pl. 42a, p. 174, calls the nongrazing horse a "colt" to distinguish the two types.

excavations and does not seem to belong to the animal stand assembled above (Pl. 11).[86] First attributed by Karouzou, it shows a human profile next to a bird and a dot rosette that leave no doubt as to the artist. The incised divisions of the hair, in contrast to the painted white lines used on the Peleus amphora, the Ram Jug, and the Hoplites bowl, suggest an advanced date, although the profile does not curve into a proper jaw as on the faces of Peleus and Cheiron. A date midway through the painter's career, as suggested by Karouzou, is appropriate; original shape and scene (a figure of unknown sex facing right, holding a bird resembling a Rhodian swallow) are impossible to reconstruct. This tantalizing fragment promises another major piece from the Acropolis by the Ram Jug Painter.

This concludes the extant oeuvre of the painter: a total of five vases from Aigina and two from the Acropolis. The elimination of a number of attributions (below, 3.3 and 3.6) reduces the variety of shapes, techniques, subjects, and influence previously assigned to the Ram Jug Painter. The maximum range of his career cannot exceed two decades, most comfortably between 660 and 640 B.C., although it seems contrived to spread so few vases over more than a decade, to fill a "career." If a total of seven vases seems few, one should remember that only seven vases are attributed to the Dipylon Master and that the personality of the Ram Jug Painter has been expanded through modern affection.

In this study the Ram Jug Painter emerges as an artist more modest and less influential than the Polyphemus Painter, whom he clearly admired. As a potter, he was attracted to exotic shapes and strong curves which often compromised, or at least complicated, his painting. He used those shapes thoroughly, spanning both sides of a vase with his scenes, without regard for the boundaries of sides; this closely resembles Protocorinthian rather than Protoattic tradition. He was more comfortable with a brush but gradually introduced incision; he also began as an animal painter and graduated to figures and narrative, features which apparently increased in the lifetime of the Polyphemus Painter. Finally, his name vase is not of Attic fabric, which was the original clue to a non-Athenian painter. That distinction is reinforced by a style at moments perversely unique; even within the company of the Aigina workshop he is consistently different, and represents that element of the exotic essential to Orientalizing art.

3. THE ORESTEIA PAINTER

Among artists usually identified with the Ram Jug Painter is a separate master from Aigina so closely influenced by his work that it may seem unnecessary to define a separate painter. Only three works can be associated with the Oresteia Painter, and it would be

86. J. M. Cook, "Archaeology in Greece, 1951," *JHS* 72 (1952): 93, pl. VI. 4b; Karouzou, *ArkhEph* 1952, pp. 160–61, pl. 9:3; p. 166, no. 8.

more convenient to classify them as works of the Ram Jug Painter, who could then claim a more substantial oeuvre. But important distinctions, however subtle, argue for a sep-

60   arate status.

This follower's most celebrated work, and his name vase in this study, is an ovoid krater in Berlin attributed to the Ram Jug Painter in the original publication (Pl. 13).[87] An immediate objection to identifying the Ram Jug Painter as the maker of this vase is its shape: the large krater with its wide, flat field was never attractive to the Ram Jug Painter, who preferred more tightly articulated ceramic profiles. As with many of the Aigina vases in Berlin, most of this krater is missing; much has been made of what is preserved. The more complete side is dominated by an interlocked pair of male figures in dotted scale cuirasses. The black figure on the left points a sword at the back of the head of the white figure on the right, and grasps his victim's forelock with his free hand. The white man reaches back to grasp his captor's beard in a suppliant gesture. Two female figures, both in white, flank this grim scene with appropriate cheek-tearing gestures of despair, as all four figures face right.

This dramatic scene may be one of the most overworked in Greek art. It is commonly interpreted as a specific epic murder, either the death of Aegisthus at the hands of Orestes or the murder of Agamemnon by Aegisthus.[88] The latter argument hinges on a claim that the wavy lines flowing out of the white victim's hair into the black captor's fist indicate the net traditional to the murder of Agamemnon.[89] Other interpretations include the slaying of Memnon by Achilles, witnessed by Thetis and Eos.[90] The most sensible explanation seems to be that of Rumpf, who suggested, two years after the vase was published, "das eindrucksvolle Bild eines Gefangenentransportes."[91] The scene is a vivid image of capture in warfare: the enemy (in black) killing a defeated warrior (in white); two women of the defeated city lamenting their loss and anticipating their capture. Such a piteous scene is what Kleopatra described to Meleager, as Phoinix recounts in his appeal to Achilles in the Embassy (*Iliad* 9.590–94). The use of black and white to make a subjective distinction between conqueror and captives introduces symbolic color to a formulaic scene and reveals how a technique (white paint) has become a narrative device. Recast as a genre scene instead of a specific mythological episode, this krater reinforces the role of epic formulas during a period when myth is too readily identified

87. *CVA Berlin 1*, A 32, p. 7 (no. 3), pls. 18–21; attribution rejected by Cook, "Protoattici vasi," 501, Kraiker, *Aigina*, 90 (no. 582); Davies, *BCH* 93 (1969): 252, n. 1 (bibliography).

88. Davies, *BCH* 93 (1969): 252ff., with summary of earlier arguments.

89. Ibid., 254, Schefold, *Myth and Legend*, 43. However, the lines make better sense as a lock of hair by which men grasp an opponent, as on the New York Nessos amphora (Pl. 15, *left*): Cook, *BSA* 35 (1934/35): 192, n. 4.

90. Cook, "Protoattici vasi," 502 (any scene with a duel flanked by two women lends itself to this interpretation: e.g., the Late Geometric stand in Munich, cf. above, chap. 2, n. 35; *MJb* 18 [1967]: 241ff.).

91. A. Rumpf, review of *CVA Berlin 1*, *PhilWoch* 60 (1940): 27 (although Rumpf later proposed an episode from the labors of Herakles: *Malerei und Zeichnung*, 25).

by scholars. Despite this conservative reinterpretation of the subject, it seems advisable to retain the name Oresteia krater, and Oresteia Painter, for the sake of its familiarity to scholars.

61

The other side of the krater is missing its center, preserving only two flanking figures. The male figure on the left may be connected with floating fragments of a lyre and chariot reins; the female figure opposite and facing him wears a quiver of arrows and brandishes a bow. These attributes, plus the elaborate costumes they wear (the man's chiton is bordered with rays, the woman's skirt is of dotted material and also bordered) and their ornamental ears, suggest a divine pair such as Apollo and Artemis.[92] Seventh-century parallels for such an epiphany scene compare closely.[93] On the reverse of the epic capture scene on this krater, Apollo and Artemis represent the immortal backdrop to human action, much as an episode on Olympos is juxtaposed with the Homeric battlefield in epic poetry.

The most enigmatic figures on the krater are under the double handles, two under one handle, a single figure under the other, clearly separated from the main scenes by borders. These figures are all black, the single figure covered with hair from head to toe but humanoid in other respects, his beard, hair, and limbs articulated by the same conventions (ankles, knees, and thigh ornaments) as the other male figures. He holds a black ball in each hand, presumably to hurl at his counterparts under the opposite handle. Those two are engaged in a chiastic confrontation fitted under the double arc of the handles: each leans out but faces back to throw the black ball in his hand. The two figures are bald of head as well as of body hair, and also have humanoid features and limbs.

These original monsters have inspired a host of speculations as to their source and significance; the most attractive interpretation makes them early comic figures or protosatyrs.[94] Their effect, however, is primarily decorative and explicitly non-Greek; identical monsters cavort on Phoenician silver bowls, of the sort cited above (n. 82) as a parallel for the mounted archer delivering a parting shot.[95] Thus these monsters func-

92. The attempt to identify Aegisthus as the male figure, on the evidence of the lyre, *CVA Berlin 1*, pl. 19, ignores the chariot reins: Davies, *BCH* 93 (1969): 256, n. 2.

93. The Oresteia krater may be the earliest in the seventh-century epiphany scenes which include the Melian amphora with Apollo and Artemis (Conze, *Melische Thongefässe* pls. 3, 4) and the Crowe cuirass from Olympia (Mallwitz and Herrmann, *Die Funde aus Olympia* [Athens, 1980], no. 59), both of the later seventh century.

94. Beazley, *Development*, 9; T. B. L. Webster, *Greek Theatre Production* (London, 1956), 133, 157, 192. Alan Boegehold has suggested (pers. comm., October 1980) that these figures are a pair of slaves pelting the audience with fruit or sweetmeats in a Greek comic production (Aristophanes, *Wasps* 58–59; *Wealth* 797–801). This attractive interpretation would make the krater the earliest representation of Greek comedy as well as the earliest illustration of Greek tragedy, but it seems premature in the history of theater, as well as less convincing than Oriental parallels.

95. See such a silver bowl from the Bernardini tomb (O. Montelius, *La Civilisation primitive en Italie depuis l'introduction des métaux* [Stockholm, 1895–1910], vol. 3, pl. 368, 5), with its hairy apes or monsters in the royal hunt scene. A recent discussion of these bowls is Barnett, *RDAC* (1977): 157–69. "Monkey" identified by Young, *AJA* 43 (1939): 715.

62

tion as subsidiary decoration, like the grasshopper climbing the border to the left of the single monster, and their inspiration should be sought among the Near Eastern minor arts in circulation during this period.

The lower frieze on the krater presents another subsidiary theme, this time one from Attic tradition. Grazing horses with outline heads and ladder manes on dark bodies, their long tails incised in a herringbone pattern, carry on the Analatan tradition noted for the Polyphemus Painter and the Ram Jug Painter (Pls. 2, 5, and above, n. 67). The horses on this krater are more liberally incised at joints and muscles, tail and hooves, and where limbs overlap—places where the Ram Jug Painter would have used white paint. Like the Peleus amphora, the Oresteia krater exhibits an interesting distribution of techniques. The main scene of murder or capture has no incision, all details (fingers, toes, hair, tattoos) being painted in white. In the reverse scene, however, in the lower and handle zones, incision is used in alternation with white paint (painted scales but incised hair, for example).

There are distinct departures in ornamentation from the style of the Ram Jug Painter. Although the dot rosette, multiple lozenge, spiral ray, and pendent zigzag are from his repertoire, their execution and placement on this krater are different. The rosettes are overgrown, even sloppy, with clusters of rays; the spiral rays are pendulous rather than pendent. Certain motifs—stacked zigzag, dotted cable strand—are ones he never painted. Nor did he ever add extraneous cartoon figures, such as grasshoppers or monkeys, to his scenes.

The figural conventions show a comparable difference in execution, although the same ones were practised by the Ram Jug Painter. The stylized rings at ankle, wrist, and throat have spread to elbows and knees (on the male figures); the cable ornaments on the black warrior's thigh are a convention shared by the Ram Jug Painter (Pl. 11), but not the rosettes on male buttocks, borrowed from the Polyphemus Painter (Pl. 6). The scale torso suggests plate cuirasses on the male characters but also is converted to corsetlike garments on the women.

Most effective in distinguishing a separate painter are the faces. The flat-topped heads on this krater have a square appearance, emphasized by the horizontal mouth, lower eyelid, base of nose, and the vertical axis of the tall head and long ear. The only profile facing left—that of Artemis—looks like a caricature of the Ram Jug Painter's style, not an evolved stage of it.[96]

Despite some resemblances to the Ram Jug Painter's style, the Oresteia krater also shows the influence of the Polyphemus Painter, particularly in ornamentation. Additional examples of the Oresteia Painter's work document a full personality that cannot simply be absorbed into the oeuvre of the Ram Jug Painter.

96. For a comparison of Protoattic profiles see Mylonas, *O protoattikos amphoreus*, 105, fig. 37; Beyer, *AA* 92 (1977): 73, fig. 33.

The most important other work by his hand is a krater with centaurs from the Kerameikos of Athens, incomplete but restored from sherds recovered from three late contexts (Pl. 14).[97] Presumably the krater once marked the mound which the three burials containing the sherds intersected; it is a great pity that the complete shape and original context are a matter of conjecture, as this is the only substantial candidate of the Aigina workshop from the chief cemetery in Athens (above, 1.2).

63

Most of the lower body is missing: the vase could have been a kotyle krater, with stand or foot, or even a conical stand with flaring bowl-shaped rim like those made in the same workshop (Pls. 8, 11). The rim inclines inward, representing a stage of imitation between the eighth-century bronze prototype and its developed ceramic counterpart.[98] The preserved portion (some fifteen fragments, a tiny fraction of the original) shows three centaurs, alternately black and white, moving right in a formal frieze. They carry a triple spray of piney branches in each outstretched arm, one before them and one behind held over their backs. This scene is reconstructed from two tails, two heads, and four legs; even the best-preserved face is missing below the chin, leaving no evidence of hair or beard.[99] The white centaur is especially dubious, as only his tail is preserved, but presumably he looked like his companions, with details painted black instead. The black centaurs have fingers, muscles, hair, and tail, and thigh tattoos painted white—no incision is preserved in the fragments.

The ornaments (dot rosette, stacked zigzag, dotted cable strand, and spiral ray) resemble those of the Oresteia krater, and the figural conventions (profiles, "tattoos," and "bracelets") also indicate the same painter.[100] The Centaurs krater forms a reasonable antecedent to the more ambitious one in Berlin, beginning with the evidence of subject. The main frieze—and perhaps the only one—is a conventional Late Geometric scene of centaurs with branches, exotic but static, old-fashioned by the middle of the seventh century.[101] As with the grazing horses (Pl. 13), an older motif is enlivened with new techniques, here by the contrast of black and white paint; but the choice of subject still suggests a less adventurous period than the one which produced the Oresteia krater.

The second feature of the Centaurs krater making it earlier than the Oresteia krater is its figural style. The simian profile of the black centaur is still a single painted line from forehead to chin, with an added stroke for the mouth. Later, for the figures on the

97. Kübler, *Kerameikos VI, 2*, 447–48, no. 35 (inv. no. 98), fig. 49, pl. 29, with a description of the context in Kübler, *Kerameikos VI, 1*, 2, 21, 34ff., 43.

98. Kübler, *Kerameikos VI, 2*, 164, n. 74.

99. The restoration (Kübler, *Kerameikos VI, 2*, 447, fig. 49) is disputed by Schiffler, *Die Typologie des Kentauren*, 18, as there is no evidence for beard and hairstyle.

100. In recognition of these similarities, both the Oresteia krater and the Centaurs krater were attributed to the Ram Jug Painter in the Berlin *CVA* fascicle. *CVA Berlin 1*, p. 7, nos. 3, 5; even Kübler, *Kerameikos VI, 2*, 331, acknowledges the resemblance, although he refuses to attribute, as usual.

101. Kübler, *Kerameikos VI, 2*, 251–52, discusses older parallels but suggests these centaurs are Lapiths, specifically (*pace* Knigge, *Gnomon* [1974]: 206).

Oresteia krater, the painter articulated profiles by separate strokes, with a loop for the nose and a V-indent for the two lips.

64   Last, changes in technique correspond to the development suggested in the careers of other painters (above, 3.1–2). On the early Centaurs krater the Oresteia Painter added in white paint those details he incised on the later krater; this increase in the use of incision, at the expense of white paint, was noted in the works of the Polyphemus Painter and the Ram Jug Painter.

With this tidy pair of an early and a late piece by the Oresteia Painter, one hopes for some additions to his distinctive style, but they are few. A fragment with a sphinx from Aigina is the only candidate; it was originally attributed to the Ram Jug Painter by Cook and Eilmann.[102] The flat fragment is unpainted inside and presumably belonged to a third large krater by the Oresteia painter. On the fragment is the head of a sphinx, crowned with a palmette and two long tendrils ending in palmettes. Just visible is the tip of the sphinx's sickle wing with colorful petal-feathers, alternately white and dotted. This type of sphinx is Protocorinthian in origin and rare in Athens during the Middle Protoattic period. The finest parallel to this sphinx is another one from Aigina, on the name kotyle of the Bellerophon Painter (Pl. 25).[103]

The upper zone above the sphinx is preserved only in a white foot, facing left; such scanty evidence cannot be coaxed into any convincing interpretation. Presumably a figural scene was bordered by a frieze of sphinxes below, in the manner of other vessels in this workshop (see the conical stands in Berlin: Pls. 7, 8).

An interesting detail on this sherd provides technical evidence for the Black and White style. The sphinx's face is painted white, but her hair is separated by incised horizontal strokes, suggesting a later rather than earlier date. In addition, problems in the application of white can be observed on the face. A shadowy second profile is visible to the left of the throat as a *pentimento*, as if the artist had painted over the first profile with white, then added a second profile safely outside the white paint. (This evidence is complicated by the deterioration of features such as eye and ear, which have now flaked off the unstable white, and of the hairline.) Details such as these illustrate the intransigence of the Black and White technique, explaining why such an attractive "style" was abandoned.

With the definition of the Oresteia Painter in these three pieces, one expects more. Or is there still room for these works in the later career of the Ram Jug Painter? If so, one must presume a radical change in his style, a new orientation toward larger shapes, perhaps a new employer like the Polyphemus Painter. This phase of the Ram Jug

102. Cook, *BSA* 35 (1934/35): 189, n. 6; *CVA Berlin 1*, p. 7, no. 13. It was Kraiker who published the sherd properly fifteen years later, and associated the sphinx and the Oresteia krater with a personality separate from the Ram Jug Painter (*Aigina*, p. 90, no. 582, pl. 43).

103. Kraiker, *Aigina*, p. 48, no. 253, pls. 18, 20, B (attributed by Dunbabin and Robertson, *BSA* 48 [1953]: 177).

Painter's career could grow out of his most monumental work, the Peleus amphora, where he already follows a Polyphemus Painter topic, on a new scale with a try at overgrown floral ornaments. But the three works make sense in their internal development and would be hard to coordinate with the late style of the Hoplites bowl.

4. THE WILD STYLE

4.1. The New York Nessos Painter

Since 1912, the painter of the colorful amphora acquired by the Metropolitan Museum has been familiar, although his oeuvre has hardly grown in the past seventy years. The tendency in scholarship has been to place the painter at an early stage of the Black and White style, in a phase affectionately known as the Wild Style.[104] The second-rate draftsmanship of many of these works has suggested an "early" status; but dating the inferior products of the Middle Protoattic period to an early and tentative phase is better resisted. Experiments in technique and style can be observed among even the leading painters of this short-lived Black and White workshop, and are a symptom of the early archaic period. The New York Nessos Painter and his associates belong to a mature stage of the Black and White style, under the influence of the leader, the Polyphemus Painter.

Until the discovery of the Eleusis amphora, the New York Nessos amphora was the finest specimen known in the Black and White style (Pl. 15). The amphora shape, the most popular one in this workshop after the ovoid krater, is similar to those by other Middle Protoattic painters (Pls. 6, 12); its decoration points to three sources of influence consistent in this workshop—Early Protoattic, Middle Protocorinthian, and Oriental.

The scene on the neck, a lion attacking a deer, shares the animal conventions of the Polyphemus Painter: the mule-eared deer, for example, appears on the bowl of the Menelas stand (Pl. 7), the lion's scale mane on the Acropolis fragment (above, n. 47). More eccentric versions appear in the Checkerboard Circle when lions attack deer in imitation of this scene (Pls. 19, 20). A comparison of such details demonstrates the proximity in which the major artists—the Polyphemus Painter and the New York Nessos Painter, in this instance—were at work. Furthermore, the common source for these kindred animal fights may have been Corinthian. An aryballos by the Ajax Painter is a classic example of the frontal lion attacking a deer.[105]

The shoulder scene on the New York amphora, two grazing horses with ladder

104. Brann, *Agora VIII*, 10–11, 20; Cook, *BSA* 35 (1934/35): 192, "Protoattici vasi," 501–02.

105. Payne, *Protokorinthische Vasenmalerei*, pl. 11:5, for the aryballos by the Ajax Painter (attributed by Dunbabin and Robertson, *BSA* 48 [1953]: 176); for an Attic imitation outside the Black and White style, see the oinochoe from the Kerameikos: Kübler, *Kerameikos VI, 2*, pls. 1, 2, pp. 509–10, from the north bank of the Eridanos.

manes, is the familiar Analatan frieze maintained by every major painter in the workshop (cf. Pls. 2, 5, 13). On this same amphora, the other type of horse with upright head and incised mane appears in the mythological scene below the grazing horses, a reminder that the two types of horse are formulaic motifs with a contemporary function.

The mythological scene on the belly of the amphora is a specific version of the man-and-centaur battle popular elsewhere (Pl. 19) as a genre scene. The presence of Deianeira on the New York amphora identifies the subject as the victory of Herakles over Nessos.[106] The centaur fills the area under the handles in this wrapped panorama in a manner similar to the disposition of the Perseus narrative on the Eleusis amphora (Pl. 6), as both subjects were too large to fit on the front of the vessels. Nessos is falling to the ground but not yet on his knees, like the centaur on a contemporary ivory seal from Perachora.[107] The human forelegs of the centaur are extended in a remarkable stretch to support the falling torso. This pose is also a direct quote from Protocorinthian centaurs (Pl. 23) and is shared by other Middle Protoattic centaurs from the same workshop (Pl. 4).

In falling, Nessos has dropped his weapon, a branch; at least it topples behind him and seems to be growing out of his back. This image captures the origin of branches in the hands of Greek centaurs, misunderstood from wings on Near Eastern monsters.[108] Greek artists transformed these wings into either a weapon for hostile centaurs like Nessos and Pholos or a hunter's game pole for friendly centaurs like Cheiron (Pls. 4, 12).

The centaur's hair, long and incised where it floats free of his head but a solid black cap for skull and beard, helps illuminate the peculiar hair of the white victim on the Oresteia krater (Pl. 13). Below this continuous black hood of hair is an awkward transition to the shoulders, then a right arm resembling the deltoid muscle of an animal, not a human arm.

The owl floating above the falling centaur has been interpreted as both a bad omen for Nessos and a good one for Herakles.[109] However, in this workshop, and especially in this heavily incised form, it is simply another Protocorinthian motif borrowed for

106. Recognized and described by Richter, *JHS* 32 (1912): 373, n. 9; the amphora illustration does not follow the tradition behind Sophocles' *Trachiniae* (555f.), unlike the Argive Heraion stand (Pl. 17; below, 4.2).

107. Payne and Dunbabin, *Perachora II*, no. A 65b, pl. 180; cf. an ivory relief from Sparta (Dawkins, *Artemis Orthia*, 210, pl. 101).

108. The common claim in scholarship (Schiffler, *Die Typologie des Kentauren*, 16; Hurwit, *AJA* 81 (1977): 27, n. 129) is that Greek artists planted branches in the backs of centaurs; actually, the Greek imagination transformed wings to weapons, accompanied by a narrative explanation. In the seventh century one can still find centaurs who both wear branches in their backs and carry them as weapons: see the bronze Kaineus relief from Olympia (above, n. 66).

109. For modern Greeks, the *koukouvayia* brings bad luck (Karouzou, *Angeia*, 110), but in the western world the owl brings good luck (Beazley, *Development*, 7). It is unlikely that in the Middle Protoattic period the owl was already an attribute of Athena, as Richter (*JHS* 32 [1912]: 374) would have it.

decorative purposes from pottery or ivory seals.[110] This particular form, with a perfect circle for the head, appears as a shield device on the MacMillan aryballos.[111] Its adoption by Protoattic artists is limited to the Aigina workshop, as on the Argive Heraion stand, where it appears in the field of the animal fight scene (Pl. 17).

To the right of Nessos on the New York amphora stands Herakles in a short tunic and sandals, sword drawn as he seizes the centaur by the forelock with his free hand. He is decorated like other Protoattic figures, with an Oriental rosette on his buttock over the decorated tunic (cf. Pls. 6, 13). His face shows the same affinity to a Protocorinthian protome suggested by the style of the Polyphemus Painter (above, n. 54); the figure also anticipates archaic Attic conventions for sculptural figures, with its swelling thigh and upper arm, volute ear and stylized joints (the elbow).

To the right of Herakles waits a four-horse chariot, with a skirt hanging over its back edge facing the hero and a figure holding the reins, also looking back. A large portion of the vase between skirt and face is missing; it seems impossible to see a single figure both wearing the skirt (seated?) and holding the reins (standing?). The long flowing hair is more appropriate to a woman than to a charioteer (contemporary drivers tie their hair back: Pl. 8); although Deianeira had a reputation for driving chariots, her position, according to these fragments, would make her a contortionist, too.[112]

Her chariot is drawn by four horses in typical stacked formation, the inevitable counterparts to the grazing ones in the shoulder frieze (Pl. 15, *right*).[113] As with the centaur, the artist's fidelity to figural conventions is mixed with more imagination than understanding. Each horse's head has a different shape and a different kind of eye; there are eight forelegs among the four horses, but only two hind legs; the attempt to represent eight separate hindquarters dissolves into two meaningless lines; the reins disappear into the manes, never reaching the horses' mouths.

The last figure in this scene is placed under the right handle but is still in the frame, "as if he were in danger of not getting into the picture" (Pl. 15, *right*).[114] He is headed for collision with the four horses, his front foot overlapping their forward hooves. His back leg is raised in an unusually agile gesture for a period not yet acquainted with

---

110. The owl was a favorite of the Head-in-Air Painter: Payne and Dunbabin, *Perachora II*, no. 88, pp. 22–23, with a useful bibliography on owls in early Greek art. Compare also the ivory seal from Perachora in Payne and Dunbabin, A 83a, pl. 181.

111. Matz, *Geschichte der griechischen Kunst*, pl. 151a, although Beazley, *Development*, 7, explained the round head thus: "the target-like head is meant for a side view."

112. On the equestrian skills of Deianeira, Richter cites Apollonius of Rhodes (1.8.1) and assumes that a single figure is represented on the amphora (*JHS* 32 [1912]: 375, n. 21). Beazley, *Development*, 7, admits the difficulty of restoring two figures from the fragments but cannot reconcile what is preserved with a single figure.

113. Brann, *Agora VIII*, 86 (no. 492), discusses the stacked team in the seventh century; see also Kardara, *AJA* 59 (1955): 52, pl. 32, for the relationship between Attic and Cycladic quadrigas of this type.

114. Beazley, *Development*, 7; Fittschen, *Untersuchungen*, 116 ("Kobold").

68   the *Knielauf*. The animation of this figure might not necessarily be related to the action of the main scene; his function could be as an Oriental cartoon figure in a subsidiary area, like the humanoids on other works (Pl. 13). If this running figure, noticeably smaller than the main characters, belongs in the main scene, his significance must be hidden in the obscure scenario of the myth.

Finally, the ornaments on this vase deserve some attention. In the field, stuffed and dotted trefoils are typical descendants of Early Protoattic motifs, distinctive enough in the hands of this painter to attribute fragments from the Agora to him. The feeding water birds along the ground line reappear on his krater in Boston (Pl. 16). Other ornaments establish this painter's connections to the Checkerboard Circle and the Polyphemus Painter, through similarities in the outline cable, enclosed cross and S-chain, and the more common lozenges, tongues, and stacked zigzags.

More unusual is the lower zone of curious black silhouettes below the main scene, where one would expect a band of rays. They have the shape of a cone topped by an echinus cushion and a sphere, the three sections separated by double incised lines. Richter recognized in them imitations of Orientalizing cauldrons on stands, but she knew no parallels.[115] With the appearance of the rest of the workshop of the New York amphora, parallels for such representations of cauldrons and stands emerged in the work of both the Checkerboard Circle and the Polyphemus Painter (Pl. 8). The ultimate source of these explicit representations of metal vessels may be Protocorinthian, as executed by those painters who influenced Protoattic artists in a number of other motifs.[116]

The technique of this vase was called "semi-black-figure" by Beazley: incised details are still unskilled, but white was applied selectively, to the sword, skirt, and ornaments, but not for human flesh.[117] As in the New York Nessos Painter's other work, misfired (red) color appears over much of the painted area, but whether this was accidental or intentional cannot be determined.

The only other major vessel by his hand is a fragmentary ovoid krater on loan to the Boston Museum of Fine Arts (Pl. 16; above, 1.3, n. 72). The shape is a welcome addition to the painter's repertoire, for it is the second favorite in this workshop (above, 2.3). The condition of the upper rim has been interpreted as evidence for reuse of the vessel in antiquity; however, as in the case of the Menelas stand, it rather suggests damage since antiquity.[118] In technique, this krater has been interpreted as a later phase

---

115. Richter, *JHS* 32 (1912): 378, first proposed "a further variation of [this] loop pattern" for these objects and later suggested that tripods with bowls were meant.

116. For a Protocorinthian picture of a cauldron on a stand, see the aryballos in Boston by the Ajax Painter (Pl. 23) or the Cumaean oinochoe in New York (N.Y. 23.160.18, in *Aspects of Ancient Greece*, ed. G. F. Pinney and B. S. Ridgway, Allentown Art Museum [1979], 120–21, no. 57).

117. Beazley, *Development*, 7, 12.

118. Vermeule, *AJA* 75 (1971): 286, n. 5, cites the advice of Homer Thompson for this interpretation. Cf. Karo's comments on the Menelas stand, above, n. 16.

of the painter's career, but the red color which has been called polychrome is more likely a misfiring of the dark glaze than a deliberate attempt at "two tones of red with brown."[119] Distinctive on the Boston krater is the profusion of ornament, exaggerated by the preservation of the handle area at the expense of the major scenes. The palmette chains and tendrils recall the extravagant style of the Polyphemus Painter on his animal vases (Pls. 2–5).

Too little is preserved of the figural scenes for close analysis or even identification. One side presented a young woman carried to sacrifice by young men, and the published suggestion of Iphigeneia's sacrifice at Aulis is the strongest possibility for a vase from a workshop sensitive to epic themes. As with all fragmentary or ambiguous mythological illustrations, other interpretations will continue to suggest themselves,[120] but without a greater proportion of the original krater preserved, speculation is useless. The most attractive interpretation, the Iphigeneia story, complements the House of Atreus theme on the Menelas stand.[121] As well as in shape, subject, and ornament, the Boston krater agrees with other Black and White vases from Aigina in its evidence for Protocorinthian influence. The bearded face lost in ornaments on the reverse bears a resemblance to that on the Protocorinthian oinochoe from Aigina (above, n. 54), also compared above to the face of Herakles (Pl. 15).

The lower frieze of sea monsters on the Boston krater reflects two sources of influence: from the Orient and from Corinth. Three-headed marine creatures are a species popular in early archaic Greek art but were influenced by the Oriental bestiary; the gold bowl discovered at Hasanlu forms an attractive Near Eastern prototype for the Protoattic version.[122] But the sea monsters by the New York Nessos Painter also recall a Protocorinthian convention in the execution of their tails. The loop which doubles over on itself has no good parallels in the marine world, or in other Protoattic painting; the closest source may be an abstract Protocorinthian motif popular on Early and Middle Protocorinthian oinochoae, of the same class to which the protome oinochoe belongs.[123]

119. Vermeule, *AJA* 75 (1971); 285, 289; see above, 2.4.

120. An attractive if unlikely possibility is the obscure Makaria, daughter of Herakles and Deianeira, a voluntary sacrifice for the sake of an Athenian victory in the tradition surrounding the children of Herakles (Pausanias 1.32.6). She is unnamed in the Euripidean version of the *Heraklidae* and named only "the daughter of Herakles" in the classical painting inspired by the tragedy (scholiast to Aristophanes, *Wealth* 385). Her name suggests an abstract personification of a later date, but her character belongs to an early tradition. On Makaria in fourth-century vase painting, see Margot Schmidt, "Makaria," *AK* 13 (1970): 71–73. This interpretation would make the Boston krater a convenient sequel to the rescue of Deianeira by Herakles on the New York amphora, with the distressed Herakles witnessing (from Olympos?) the misadventures of his children on the second vase.

121. Vermeule, *AJA* 75 (1971): 292; however, since the Oresteia krater probably represents an epic genre scene rather than the murder of Agamemnon or Aegisthus, it no longer belongs to the same mythological cycle.

122. Porada, *Ancient Iran*, 96–102, figs. 63–64, pl. 24, on the Hasanlu bowl; K. Shepard, *The Fish-Tailed Monster in Greek Art* (New York, 1940), chap. 1, for other Oriental prototypes.

123. The oinochoe class in question: Dunbabin and Robertson, *BSA* 48 (1953): 174; an example from the Kerameikos: Kübler, *Kerameikos VI, 1*, pl. 57.

Although the resemblance may appear subtle, in the context of other such tricks picked up by this painter (e.g., the imitation cauldrons, Pl. 15) and his colleagues, the connection is significant.

The vividly personal style of the New York Nessos painter cannot be traced outside these two vases in American collections, except for scraps from the Agora.[124] In scholarship, this personality has been associated with an early and awkward phase, as an artist instrumental in introducing the Wild Style. Rather, he suggests the developed style of an established workshop, and his influence on the Checkerboard Circle serves as evidence of his professional impact. Reflections of his style among painters of the Wild Style also establish a chronological framework for his career, for his imitators were also exposed to the Polyphemus Painter, and all these artists must have been at work in the middle of the seventh century.

4.2. The Argive Heraion Stand

An important if isolated example of this Black and White style workshop demonstrates both the influence of the New York Nessos Painter and the firm Middle (rather than Early) Protoattic associations of the Wild Style. The fragmentary stand from the Argive Heraion (Pl. 17; above, 1.2, n. 56) has suffered an early classification but also belongs in the second quarter of the century on these newly determined stylistic grounds. Since its original publication as "local" (i.e., Argive), the stand has found parallels in shape and style in the Berlin collection from Aigina.[125]

Most of the bowl, above the join with the conical stand, is missing (as is common with other examples of the shape: cf. Pls. 7, 8, 11), unless two rim fragments, the only other Protoattic sherds from the sanctuary, belong.[126] The conical base presented the main narrative scenes of the vessel in three friezes, in the tradition of other stands from Aigina (Pls. 7, 8, 11). A scrap from the uppermost scene, joining the only preserved fragment of the bowl, shows a centaur holding a woman in a dotted skirt, both figures moving right but facing left. The woman's left arm is out of sight, probably behind the centaur, but her right arm is flung up, apparently in a gesture of appeal. The scene was identified as Nessos and Deianeira in the original publication, perhaps with the help of the Metropolitan amphora, already on the market. Even without such a parallel, the

124. Brann, *Agora VIII*, 11, 83–84, nos. 463–66.

125. Cook was the first to rescue it from Argive Orientalizing ("a home away from home for orphans") and to compare it to the "uncouthness" of the New York Nessos amphora: *BSA* 35 (1934/35), p. 191, n. 3, p. 192, pl. 52 (a more complete illustration than the original publication plate, as additional fragments of the animal scene were included). Courbin still maintains that the stand is Argive: *BCH* 79 (1955): 1ff.

126. Waldstein, *The Argive Heraeum*, pl. 62, 1a, b; compare the palmette chain with the work of the New York Nessos Painter (Pls. 15, 16). The two suggested rim fragments would give the stand an ornamental chain of large palmettes around the upper edge.

details on the stand closely follow Sophocles' *Trachiniae* (566–68), where the centaur is also struck by an arrow (here visible between the arms of Deianeira and Nessos). In a Protocorinthian illustration of Herakles' bowmanship against Pholos (Pl. 23), four examples of stricken centaurs include three struck in the small of their backs and reaching behind them to extract the arrow, a gesture imitated by Nessos on the Argos stand.[127] Like the Nessos on the New York amphora, the Heraion centaur wears human forelegs in front of his horse's body, out of respect for the Protocorinthian species (as on the MacMillan Painter's aryballos: Pl. 23).

In addition to the arrow which has met its mark, there is a sword in the field behind Deianeira's head. It seems that the theme of a sword fight between man and centaur, also traditional to the Protocorinthian repertoire (above, n. 107), has been conflated with the archer hero of the Pholos episode; the painter of the Argive Heraion stand may have been exposed to multiple Protocorinthian traditions through a variety of minor arts.

The hero Herakles himself is missing from the unresolved scene on the Argive Heraion stand, where Deianeira has not yet reached dry land, unlike on the New York amphora. Nor do the nonjoining fragments from the same narrative frieze contribute to a restoration of the scene.[128] Whatever their significance, this second group of fragments bear a dubious relationship to the Nessos story, unless they represent a chariot and small figure waiting for Deianeira on shore, in analogy to the New York amphora (Pl. 15).

Below the epic and mythological scene(s) on the Heraion stand is a colorful battle frieze. The most coherent group of fragments shows the traditional group of four warriors fighting over a fifth, who has fallen; other floating fragments display a variety of warriors moving in both directions. Their helmets with checkerboard crest holders, black and white shield devices, and curious helmet faces are familiar in this workshop (Pls. 8, 11, 18); the crowded, overlapping figures unrelieved by filling ornaments except for flying birds are vividly Protocorinthian, especially with the polychrome effect of added off-white paint for armor. Individual motifs, such as the fallen warrior clasping an opponent's knees, are a direct reflection of Protocorinthian images.[129] The usual problems arise

127. The aryballos by the MacMillan Painter in Berlin (Pl. 23) was also cited for the boots and bow of Herakles, as reflected by the Ram Jug and Polyphemus painters (Pls. 6, 11), as well as for the hairy centaur (Pl. 4: 583) by the Polyphemus Painter.

128. The latest suggestion is that they illustrate an Achilles and Cheiron episode, a welcome third addition to the two other examples from this workshop (Pls. 4, 12): Cook, "Protoattici vasi," 502. However, Cook's "centaur" has equine forelegs and must be a horse (unlike the Nessos figure on the same stand, who has human forelegs) and wears reins connected to a charioteer; behind the horse stands a hoplite with two spears and a shield. In addition, two figures in front of the horse demand identification: a small figure in dotted, full-length chiton with embroidered border and a larger figure in boots (?) presumably suggested Peleus and the young Achilles to Cook. The sex of the small figure cannot be determined, and the context suggests that if he is male, he may be a flautist among warriors.

129. Lorimer, *BSA* 42 (1947): 103, n. 2.

with the transformation of Protocorinthian models into the Black and White technique: overlapping forms filled with white, such as intersecting greaves, become entangled when outlines show through white paint.

Into this battle scene overflows the lowest frieze on the stand, an animal fight of black lions over a white victim. The large, generously incised paws of the lions, their net-pattern manes, and big hoop of a ringed tail curving up into the next scene are all Protocorinthian in origin, as is the owl in the field above the fight.[130] The animal fight establishes the stand as a member of the same workshop that included the Menelas stand, the Munich krater, the New York amphora, and the Checkerboard Circle, which repeat the same subject in all its Black and White glory (Pls. 3, 7, 15, 19–20). The black and white cable pattern finishing the lower edge of the stand is a final link to the same works; within the scenes there are few filling ornaments, persuasive of an advanced date under Protocorinthian influence rather than the early date proposed in scholarship.

The painter of this stand was generous with white paint, for horse and human flesh in the mythological frieze and for armor in the hoplites scene. Ornaments such as the black and white cable strand, normally rendered with added white, are executed in reserved and black areas only.

The faces of Nessos and Deianeira on the Argive Heraion stand recall those on the New York amphora, especially the small figure under the amphora handle (Pl. 15, *right*). The round, floating eye also appears on the sphinxes by the Polyphemus Painter (Pl. 8). Other painters are recalled with different motifs: the dotted clothing is typical of the Ram Jug Painter, for example, while the animals, hoplites, and cable ornament are common to a larger circle of painters.

In many details, therefore, the Argive Heraion stand belongs to the tight circle of Middle Protoattic painters under Protocorinthian influence isolated in this study. However, it too has been dated to an early and transitional phase, "not much later than the [Vlastos] sphinx fragment."[131] Yet the strong Middle Protoattic (and Middle Protocorinthian) connections of this stand preclude its being the direct successor of the latest Mesogeia works, as proposed: the open field free of ornaments is not an immediate development from the close style of the Mesogeia Painter.[132] Given the manifest influence of the Polyphemus Painter, the stand testifies to his stylistic leadership and is not derived independently from other Early Protoattic painters.

130. Compare the ringed tail on the Chigi vase lion (Robertson, *Greek Painting*, p. 49); the net-pattern mane on ivory seals from Perachora (Payne and Dunbabin *Perachora II*, nos. A 30b, A 35b, A 40b, pls. 176–77). The owl is discussed above, n. 110.

131. Cook, *BSA* 35 (1934/35): 191, also called it "the earliest definitely recognizable mythological scene on any Attic, almost the earliest on any archaic Greek, work of art."

132. Cook, "Protoattici vasi," 502, connects the Argive stand with the Mesogeia Painter; cf. Brann, *Agora VIII*, pl. 26, for the close-style ornaments of the Mesogeia workshop.

4.3. The Checkerboard Painter

Outside of the distinctive personalities of the New York Nessos Painter and the Argive
Heraion artist, manifestations of the Wild Style are common but rarely reveal individual
or prolific artists. Nevertheless, such imitative works are important for the workshop
from Aigina, as they reveal the extent of its activity and its milieu.

A third conical stand in the Berlin collection from Aigina exemplifies the style
called "early" but in reality late (Pl. 18).[133] The main scene on the lower stand is an
enlargement of the Flowery Ornaments stand's minor scene: warriors fighting in sword
or spear engagements of two. They wear the same white helmet faces and black crest,
and carry the same "three-quarter" shield; all the "white" details are reserved, although
one greave is actually painted white. The ornaments surrounding them point to the
Polyphemus Painter; Cook went so far as to suggest that a younger Polyphemus Painter
made the stand.[134] Such an attribution, however, would be hard to reconcile with the
youthful personality of the painter, as identified in his earliest works (Pls. 1–5; above,
3.1). Furthermore, other motifs on this "early" stand point in different directions. The
row of sphinxes above the warriors, for example, are not identical to those by the Polyphemus Painter (Pl. 7): these have floating eyes, not attached "goggles," and a different
shape of head. The stand's torus molding is decorated with alternating light and dark
rosettes, their petals defined in contrasting paint (Pl. 18). This motif must have been
imitated from the Ram Jug Painter's stand from the Acropolis (Pl. 11: 370), which bears
a similar chain of rosettes below the torus molding, not on it. The rosettes on the Berlin
stand are not as fine, and resemble blobs between hasty versions of the neat separations
by the Ram Jug Painter; one assumes that the painter of the Berlin stand followed the
example of the Ram Jug Painter, but with less care. If the stand imitates rosettes by the
Ram Jug Painter, filling ornaments and a warrior type from the Polyphemus Painter, the
vase becomes a school piece of the workshop, produced around the middle of the seventh
century.

A surprise of this school piece is the goblin figure squatting between the legs of
a warrior and gesturing with an upraised thumb (Pl. 18). His ancestry is Oriental, not
Greek; such a figure is found in Elamite cylinder seals and Luristan bronzes, thus on
portable arts of the East which might have reached the Greek world.[135] Such Orientalizing
monsters appear even on minor pieces of this period: a hybrid amphora from Aigina
shows such a simian figure (munching fruit? Pl. 22, *right*; see below, 3.5). Thus the
stand displays Oriental motifs as well as those borrowed from the developed Black and

---

133. *CVA Berlin, 1*, A 40, p. 23, pls. 28–29; Kübler, *Kerameikos VI, 2*, 300.

134. Cook, "Protoattici vasi," 501 (Kübler, *Kerameikos VI, 2*, 305, objects).

135. Porada, *Ancient Iran*, p. 38, fig. 13; p. 48, fig. 23; p. 78, fig. 49; p. 88, n. 23, fig. 60; cf. *Artemis
Orthia*, pls. 9, 10 (above, 2.6, n. 66).

White style painters; such sources point to a later imitative piece rather than an early experiment. Its artist remains elusive; but among the remaining vessels in Berlin there **74** are more vivid examples of the Wild Style, which can be grouped under a single painter.

Two ovoid kraters and a lid were isolated as the work of the Checkerboard Painter when the Berlin collection was published (Pls. 19, 20).[136] His name celebrates the triple rows of black and reserved squares framing most of this painter's scenes, a persistent juxtaposition which epitomizes the Black and White style. The popularity of the checkerboard motif can be traced to Protocorinthian pottery but is rarely picked up by Attic painters outside of the vases from Aigina.[137] As usual, Middle Protocorinthian models with this motif are abundant on Aigina, suggesting that this painter's favorite motif is as diagnostic as the letters and dialect of the Menelas stand.[138] The Checkerboard Painter uses the motif in the same manner as on Protocorinthian vases: as a border either below or along narrative scenes.

Only one side of one krater by this painter has a mythological scene, and its inspiration is undoubtedly Protocorinthian. Between the handles on the front (?) of the krater a man fights a centaur, attacking from the right with a sword while the centaur, armed with a branch, grasps his opponent's chin in supplication (Pl. 19). The style is splashy, an exaggerated version of more refined Middle Protoattic work. The elongated body of the centaur reflects the ectomorphic type by the Polyphemus Painter (Pl. 4), with the same painter's boots (Pl. 7). The awkward paws of both man and centaur show a certain distance from more skillful models (e.g., Pls. 6, 7). The faces are equally eccentric: no ears were deemed necessary; the hero's eye is free floating, whereas the centaur's is enclosed like a goggle eye; the centaur has a shaggy beard to offset the smooth chin of his youthful aggressor. Even in this primitive version, it may be fair to read that deliberate differentiation between men and giants which is traditional to Greek art.

The man-and-centaur motif as portrayed by the Checkerboard Painter shows a particularly close relationship to the earliest versions in Greek art.[139] The theme first appears among Middle Protocorinthian artists, the same ones whose work may have inspired the New York Nessos Painter.[140]

On the reverse of this krater by the Checkerboard Painter, the entire field is filled

136. *CVA Berlin 1*, p. 7: A 21–A 23, pls. 10–14.

137. Kübler, *Kerameikos VI, 2*, 112, on the neglect of the checkerboard in Early Protoattic pottery; p. 346 on its popularity among the Wild Style painters but absence in the contemporary Kerameikos.

138. For examples of the checkerboard from Aigina, see Kraiker, *Aigina*, no. 254, pl. 17 (by the Head-in-Air Painter), no. 265, pl. 20 (by the Ajax Painter), no. 282, pl. 23 (by the Sacrifice Painter)—all painters whose influence reveals itself through other motifs (boar, shield interior, hairy centaur, owl).

139. For example, on stone and ivory seals: Boardman, *Island Gems*, 120 C 14; von Steuben, *Frühgriechische Sagendarstellungen*, 23–26 (ca. 700 B.C.?); Payne and Dunbabin, *Perachora II*, no. A 29, pl. 175.

140. Above, 4.1; von Steuben, *Frühgriechische Sagendarstellungen*, 24–25 (MPC oinochoe from Syracuse).

with the figure of a bull, an imitation of finer beasts by better painters (Pl. 19, *right*). The head belongs on a deer; it is dwarfed by the enormous body with its emphatic genitals, and one hoof is raised like that of a prancing lion. Under the krater's handles are animals in similar guise: the one to the left of the centaur is headless but presumably was a deer, judging by its short tail.

The ornaments on this krater are as wild as the animals: around the bull, for example, they are crowded into a row above his back, while a bird picks at the lozenge star below his belly. The motifs are clearly debased favorites of the Polyphemus Painter—black and white rosettes, multiple lozenges which have become a mass of trefoils, random squiggles derived from zigzags, and an occasional eccentricity such as the huge white hook with palmette, hanging behind the hero's head (Pl. 19).

The use of white on the krater is restricted to ornaments (rosettes); it is more abundant on another krater by the same painter, with an animal fight repeated on both sides (Pl. 20).[141] Lions attack a deer from behind, sinking paws into the hindquarters, jaws open. The animals in both scenes are black with white markings: white circles and dots for the deer, white face, paws, and muscles for the lions. This taste for white has spread to most of the ornaments in the field. For example, black lozenges are crossed in white, rosette petals are erratically filled with white. The lower half of the krater is covered with two broad bands devoted to black and white ornaments: a palmette chain and a band of rays with rosettes in between. Huge birds with tiny heads fill the area beneath the handles; small birds perch among the copious filling ornaments in the field.

This krater epitomizes the bold intentions and wild results of the Black and White style among the eccentric fringe, where exaggerations illustrate the principles of the tradition in a colorful manner. Typical is the affection for exotic flora and fauna, imperfectly understood: the attempt at a ruff behind the lion's head, the deer markings which have spread over the entire body, the extended lions' tongues of the deer, the deers' heads placed on bulls.

Other vases, chiefly from Aigina, belong to the same eccentric branch of the Black and White style. Attributions to the primary artist, the Checkerboard Painter, include a lid with a lion-and-deer scene whose details are diagnostic of the same hand (dotted lion's face, extended deer's tongue, and typical ornaments).[142]

Tentative attributions proposed in the first publication of the Berlin collection include two fragmentary ovoid kraters with extravagant black and white ornaments below animal scenes.[143] Other ovoid kraters from Aigina in Berlin belong to the Wild

---

141. *CVA Berlin 1*, A 22, p. 7, pls. 12, 13; Brein, *Der Hirsch*, 204–05.

142. *CVA Berlin 1*, A 23 (once East Berlin, now lost), p. 7, pl. 14:1; Brein, *Der Hirsch*, 205–06. Unfortunately the lid does not fit either krater by the Checkerboard Painter in the same collection, but it must be by his hand.

143. *CVA Berlin 1*, A 24 (once East Berlin, now lost), pl. 15; A 25, pl. 37:3; both "vielleicht anzuschliessen" (p. 7).

Style, although not necessarily to the same painter. One has a typical scene on the shoulder, a lion attacking a deer, with an interesting attempt at incision.[144] Another krater is missing most of its shape except the handle zone, with a bird underneath and an outline cable on the handle that both represent exaggerated versions of Checkerboard motifs.[145] These two kraters demonstrate how limited the Wild Style painters were in technique; perhaps they were potters who turned their skills to painting only on rare occasions.

A third ovoid krater in the Wild Style is devoted to ornament: a tall lyre chain linked by white triangles, over a band of large black dots in metopes.[146] Under the handles of this krater, or at least under the one preserved, is a representation of two black cauldrons on conical stands, complete with a torus molding; it compares to the more abstract cauldrons on the New York Nessos amphora (Pl. 15).

In addition to ovoid kraters and cauldrons on stands, the Wild Style painters also show an acquaintance with the amphora, the third of the three favorite shapes among the vases from Aigina (above, 2.3).[147] Other miscellaneous vessels from the same context demand consideration. For example, a standed bowl in Berlin looks at first glance to be a standard Early Protoattic product; but the thick brushwork and slight distortion of traditional style suggest it belongs among the wild versions of Middle Protoattic painting.[148]

Examples such as these illustrate the range of efforts from minor painters under the influence of leaders such as the Polyphemus Painter. Motifs isolated in the work of the Checkerboard Painter and his circle establish the Wild Style as an enthusiastic imitation of the mature Black and White style, not its antecedent.[149] The limits of the Wild Style, the distinctions between early and simply second-rate work, are not always easily recognized and have been as casually treated as the material. In their preoccu-

144. Ibid., A 26, pl. 16. Note how the line between the hindquarters runs into the line separating tail and back; the incised deltoid muscle meanders all over the shoulder; the deer's foreleg runs into his shoulder, then into the lion's paw and shoulder (Brein, *Der Hirsch*, 206).

145. *CVA Berlin 1*, A 27, p. 16:2.

146. Ibid., A 30, pl. 16:3.

147. In the first publication of the Berlin pottery, Eilmann and Gebauer grouped a number of eccentric amphorae under the rubric of the Painter of the Wild Amphoras: *CVA Berlin 1*, p. 7, nos. A 7 (once East Berlin, now lost) A 8 (to which one should probably add A 5 and A 6 [once East Berlin, now lost], pl. 3).

148. *CVA Berlin 1*, A 39, pl. 24:2–3; compare the standed bowls from the Analatos workshop, found in the Kerameikos, which must have served as prototypes (Kübler, *Kerameikos V, 1* [Berlin, 1954], pl. 126).

149. Both Brann (*Agora VIII*, 10–11, 20) and Cook ("Protoattici vasi," 500–01) date the Wild Style to the first quarter of the seventh century, to fill the gap between Early and Middle Protoattic. Only Brein, *Der Hirsch*, 204–06, arranged the Wild Style sensibly, dating the Checkerboard Painter slightly later than the Polyphemus Painter (ca. 660), the New York Nessos Painter after the Ram Jug (ca. 640 B.C.). For another example of the Wild Style, without provenance, see *CVA Cambridge 1*, III H, pls. 2, 7 (7/25): Cook *BSA* 35 (1934/35), p. 170; Kübler, *Kerameikos VI, 2*, p. 259.

pation with figured and fine vases of the Orientalizing period, scholars have neglected the less distinguished pottery, which can often reveal important connections among leading painters as well as regional affiliations.

5. ANONYMOUS ARTISTS FROM AIGINA

Outside the distinctive Black and White style vases, few of the remaining pieces from Aigina can be classified by painter. Many are poorly preserved or bear few figures and narrative scenes, their chief decoration being ornamental. Yet all three shapes favored by this workshop (above, 2.3) are represented, in a variety of styles ranging from Subgeometric to the Wild Style to the quality demonstrated among the major painters. As individual pieces, the miscellaneous vases from Aigina are insignificant; but together they demonstrate an active local industry rich in Orientalizing experiments. Focus on the vanguard of these artists has neglected less exciting works, the most persuasive evidence of local enterprise.

Most unusual among the anonymous vases from Aigina is a fragmentary standed bowl in Berlin, a miniature cauldron on a stand made in one piece, not unlike contemporary examples from the Kerameikos (Pl. 22, *above*).[150] Its vertical shaft has two friezes, the lower one larger, with figures, and the smaller, upper one decorated with animals— the same format used on other Protoattic stands from Aigina (Pls. 7–8, 11). The upper frieze alternates running deer with flying birds, without filling ornaments, and is closer to Protocorinthian than to Attic compositions.[151] The lower frieze has a circle of dancers on tiptoe, their uplifted hands linked as they move. The bowl of the vessel is barely preserved; only the hind leg of another running deer is visible.

This standed bowl is a curious mixture of Attic and Corinthian motifs and techniques. The birds, for example, have painted white dots on their backs, contrasting black dots on their reserved tails, and suggest the Black and White style proper; the dancers are silhouettes outlined by incision, with Attic incised tattoos and genitals but reserved heads with painted features and beards. The nearest relative of these figures is a dancer on an amphora found with the Ram Jug on Aigina, published as Protocorinthian

150. *CVA Berlin 1*, A 46, pl. 37:1–2; cf. Kübler, *Kerameikos VI, 2*, pls. 44–46, for parallels in shape from the Kerameikos.

151. Kübler, *Kerameikos VI, 2*, 224, 232, on the infrequency of the running deer and flying bird in Attic, as opposed to Corinthian (or Boeotian), vase painting; the exceptions appear, significantly, in this Black and White style workshop (the New York Nessos amphora, Berlin A 18, e.g.). For Protocorinthian flying birds, see examples from Aigina (Kraiker, *Aigina*, no. 339, pl. 26) and Perachora (Payne and Dunbabin, *Perachora II*, no. 185, pl. 16, and nos. 254, 261, pl. 15), or as a shield device (Matz, *Geschichte der griechischen Kunst*, pls. 151a, b and 152a).

and later as Argive (Pl. 22, *right*).[152] Its smooth yellow fabric with pink core might be mistaken for Corinthian, but never the style and the mixture of outline and silhouette techniques. The dancer's silhouette body outlined by incision, and his reserved face, recall figures on the standed bowl, as noted above; the lion on the belly of the amphora, with his dotted-scale mane and incised paws, has been called an "unsuccessful" synthesis of Attic and Corinthian lions.[153] The horse menaced by the lion is a similar hybrid, with reserved ladder mane appropriate to the grazing Attic horse but a springing forelock and incised halter from a Protocorinthian source. On the amphora's shoulder a painted chain of ornament recalls both the "Big Style" motifs of Protocorinthian pottery and the extravagant Middle Protoattic jungles; both classes of pottery are represented on Aigina, and this hybrid amphora synthesizes their ornament styles in an eccentric technique without white paint or incision. On a belly fragment a monkey holding a rattle perches among ornament tendrils, in the comic spirit of other Middle Protoattic creatures of Oriental inspiration (cf. Pls. 13, 18).

The amphora on Aigina and the standed bowl in Berlin are close enough in style to suggest the same painter, yet one is in Attic fabric and the other in a material which seems to be local. One could compare this evidence with the oeuvre of the Ram Jug Painter, who also potted Attic shapes in Attic clay for the necropolis of Aigina but produced a foreign shape, the Ram Jug, for the Kolonna sanctuary (above, 3.2). Thus at least two painters worked in more than one kind of fabric during the Middle Protoattic period, and potters on Aigina used material resources as varied as their sources of inspiration in painting.

Few other vases on Aigina are so distinctly Orientalizing in style. Most are fragmentary kraters, of the standard ovoid shape (above, 2.3), and often wearing a black collar around the rim. A conservative estimate of the fragments in Aigina and Berlin suggests at least fifty kraters once served as grave markers or offerings in the necropolis of Aigina in the early to mid-seventh century.[154] When compared with the large number of unstratified kotyle kraters from the Athenian Kerameikos (below, 6.3), the kraters from Aigina represent an equivalent in local funerary practise.

Two of these ovoid kraters in Berlin are fine enough to have suggested the work of the Ram Jug Painter to the editors of the *CVA* fascicle (Pl. 21).[155] One (A 33) was decorated, on the side best preserved, with two zones of marching hoplites moving in

152. Pallat, *AthMitt* 22 (1897): 308ff. (Protocorinthian); Kraiker, *Aigina*, no. 484, pp. 77–78 (imitation of Protocorinthian, under Attic influence); Cook, *BSA* 35 (1934/35): 191, n. 3 (Argive); Dunbabin, *Gnomon* (1953): 244 (Argive, following Payne, *Perachora I*, 32, n. 2, who cites Johansen, *Les Vases Sicyoniens*, 111).

153. Kübler, *Kerameikos VI, 2*, 265, n. 403, suggests a Corinthian potter in an Attic milieu to account for the hybrid style (he suggests a date of 670–660 B.C. for the amphora). Robertson, *JHS* 73 (1953): 185, questions the descriptions of the fabric and suggests a later (and more sensible) date, after the middle of the seventh century.

154. *CVA Berlin 1*, pl. 39, illustrates 36 krater sherds, in addition to more than a dozen analyzed individually in the fascicle and below, 3.6.3. *CVA Cambridge 1*, pl. 2, no. 7 (7/25), of the same class.

155. *CVA Berlin 1*, A 31, p. 7, pl. 18, and A 33, p. 7, pl. 17:2, both "possible late works"; Cook, *JHS* 59 (1939): 151, called these attributions "convincing."

two different directions. The hoplites resemble those on the Ram Jug Painter's bowl but are clearly the work of an admirer, judging from significant discrepancies. The krater hoplites are all black, rather than alternately white; they wear no greaves, their helmets lack the checkerboard crest-holder, and the shield is more accurately rendered. Not only is the shield clearly carried on the far side of the hoplites marching right, exposing the wickerwork interior, but both central strap and handgrip at the rim are appropriately placed. The shield interior, a patchwork of concentric hatched triangles, imitates Protocorinthian shields exactly (compare Pl. 24), in distinction to the cruciform shield interiors on the Kerameikos mugs (Pl. 26; below, 3.6.1). An amphora fragment from the Kolonna sanctuary on Aigina, found with the Ram Jug Painter's bowl, duplicates this Protocorinthian pattern in the scene of a hoplite triumphant over a fallen warrior (Pl. 11: 554).[156] The fallen warrior's shield reveals the same concentric triangles; the victor, facing left, carries a shield painted white that once bore a Protocorinthian device. The fragment suggests that the upper row of hoplites on the Berlin krater may have once featured similar shield devices (not enough is preserved to tell). Such a design, with stacked friezes of warriors, may be Oriental; Phoenician silver cauldrons, like the one from the Bernardini tomb in Etruria, are decorated with such superimposed warrior friezes.[157] Thus even anonymous works from Aigina reveal that debt to the Orient which identifies the island workshop.

The reverse of the hoplites krater shows a sprawling animal fight of two lions over an unidentified victim. The type of lion (with dotted muzzle and heavily incised paws) has been compared to other Aiginetan lions; the fight is an imitation of finer scenes, expanded to cover the wall of a krater.[158] Thus on both sides, as well as in the ornament zones (enlarged step-pattern, spiral rays), the krater participates in the absorption of Attic, Corinthian, and Oriental motifs which characterizes the workshop from Aigina. Even its fabric is probably local, as the editors of the *CVA* fascicle acknowledged when they classified it in their third group of fabrics.[159]

The other krater attributed to the Ram Jug Painter (Pl. 21, *right*) is preserved only in one side; it glorifies the stuffed and dotted-leaf palmette, whose resemblance to the rosette by the Ram Jug Painter (Pl. 12) must have inspired the attribution. Again, fabric and shape distinguish it from the Ram Jug Painter's other works, as does the concept of a vase entirely devoted to ornament.[160] This krater, however, is important in connecting

156. Kraiker, *Aigina*, 86, no. 554, pl. 42, probably found at Kolonna by Furtwängler (above, 1.2).

157. Phoenician bowl: Montelius, *La civilization primitive*, pl. 367:4 (line drawing).

158. Kübler, *Kerameikos VI, 2*, 262, compares lions by the Ram Jug Painter (Pl. 12), the Polyphemus Painter (Pls. 3, 7), and in the Wild Style (Pls. 17–21).

159. *CVA Berlin 1*, p. 6, for a description of the green clay, yellow surface, and pink slip (not a true added white but an iron-based slip); R. Young, *AJA* 43 (1939): 714, pointed out the discrepancy between clay groups and attributions.

160. Young, *AJA* 43 (1939): 714, discussing the fabric groups presented in *CVA Berlin 1*, pp. 5–7; cf. above, 2.2.

80   the Aigina hoard in Berlin to a provenance on the island, as a fragment is still in the Aigina Museum (cf. above, 1.2). The fragment preserves the end of a tendril with palmette, in a size which excludes it from belonging to the side of the vase preserved in Berlin, and suggests that the missing reverse side bore a similar ornamental decoration. Flanking the large palmette were two water birds (only one is preserved) with long legs, a type found on kraters attributed to the Ram Jug Painter (Pl. 13; below, 3.6.2). Within the oeuvre defined in this study there are no birds except for the "swallow" on the Acropolis sherd (Pl. 11, unnumbered fragment) by the hand of the Ram Jug Painter. Although the quality of brushwork on this krater rivals that of the Ram Jug Painter, the vase is simply not by his hand but by another artist from Aigina.

Both water birds and palmette are derived from Early Protoattic motifs, transformed in the manner typical of the Middle Protoattic Aiginetan workshop.[161] The earliest vessels from Aigina in the Berlin collection, and the last imports to the island before the late seventh century, are from the Analatos workshop, including two hydriae with figural processions on their necks.[162] Middle Protoattic kraters from Aigina, such as one with palmette chain and wire birds, reflect the works of the Analatos Painter found on Aigina, suggesting that island painters were inspired by imports.[163] Another ornamental krater in Berlin, preserved only in rim and foot, had ornament panels on the shoulder: one bore a palmette tendril recalling the one by the Ram Jug Painter (Pl. 12, *left*), but the neighboring panel shows a reserved cable in a dark field, in a technique closer to red figure than to outline style.[164] In addition to reservation and silhouette painting, this krater was also decorated with white paint: a white line circles the vase below the joint of shoulder and rim. The main motif, on the belly, must have been a huge volute ornament with palmette (only a corner is preserved). On the basis of these few ornaments, Kübler assigned this fragmentary krater to his second group of ornament style (above, 1.3), while admitting that it belongs among variants not duplicated in the Kerameikos.[165] Were more of the krater preserved, or related pieces extant, one could venture some comparisons with the ornament style of the Kynosarges amphora (the focus of Kübler's second group) and explore a possible connection between the Aigina vases and the Kynosarges workshop.

Other kraters are less progressive but mark the origins of the Wild Style on Aigina. An eccentric krater, dated early by Kübler, suggests this link.[166] Its single figure, a bull

---

161. For the palmette with dotted petals, see the Louvre amphora by the Analatos Painter (*CVA Louvre 18*, pl. 30: CA 1960) and the reverse of the Analatos hydria itself (Cook, *BSA* 35 [1934/35], pl. 38b); cf. above, 2.5, for a summary of Middle Protoattic transformations of earlier motifs.

162. *CVA Berlin 1*, A 1, pl. 1, and A 2, p. 15, fig. 2.

163. *CVA Berlin 1*, A 68, pl. 38:2; cf. Kraiker, *Aigina*, no. 540, p. 84, pl. 40, by the Analatos Painter.

164. *CVA Berlin 1*, A 28, pl. 38:1 (cf. Kraiker, *Aigina*, no. 590, pl. 41, for a lid which might fit the krater).

165. Kübler, *Kerameikos VI, 2*, 336, n. 2.

166. *CVA Berlin 1*, A 18, pl. 8:2; dated around 660 B.C. by Kübler, *Kerameikos VI, 2*, 226.

surrounded by careless versions of conventional ornaments, offers an attractive antecedent to the bull scene by the Checkerboard Painter (Pl. 19, *right*), with the same exaggerated genitals and stringy tail. The white circle for the bull's eye on the anonymous krater suggests an early substitute for reservation, as practised by the Polyphemus Painter (Pl. 1). The enormous spiral hooks around the belly zone, filled with white, are a more developed sign of the Black and White style. If this is the earliest krater from the Checkerboard Circle, it proves how early the Polyphemus Painter was admired.

Conveniently juxtaposed with this early Checkerboard krater is an ovoid krater which heralds the Subgeometric style popular on Aigina.[167] On the shoulder a horse race is represented, both riders leaning forward with one hand at the reins and the other whipping their horse's hindquarters; the belly has a frieze of grazing horses. Both scenes are executed in an expanded Geometric style with enormous filling ornaments, which does not belong in the eighth century yet shows less innovation than true Orientalizing efforts of the Protoattic period. This anachronism, presumably, forced Kübler to date the krater before 700 B.C., but its style should be considered with care. The persistence of the Geometric tradition is a vital component of the seventh century, and a number of pieces from Aigina represent such a Subgeometric style.[168] Many are diminutive and decorated with typical debased versions of Late Geometric and Early Protoattic motifs.[169] The examples of this Subgeometric class now in Berlin are too fragmentary for close dating or identification of artists. Details such as painted white spots on a lion (A 57) or painted white ribs on an ornament (A 77) distinguish a few in technique, but most would be classified as "plain, probably Middle Protoattic." A few have been classified as "Boeotian," including a krater foot in Aigina which matches a sherd in Berlin.[170] The Aigina fragment preserves a single grazing horse (or deer) on a panel from a stand with open-worked slots; the elongated animal and overgrown floral ornaments connect it to the specific fragment in Berlin cited above, but also to the wider group of Subgeometric kraters. Less diagnostic contributions from Aigina which supplement the Subgeometric kraters in Berlin include rims, lids, and feet of kraters, many from Welter's necropolis

167. *CVA Berlin 1*, A 16, pl. 8:1.

168. Kübler, *Kerameikos VI, 2*, p. 37, n. 44, p. 48, n. 88, for the date of A 16 (720–710 B.C.); on the Subgeometric tendencies of the seventh century, see Burr, *Hesperia 2* (1933): 626, 631; R. Carpenter, "The Greek Alphabet Again," *AJA* 42 (1938): 61, on the "Geometric Overlap"; Young, *Late Geometric Graves*, pp. 195, 197, 212–13, on Protocorinthian Subgeometric; Payne and Dunbabin, *Perachora II*, pp. 8–9.

169. *CVA Berlin 1*, A 17, pl. 9: 1, with running dogs derived from the Athens 897 workshop (cf. Kraiker, *Aigina*, nos. 52, 53, pl. 3, and Cook, *BSA* 42 [1947]: 146, for examples of the Athens 897 workshop from Aigina) and Late Geometric leaf motifs; A 19, pl. 9:4, with early Protoattic birds and stuffed palmettes; A 20, pl. 9:2, with a single horse and two series of loops; A 67, pl. 1, a shabby version of the latest Geometric style; A 72, pl. 37:4, with a traditional deer motif updated by incision (dated by Kübler, *Kerameikos VI, 2*, 224, to 670–660 B.C.).

170. Kraiker, *Aigina*, no. 64, p. 30, pl. 4, from the Iriotou sounding (sherd labeled "10.3.29"; cf. above, 1.2, p. 7; cf. *CVA Berlin 1*, pl. 39, no. 25 (A 69).

82 soundings.[171] Others were once classified as "Argive," for lack of reasonable Attic parallels, and are still of disputed origin.[172] The classification of these and other fragments from Aigina, as early as the Geometric period, will be best evaluated with the publication of the new Geometric pottery from Kolonna. For the moment, the number of anomalous Geometric and seventh-century sherds from Aigina, which do not fit into the known typologies of neighboring states, reinforces the evidence for local manufacture.

Next to these examples, eccentric in style and size, conditions of fabric distinguish a separate class of Aiginetan krateriskoi in Berlin, still unpublished; they were isolated from the Protoattic finds in the same collection and are currently under study for a *CVA* publication.[173] Color (pale buff, firing from green to gray to pink), texture (coarser than Corinthian, almost sandy in feel), and careless manufacture separate them from standard Attic and Corinthian pottery.[174] Their diminutive size (they average from 0.15 to 0.25 m in height, none exceeding 0.30 m) makes them imitations of the larger kraters, hence to be classified as "krateriskoi." Technically these are not "miniatures" like the tiny Corinthian replicas of kraters, hydriae, and kotylae but simply smaller vessels for a modest burial or an infant's grave.

In style the fragments of krateriskoi suggest a hasty Subgeometric decoration with little variety: banded foot, ray-based lower body, and bands around the belly, with isolated motifs only on the shoulder (loops, spiral hooks, or even a Laconian pomegranate net).[175] Confusion arises in the resemblance of these Aiginetan krateriskoi to the Subgeometric kraters from Aigina discussed above. For example, what distinguishes a krater only 0.28 m in height, decorated with bands, loops, and a single figure (a horse) in the handle zone, of a fabric classified with the local krateriskoi, from those imitations?[176] Does such a vessel belong among the largest of the local imitations or the smallest of the Attic imports? The forthcoming publication of the local krateriskoi may re-evaluate those kraters from Aigina which are uncomfortably close in size and style, if not in fabric, to those in local fabric.[177]

171. Kraiker, *Aigina*, no. 573, pl. 41 (from "Pyrg. 29"); no. 574, pl. 41 (a lid from "Ir. 29"); no. 579, pl. 41 (openwork foot); no. 591, pl. 41 (lid, from "Pyrg. 29"). Cf. above, 1.2, on the exploration of the necropolis.

172. Courbin, *Céramique géométrique de l'Argolide*, 552, nn. 1–2, rejects more than 10 of the 14 sherds from Aigina which Kraiker, *Aigina*, nos. 66–89, called "Argive."

173. *CVA Berlin 1*, pp. 5–6; cf. above, 1.3. The Protocorinthian and local material is currently being prepared for publication by Christiane Dehl, and is mentioned here with her kind permission.

174. For a description of this fabric see *CVA Berlin 1*, p. 5; Kraiker, *Aigina*, 77 (nos. 484–96).

175. Compare other Subgeometric vessels with a similar banded body and a curvilinear motif in the handle zone: Brann, *Agora VIII*, 88, no. 499, pl. 31, with references to similar Subgeometric vessels from Ithaca (or Argos: cf. J. Deshayes, *Argos: Les Fouilles de la Deiras* [1966], 214–19, xxiv, xxxi, lvi).

176. *CVA Berlin 1*, A 20, pl. 9: 2, p. 6, for a description of its fabric.

177. Half a dozen candidates in this category were published in the *CVA* fascicle, some even dated to the late eighth century (by Kübler), but most belong to the seventh century and should be compared with the local imitations: A 12 through A 15 (Kübler, *Kerameikos VI, 2*, 45, 116, for the early date on A 12); A 37 and A 38 (attributed to the Mesogeia Painter by Cook, *JHS* 59 [1939]: 151).

Fabric distinguishes several pieces in Berlin published as "Attic"; they exhibit a peculiar, thick, sulfur-yellow slip, unlike even an abnormal result in the firing of Attic clay. The hoplites krater once attributed to the Ram Jug Painter, for example (Pl. 21, *right*), and other fragments in Berlin, display this curious color of slip.[178]

Beyond the Black and White style, seventh-century Aigina thus produced an impressive variety of fine wares which should no longer be classified as imports. All the personalities characteristic of Orientalizing Greece can be recognized: progressive innovators, craftsmen faithful to the Geometric tradition now centuries old, prolific imitators on a more modest scale, even a few mischievous ones, and perhaps potters who turned their hand to painting on a spontaneous and humorous occasion. Much activity was inspired by a stream of imports, not only pottery from Athens and Corinth but more exotic trinkets from farther abroad (below, 4.1).

As a corpus of pottery from the Orientalizing period, the evidence from Aigina compares to that from other sites which imported Attic or Corinthian pottery and responded with local efforts of their own (for example, Megara Hyblaea in Sicily, Ithaca, Euboea).[179] What distinguishes Aigina from other Orientalizing sites is the high quality of its Black and White style. In other periods and other art forms, Aiginetan artists were renowned; in this century of ceramics Aigina actually outranked Athens, and with the help of history (below, chapter 4) this imbalance finds a cause.

6. ATHENIAN PAINTERS

The vivid personalities of the Aiginetan painters have been extended to many Athenian vase painters of the Middle Protoattic period, by scholars eager to synthesize the Black and White style. The Ram Jug Painter, especially, attracted more attributions than he deserves; the Polyphemus Painter was traced to a specific Early Protoattic workshop in one scholar's analysis.[180] Disagreements in attribution are to be expected in scholarship on vase painting; but here, reattribution serves to define the borders of the Aigina workshop and to separate what is Athenian in Middle Protoattic from what was produced on Aigina. Kübler's classification by groups initiated this process (above, 1.3) by isolating

---

178. Fragments of peculiar fabric from Aigina, as noted by this author in Berlin: *CVA Berlin 1*, A 61 (pl. 39), A 71 (p. 29, fig. 5), A 75, A 78, A 80, and A 88 (pl. 39).

179. On Megara Hyblaea, see G. Vallet and Fr. Villard, *Megara Hyblaea II*, 190–99, and Tréziny, *MEFR* 91 (1979): 7–12; for Ithaca, M. Robertson, *BSA* 43 (1948): 60f.; on Eretrian Orientalizing, see J. Boardman, *BSA* 47 (1952): 1–48 (20–30 on local Orientalizing); for local Corinthian on Corcyra: Dontas, *Hesperia* 37 (1968). Local Corinthian fabrics are summarized by Payne, *Necrocorinthia*, 181–209.

180. For criticism of this characterization, by Brann, see reviews by Cook, *Gnomon* 34 (1962): 822–23; Coldstream, *JHS* 82 (1962): 217.

the mainstream tradition from a provincial but influential style. Middle Protoattic painting
from Athens exhibits a new personality, once separated from that on Aigina, and deserves
84   an exclusive analysis, if only to emphasize what sets it apart from Aigina.

6.1. The Kerameikos Mugs Group

At the time of Cook's first article on Protoattic pottery in 1935, three vases from an
offering channel in the Kerameikos had been publicized: two mugs (Pl. 26) and a lidded
pyxis.[181] In total, the offering channel produced the richest hoard of Protoattic pottery
retrieved from a single burial. Five mugs, four pyxis lids and one pyxis bowl, and two
standed bowls were decorated in the mixture of outline and silhouette, incision and
added white which distinguishes the Black and White style.[182] Several other vases—a
kotyle, three oinochae, and the only Protoattic plate extant—were executed in an avant-
garde technique anticipating black figure a full generation before the style took over
Athens.[183] In this case, the Protocorinthian influence which glares from the "black
figure" pieces is inadequately matched by the scanty Protocorinthian sherds (a plain
pyxis and a battered aryballos) from the same burial.[184] With the Centaurs krater by the
Oresteia Painter (Pl. 14) crowning the mound associated with the offering channel, this
single burial, dated around 660 B.C., documents all the circumstances of the Black and
White style.

It was only natural for scholars to associate the exquisite painting on many of
these pieces with artists like the Ram Jug Painter.[185] But the contents of the Kerameikos
offering channel are distinct not only from the Ram Jug Painter's work but from his
whole workshop. Both groups carry on Attic Geometric traditions and pick up new ideas
from Corinth, but the results are not the same.

The shapes in the Kerameikos group—Late Geometric kantharos, Early Protoattic
pyxis—are traditional ones of modest size, while the grave markers from Aigina—Geometric amphora and ovoid krater—are conservative and large. The mugs and pyxides
are enlivened by plastic decoration which qualifies as sculpture: figures of mourning
women on the handles of the mugs, for example. Although the Ram Jug Painter can

---

181. Kübler, *AA* 49 (1934): 211, figs. 9–11; H. Payne, "Archaeology in Greece, 1933–1934," *JHS* 54
(1934), pl. 10:2; Cook, *BSA* 35 (1934/35): 189, n. 5.

182. Kübler, *Kerameikos VI, 1*, 18–21, for a description of the burial and its contents.

183. Payne's reaction to this extraordinary early imitation of Corinthian technique in *JHS* 54 (1934): 188.

184. Kübler, *Kerameikos VI, 1*, 20, with full references on these two pieces, illustrated on pls. 60, 67; cf.
above, chap. 1, n. 82; 2.8.

185. Cook cited as a connecting piece the sphinx sherd by the Oresteia Painter: *BSA* 35 (1934/35): 189, n.
5; Brann went on to identify the early Ram Jug Painter himself among the Kerameikos offering channel vases: *Agora
VIII*, 6, 11, 21, 23. Coldstream, and eventually Cook himself, expressed reservations about Brann's judgment; in the
words of Coldstream (*JHS* 84 [1964]: 217) "for the time being it might be wiser to treat the Mug Painter as a separate
hand, since we have nothing to bridge the gap between his somewhat finicky style and the broader, more assured
drawing of mature Ram Jug work"; cf. Cook, *Gnomon* 34 (1962): 822.

imitate bronze vessels (e.g., Pl. 12, *right*), he is primarily a painter and does not branch out into the production of plastic attachments.

The subjects on the Kerameikos vessels are also Geometric and funerary: mourning women at a bier, chariot races appropriate to funeral games, but never scenes from myth or epic, which appear exclusively on the vases associated with Aigina (above, 2.6). Finally, the delicate style of the mugs and pyxides is appropriate to the small, elegant shapes—vessels for placing inside graves but not for marking a burial like the "monuments" found on Aigina. Details also isolate the Kerameikos vases from the Ram Jug Painter and his colleagues. Shield interiors on the Kerameikos mugs appear as a cruciform pattern, in contrast to the Protocorinthian formula practised on vases from Aigina (Pl. 11: 554). The composition of battle scenes reveals different degrees of Protocorinthian influence. Vases from Aigina (Pls. 7, 8, 18, 21) repeat a typical Protocorinthian format: a symmetrical group of four warriors fighting over a fifth, arranged on an axis with the handle. A Protocorinthian oinochoe from Samos similar in shape to the Ram Jug (above, n. 58) illustrates the formula, with a duel on one side of the vase and a group of four (probably fighting over a fallen warrior) opposite the handle, at the vase's focal point.[186] The Ram Jug itself follows this design, with the central figure of Odysseus opposite the handle (Pl. 10). The Kerameikos mug with the warriors, however, presents the composition of four warriors fighting over a fifth on the face to the right of the handle, not opposite it.

The mugs and pyxides have lavish ornamentation, their lower portions entirely devoted to such decoration. In the figural scenes themselves there is a greater quantity and variety of filling ornament, stuffed with imagination and delight into every available space. In contrast, the vases from Aigina left open space in figural scenes, especially those under Protocorinthian influence (Pls. 11, 21).

In addition to these internal details that separate the Kerameikos vessels from the Ram Jug Painter, and from Aigina in general, other vases from Athens provide an Athenian home for the small vessels. A pyxis lid with chariot races from the Agora helps fill out the development of the lidded pyxis between the two offering channels in the Kerameikos.[187] A rim with male figures moving left is surely by the Painter of the Kerameikos Mugs; it was published as an amphora neck but clearly comes from a similar mug.[188] A third candidate from the Agora is a spouted bowl rim with bearded men in

186. For other Protocorinthian examples, see the MacMillan aryballos (Matz, *Geschichte der griechischen Kunst*, pl. 151a) or the Louvre aryballos by the Boston Painter (Matz, pl. 152a); Kübler, *Kerameikos VI, 2*, 208–12; Lorimer, *BSA* 42 (1947): 98–104.

187. Brann, *Agora VIII*, 11, 81, no. 440, pl. 26, "close to and perhaps by the Painter of the Kerameikos Mug Group."

188. Ibid., p. 81, no. 441, pls. 27, 44: "neck fragment of amphora, Early Protoattic." The diameter of the fragment must have been closer to 0.14 m (as the catalogue card indicates) than 0.18 m (as published), a size closer to the mugs, which range from 0.13 to 0.15 m in diameter (Kübler, *Kerameikos VI, 2*, nos. 20–24, pp. 428–35). Note also that the bearded men move *left* on the Agora fragment, an unusual direction in this period but one taken by the female mourners on the Kerameikos mug.

procession (only two heads are preserved), to be attributed to the artist of the Kerameikos pyxis with chariots.[189]

86   On the strength of these examples from the Agora, a krater rim from the Acropolis attributed to the Ram Jug Painter can be associated with the "miniature" workshop represented in the Kerameikos and the Agora (Pl. 11: 368).[190] Although the human profiles on these smaller vases recall figures on the larger vessels from Aigina, one cannot identify a painter by combining large and small vases, as Brann and Cook attempted.[191] To link the delicate style of these Athenian sherds to the same hands responsible for the large grave markers is a violation of workshop boundaries. Although the Aigina vases derive Black and White technique, ornaments, and subjects from Athenian tradition, they incorporate foreign elements and embody a new style.

6.2. The Pernice Painter

Another Athenian vase incorporated through scholarship into the oeuvre of the Ram Jug Painter is a large bell krater with sphinxes, found in Athens in the same decade when the Ram Jug was discovered (above, 1.3).[192] The krater is shaped like the one in Munich by the Analatos Painter, rare in the Middle Protoattic period.[193] The upper zone has a continuous frieze of marching sphinxes with narrow, elegant bodies, dotted scale wings, and oversize heads on tall necks. Below it is a frieze of feeding deer (interrupted by the handles) with lowered heads and graceful bodies. The lower krater is decorated with a band of black and reserved leaves above spiral hooks ending in palmettes.

The ornaments seem identical to those by the Ram Jug Painter: spiral hooks, dotted triangles, single row of zigzags as pendants, lozenges, dot rosettes, meander square in the field, and a band of black and white leaves. A fair number do not appear in his works—the dotted circle and the stacked zigzag—although they are common enough on vases by the Oresteia Painter (Pls. 13, 14). Furthermore, a close examination of the sphinx profiles, which at first recall the faces on the Ram Jug, reveals a significant distance in style. The

189. Brann, *Agora VIII*, pp. 11, 21, 23, 92, no. 537, pl. 33, attributed to the Painter of the Kerameikos Mug Group.

190. Graef and Langlotz, *Vasen von der Akropolis*, 368; Cook, *BSA* 35 (1934/35): 192, n. 3; Karouzou, *ArkhEph* (1952), pl. 9:3.

191. Brann, *Agora VIII*, 5, 11, 21, 23; Cook, *Gnomon* 34 (1962): 822, "Protoattici vasi," 501.

192. In the 1930s Cook hesitated to make an attribution on the basis of the Gilliéron drawing, but Eilmann identified it as the earliest work of the Ram Jug Painter, approved by Karouzou, Brann, and even Cook: *CVA Berlin 1*, p. 7, no. 1 (Cook, *JHS* 59 (1939): 151: "clearly . . . correctly assigned"); Karouzou, *ArkhEph* (1952): 149ff.; Brann, *Agora VIII*, 92 (under nos. 538, 539, 541).

193. Cook, *BSA* 35 (1934/35): 173, pl. 41, attributed the Munich krater to the Analatos Painter; Karouzou, *ArkhEph* (1952): 150, n. 2, cites fuller references for the shape. No complete examples are known outside these two, but there may be some candidates among the undiagnostic rims in the Agora (Brann, *Agora VIII*, nos. 420, 421, pl. 26) or unpublished stray finds from the Kerameikos.

sphinxes have a small neat nose, an eye with a horizontal lower lid placed directly behind the bridge of the nose, not at an angle slightly below it. The ear is less exaggerated a stylization and sits correctly near the level of the eye, not down near the mouth (as on the face of Peleus: Pl. 12). The ancestors of these sphinxes belong to the Analatos workshop, without a trace of Protocorinthian influences.[194] The style of the animals, too, is difficult to reconcile with those in the Ram Jug Painter's bestiary, with their large outline heads. The elegant heads on the Pernice krater compare with the deer by the Polyphemus Painter on the Munich krater (Pl. 3). The bold intersection of animal heads and limbs among the deer on the Pernice krater is not an arrangement favored by the Ram Jug Painter; it presumes an ease with incision that he never acquired (note the problems on the Hoplites bowl, Pl. 11: 584, 585). There is a remote possibility that this krater is a late work by the Ram Jug Painter, presuming a lacuna in the evidence for the transition toward such elegance. As the early work it has been called in scholarship it makes little sense, and related works from Athens suggest, instead, a Pernice Painter.

Several sphinx fragments from the Agora, originally attributed to the Ram Jug Painter through the Pernice krater, can now be associated with an independent Pernice Painter.[195] Even closer in style, and in context, is a fragment with pendent dotted triangle and the top of a sphinxlike head from the Dipylon cemetery, now in the Netherlands.[196] Finally, a fragment from the Peiraieus offers a similar dotted-scale wing, dot rosette, and pendent dotted triangle.[197] Although not all these sphinx fragments are necessarily by the same artist, they document a taste for sphinxes in an elegant outline style that does not spell the Ram Jug Painter but promises other fine Middle Protoattic painters in Athens. The finest and latest of these mid-century sphinxes are on the Agora oinochoe attributed to the late career of the Ram Jug Painter.[198] The oinochoe is an epitome of many Middle Protoattic developments, including some practised by the Ram Jug Painter, but they are by no means exclusive to him. The neck ornament, for example, is similar but not identical to the one on the Peleus amphora (Pl. 12) and is merely common for the period. Nor is the central ornament on the oinochoe, between the sphinxes, sufficient grounds for attribution. A fragment included in the final publication of the oinochoe from the neck of the amphora bears an ornament more appropriate to the Polyphemus Painter than to the Ram Jug Painter, suggesting a painter somewhere in between their styles. The profiles of the sphinxes

194. Early Protoattic sphinxes: *CVA Louvre 18*, pl. 33:1–2; *CVA Mainz 1*, pl. 21; Protocorinthian sphinxes: Kübler, *Kerameikos VI, 2*, 92, 249, 385.

195. Brann, *Agora VIII*, 292, nos. 538, 539, 541, pl. 33.

196. *CVA Musée Scheurleer 2 (Pays Bas 2)*, pl. 4, no. 6 (inv. 2006).

197. I. Threpsiades, *Praktika* (1935): 183, fig. 16, from the Koumoundouros hill investigations (cited by Brann, *Hesperia* 30 [1961]: 309, n. 15).

198. Young, *Late Geometric Graves*, p. 108, B1, fig. 120; Brann, *Agora VIII*, no. 53 = no. 543, pp. 5, 11, 22–23, 37, 93, pls. 4, 33, 44.

88

are considerably more advanced than even on the Pernice krater, with a small re-
troussé nose instead of the Ram Jug Painter's hook, a neat ear and small eye sensibly
placed, and an exaggerated long, slender neck with room for two triple-ring necklaces.
The lavish incision on the wings shows great progress over the engraving experiments
in the Ram Jug Painter's work; the Agora sphinxes have black figure wings, or at least
in a Kynosarges stage of black figure.[199] If this is the latest and finest work by the
Ram Jug Painter, the lacuna in his extant oeuvre is serious. Given a rich context for
the Agora oinochoe within Athenian development, one cannot neglect an Athenian artist in order to add to the Ram Jug Painter's fame.

6.3. The Kerameikos Kotyle Kraters

The heraldic scheme of the sphinxes on the Agora oinochoe is also unlike that of the
Ram Jug Painter and rare on the vases from Aigina, but it is popular in Athens. The
Burgon krater in the British Museum has a similar heraldic scheme of facing lions and
has also been taken for the work of the Ram Jug Painter.[200]

The shape of the Burgon krater, a well-articulated kotyle krater, is the hallmark of a
leading Middle Protoattic workshop associated with the Kerameikos. At least seventy-three
such kraters have been identified from fragments in the Kerameikos, mostly stray finds,
attesting to this vessel's popularity as a grave marker in the main Athenian cemetery.[201]

Several distinguished hands can be identified among the kotyle krater sherds from
Athens. In particular, three kraters from the Kerameikos plus a fragment from the
Acropolis represent an Athenian Black and White style master who worked into the
period of added red (Pl. 27).[202] The kraters present familiar subjects—black and white

199. Compare the wings of the horses on the Kynosarges amphora (*CVA Athènes, Musée National 2 (Grèce
2)*, pl. 4:4 (Athens NM 14497).

200. British Museum 1842.7—28.827; the vase has no provenance beyond the information "Athens 1813"
found on the vase itself. As one of the earliest known Attic Orientalizing vases, it figures in early scholarship like
Samuel Birch's *History of Ancient Pottery* (London, 1858), 184. Kübler, *Altattische Malerei*, juxtaposes the Ram Jug
Painter's dinos (pl. 16) and the Burgon krater (pl. 17), an association often made. Cook first declared it "closely
connected with the Ram Jug in ornament and the use of thin white lines on the varnish" but "less advanced": *BSA*
35 (1934/35): 193–94. When the *CVA* publication of the Aigina hoard in Berlin outlined the oeuvre of the Ram Jug
Painter, it included the Burgon krater, giving Cook some second thoughts: *CVA Berlin 1*, p. 7, no. 8; cf. Cook, *JHS*
59 (1939): 152. His view, that the Burgon krater is a more advanced piece by a follower of the Ram Jug Painter,
has been shared by some but not all scholars. Karouzou and Mylonas retained the attribution (though citing Cook's
objection quoted above), but most scholars, like Kübler and Matz, admit that it belongs after the lion dinos in Berlin
by the Ram Jug Painter: Karouzou, *ArkhEph* (1952): 164–65, n. 1; Mylonas, *O protoattikos amphoreus*, 59,107, n.
3; Kübler, *Kerameikos VI, 2*, 260–61; Matz, *Geschichte der griechischen Kunst*, 317.

201. Ten Middle Protoattic examples are published in Kübler, *Kerameikos VI, 2*, 156–59; 63 other fragments
from surface contexts were catalogued (pp. 515–40).

202. Kübler, *Kerameikos VI, 2*, pls. 82–84 (inv. 151), 85 (inv. 99), 86 (inv. 130); *CVA Scheurleer 2 (Pays
Bas 2)*, pl. 4:4; Cook, *BSA* 35 (1934/35): 193, n. 6 (Scheurleer fragment), n. 7 (Kerameikos lions krater); Brann,
Agora VIII, 92, no. 541, attributes the birds krater from the Kerameikos to the Ram Jug Painter, calling it "the finest
work" among Middle Protoattic bird vases.

lions, horses, and birds—in traditional arrangements, in the brushwork of a master who never used incision. None of his kraters, however, are from a context contemporary with their date of manufacture, which is especially unfortunate given this painter's influence on the Polyphemus Painter (above, 3.1).

6.4. Middle Protoattic Athens

Among other miscellaneous products of Middle Protoattic Athens, several attributed to the Ram Jug Painter should be eliminated from his oeuvre. Two pitchers with lions, one from the Agora and another in the National Museum of Athens, have been associated with him by virtue of being distinctive, but Brann herself admits that all these "lion pots" could represent a different painter.[203] The fact that the same lion vase can be called both his earliest and his latest work by different scholars suggests a dubious association, at best.[204] Other lion fragments, such as two rims from the Agora, are simply too small for convincing attribution.[205] Several pieces from the Agora with quotations from Ram Jug Painter motifs are standard school pieces from Middle Protoattic Athens, on which his style has no exclusive claim.[206] Finally, the intriguing pair of dice from the Acropolis attributed to the Ram Jug Painter by Karouzou would be an attractive addition to his personality, but they show little stylistic affinity to his work.[207]

Reflections of the Wild Style as well as of the leading painters from Aigina are manifest in Middle Protoattic Athens.[208] A common attribution to the Checkerboard Painter is a collar-necked krater with a departing warrior scene, formerly in Schliemann's possession and now in the National Museum of Athens.[209] Despite its equally provincial

203. Brann, *Agora VIII*, 309 (Karouzou, *ArkhEph* [1952]: 166, nos. 1, 2, pl. 8:2); the lion olpe from the Agora: Brann, *Agora VIII*, 93, no. 544, pl. 33.

204. Compare Karouzou, *ArkhEph* (1952): 165–66, where the earliest work is the same lion olpe that Brann, *Agora VIII*, 93 (no. 544), calls late.

205. Brann, *Agora VIII*, 92–93, nos. 542a, b, pl. 33; other anonymous lion fragments in Karouzou's list (*ArkhEph* [1952]: 166, nos. 1, 2, 5).

206. Pieces from the Agora attributed by Brann, *Agora VIII*, pl. 33, on the basis of parallels that no longer qualify as the work of the Ram Jug Painter (listed under nos. 540, 541, pp. 11, 23, 92).

207. S. Karouzou, "Der Erfinder des Würfels: das älteste griechische mythische Porträt," *AthMitt* 88 (1973): 55–65.

208. An amphora neck with a black and white lyre motif, a twin of the same motif on one of the ovoid kraters in Berlin: Brann, *Agora VIII*, no. 468, p. 84, pl. 28. Two other fragments of large vases from the Agora with animal scenes are more difficult to place than in a general manner, as "oversized Middle Protoattic": Brann, no. 451, p. 82, pl. 27; no. 471, p. 84, pl. 28; no. 473, p. 84, pl. 28. Other fragments from the Agora, attributed to the Checkerboard Painter himself, are simply not his thick brushwork but a thin spidery hand with different ornaments, complicated by added red that heralds a new phase: Brann, no. 411, pp. 20, 77, pls. 24, 44 (classified as Early Protoattic, but the style is at least Middle Protoattic and the purplish red even later). *CVA Cambridge 1*, III H, pl. 2:7 (7/25) could be Aiginetan ("said to have been acquired at Athens").

209. Still referred to by the name of the former owner, the shape is variously called amphora, krater, or stamnos, and published as a pithos: *CVA Athènes, Musée National 2 (Grèce 2)*, pls. 1, 2 (NM 17762); attributed to the Checkerboard Painter by Cook, "Protoattici vasi," 501.

flavor, and even the checkered frame which borders the scene on the Schliemann krater, it is not the work of the Checkerboard Painter.[210] It appears that although the Schliemann **90** krater shows an equivalent distance from an established style, it cannot be classified with the Wild Style vases from Aigina; it illustrates a separate moment of experiment on the Attic "road to black figure."

Other examples from Athens illustrate a Middle Protoattic "provincial" style whose province is not Aigina. Related to the Schliemann vase is an amphora from the Agora, also with a departure scene.[211] Its ornaments and frieze with grazing horses resemble details of vases from Aigina, but it could represent another reflection of the same inspiration. Likewise, an amphora from the northern extension of the Kerameikos recalls the Wild Style of Aigina but again shows a notable lack of white.[212]

Examples such as these illustrate the range of efforts from minor painters in Athens under the influence of leaders such as the Polyphemus Painter. They contribute to a rich picture of Middle Protoattic Athenian work, with a full variety contemporary with the Aiginetan Black and White style. During the middle of the seventh century, ceramic craftsmen in Athens were experimenting with monumental and miniature, polychrome and black and white, plastic figures and allusions to metal vessels. The loss to Aigina of what was once the major creation in Protoattic painting, as a result of reattributions in this monograph, should not undermine the rich resources of Athens, where the origins of black figure still reside.

210. The shape is an anomaly, and the conservative potters of the Aiginetan vases did not experiment with new shapes (above, 2.3). Nor is the subject, a warrior's departure, one that captured the fancy of the Wild Style painters. As for ornaments, the forest on the back of the Schliemann vase, although a generous selection of Middle Protoattic flora and fauna, is not the work of the Checkerboard Painter. Finally, there is not a trace of white paint on the Schliemann vase; instead, its artist used plentiful, if crude, incision.

211. Brann, *Hesperia* 30 (1961), pl. 7, H1.

212. See above, chap. 1, n. 48, for publication reference. The vase was published as a hydria, but as Kübler, *Kerameikos VI, 2*, 150, n. 5, points out, it has only two handle roots and must be an amphora. The main scene, a frieze of crouching sphinxes, is a magnified version of earlier sphinx types, grotesque at this scale; the heroic attempts to reproduce the human face, a new challenge, and to use incision, a new technique, suffer when magnified. The combination of ornaments recalls the Polyphemus Painter; trefoil, meander square, four-dot eight-point rosette, lozenge, and zigzag are the same motifs imitated by the Checkerboard Painter at an equivalent distance from the original.

CHAPTER 4

HISTORY AND THE ROLE
OF AIGINA

The Polyphemus Painter . . . was an Aeginetan, or at least he worked on Aegina. There is a suspicion that his antecedents are not to be sought among the finer exponents of Attic painting but rather in the neighborhood of the Mesogeia Painter . . . by way of the Aeginetan Black and White School.[1]

Brann did not provide details on the association with Aigina: was the Polyphemus Painter simply a native of Aigina who worked in Athens, an émigré to the island, or does he represent a school of painting resident on Aigina? Other scholars have considered the association between Aigina and Middle Protoattic pottery in a variety of scenarios, as the review of scholarship in 1.3 recalled.[2] Among the solutions, Vanderpool's presumes conditions similar to those in the contemporary Corinthian industry. Foreign craftsmen were attracted to the employment opportunities of a larger city, such as Athens or Corinth, where they trained as potters and worked in a homogeneous style but occasionally signed in their native dialect.[3] This would explain the internal contradiction of non-Corinthian dipinti on vases in a consistent Protocorinthian style. In Athens, the quantity of foreign signatures in the archaic period and the testimonia on Solon, who is said to have encouraged foreign craftsmen to settle in Athens to practise their trade (Plutarch, *Solon* 12), suggest the same situation. This phenomenon may have begun in the late seventh century, according to the evidence of a Corinthian painter who moved to Athens, or at least made "Corinthian" pots

1. Brann, *Agora VIII*, 24. For the Aiginetan Black and White school, Brann cited vases in Berlin, "especially the Painter of the Flowery Ornaments" (now identified as the Polyphemus Painter: Brann, p. 24, n. 111; above, 3.1).

2. Either Aiginetans worked for mainland workshops (according to Rumpf, Vanderpool, and Boardman), the Menelas stand was designed for a customer on Aigina (Kübler), or the inscription reflects the prototype of a monumental painting with Doric labels (Schefold). Figueira, *Aegina*, 250, n. 40, suggests Aeginetan slaves, sold abroad, account for Aiginetan letters on Attic and Corinthian pots. Only Brann imagined a "branch workshop" on Aigina, but she did not expand her almost casual remarks on this phenomenon. Cf. Williams, *AA* 1983, p. 184, for Aiginetan inscriptions on Chiote pottery.

3. Vanderpool, *AJP* 74 (1953): 322; Payne, *Necrocorinthia*, 38–39.

in Attic fabric.[4] The Nettos Painter himself, judging by his handwriting, may have been a foreigner who settled in Athens for the purpose of trade.[5] If one can assume that this situation began as early as two generations before Solon, it would neatly explain the "foreign" elements in Middle Protoattic pottery, a period when Dunbabin expected antecedents for his Corinthian émigré painter. However, such a solution would leave unexplained the export to Aigina, after manufacture, of the pottery produced in Athens—by natives of Aigina? In other words, the hypothesis of resident foreign potters in Athens would not explain the exclusive distribution of the finest Middle Protoattic pottery on Aigina. Nor do historical grounds suggest there was anything to attract a foreigner to Athens in the seventh century, a period of economic depression (below, 4.2); Vanderpool's solution thus presumes social and economic conditions which do not exist in Athens until a generation later.

Kübler's solution, that Athenian craftsmen wrote in letters and dialect to suit island customers or even commissions, presumes the same sophisticated industry oriented to export, for which there is simply no evidence in mid-seventh-century Athens.[6] Nor does Kübler account for the style of the workshop where the problem dipinto was executed, a style which he himself admits is non-Athenian, "provincial," or even "island Greek" without allowing Aigina to be the province or island responsible (above, 1.3).

Thus neither of the first two solutions—Aiginetans resident in Athens or Athenians producing for natives of Aigina—accounts for all the evidence assembled in this study. The third explanation, that the "Menelas" inscription was copied from a Doric painting, presumes the existence of monumental paintings in Greece in the middle of the seventh century, a hypothesis which has been questioned elsewhere (above, 2.4). Therefore, none of the proposed scenarios satisfies all the circumstances of the evidence, and the simplest solution—a local Aiginetan workshop—deserves a new trial.

1. EARLY AIGINA

A scholiast to Pindar's third *Nemean* (line 21), written in honor of an athlete from Aigina, quotes a fragment of Hesiod describing the people of Aigina, which ends:

οἳ δή τοι πρῶτον τεῦξαν νέας ἀμφιελίσσας,
πρῶτοι δ' ἱστία θέσαν νεὼς πτέρα ποντοπόροιο.[7]

This tribute to the seafaring skills of the islanders was famous; at least, it was quoted at another Pindaric line (*Olympian* 8.26) in another ode for a victorious Aiginetan.

4. Dunbabin, *BSA* 45 (1950).
5. A. Boegehold, *AJA* 66 (1962): 405–06.
6. Kübler, *Kerameikos VI, 2,* 328, n. 92.
7. Hesiod, fragment 205 (Merkelbach-West).

An unusual compliment from Hesiod the farmer, a most reluctant sailor, it is an impressive measure of the naval reputation Aigina had acquired by the early seventh century.[8]

Literary reflections of this reputation are most ornate in the odes of Pindar, who wrote more victory odes for Aiginetans than for any other Greeks. Either Aigina entered more athletes, trained them better, won more often, or simply could afford the best singer, all of which presume prosperity. Pindar's praises often dwell on the islanders' renown as sailors and hosts, suggesting a lively port town thronged with crew and cargo of ships.[9]

Less attractive was the impression of Aigina upon Athens across the bay, from where the island dominates the Saronic Gulf all too visibly. During the hostility between Athens and Aigina in the fifth century, the island became the "eyesore of Peiraieus" in the immortal expression of Pericles.[10] The traditional enmity between the two cities lasted until the island was defeated and subjected to an Athenian cleruchy in 431 B.C. Until this settlement, the threat of Aigina and her ships was great enough for Themistocles to persuade Athens to build a navy with an excess in state revenues.[11]

This prominence in seamanship determined the history of the island, and with it the Saronic Gulf, for some 250 years. The origins of this life-style lay in the island's limited natural resources, as both ancient and modern comments acknowledge.[12] Unlike other small, barren islands, of which Greece claims thousands, Aigina was surrounded by active mainland cities. Neighbors such as Athens and the cities of Euboea initiated early adventures abroad, according to the exports of pottery to the Near East (Crete,

---

8. Hesiod, *Works and Days* 618–22, for his aversion to sailing. For a detailed investigation of ancient sources on Aiginetan thalassocracy, see Figueira, *Aegina*, chaps. 3–4.

9. Twelve victory odes by Pindar are addressed to Aiginetans (*Olympian* 8, *Pythian* 8, *Nemean* 3–8, and *Isthmian* 5–6, 8–9), and two choral hymns (*Paeans* 6, 15). Pindar's descriptions include:

(*Nemean* 3.2–3): τὰν πολυξείναν . . . / . . . Δωρίδα νᾶσον Αἴγιναν·

(*Nemean* 5.8–9): . . . φίλαν ξένων ἄρουραν·

        . . . εὔανδρόν τε καὶ ναυσικλυτάν

(*Isthmian* 6.70): . . . καὶ ξένων εὐεργεσίαις ἀγαπᾶται,

(*Isthmian* 9.1–2): . . . κλεινὰ δὲ καὶ ναυ/σικλυτὸς Αἴγινα· . . .

(*Isthmian* 9.5–6): οὐ θέμιν οὐδὲ δίκαν

        ξείνων ὑπερβαίνοντες·

For other Aiginetan passages in Pindar, with commentary, see Figueira, *Aegina*, 168, 311–15.

10. Quoted by Aristotle, *Rhetoric* 3.10.7d (1411a), and Plutarch, *Pericles* 8.5.

11. Cleruchy: Thucydides 2.27; Athenian navy: Herodotus 7.144 (Aristotle, *Ath. Pol.* 22.7; Plutarch, *Themistocles* 4).

12. Ephorus *apud* Strabo 8.6.16 (= Jacoby FGH 70); cf. Eustathius's "The very poverty of her soil made Aigina famous," as quoted by Charles Cockerell in his excellent "History of Aegina," chap. 1 in his *The Temples of Jupiter Panhellenius at Aegina and of Apollo Epicurius at Bassae near Phigalia in Arcadia* (London, 1860). Figueira calculates that the island "could only support ca. 4000 at subsistence" (*Aegina*, 22), but in classical times 25–30,000 may have lived there (p. 41).

Asia Minor, Cyprus, and the Levant) and the West (Etruria and Sicily).[13] These early signs of contact do not last into the seventh century, for reasons which will be examined below (4.3); for whatever caused the decline of Attic and Euboean activity, it left a vacuum in the world of exploring and trading which Aigina eagerly filled, even adopting the alphabet in a form close to those used by Athens and Euboea.[14] According to the evidence of epichoric writing, Aigina was participating in commercial activity with her northern Saronic neighbors by the early archaic period, although her associations in dialect and cult indicate the island was settled from the Argolid, as Strabo records.[15]

A variety of sources agree on an early archaic date for the emergence of Aigina as independent, prosperous, and at sea. Herodotus speaks with admiration of the wealth of Sostratos, a merchant of Aigina known as the richest entrepreneur of his day (4.152). In the sixth century, Aigina is the only state near mainland Greece mentioned in Herodotus's account of Naukratis, the trading station in Egypt settled mainly by East Greek states (2.178). When Xerxes crossed the Hellespont in his invasion of Greece in 480 B.C., he intercepted ships on their way back from the Black Sea shores with grain for Aigina and the Peloponnese (7.147). Thus in Herodotus alone there is evidence for the island's commercial interest in distant markets of the archaic Greek world.

As the first homeland state to mint silver coins and establish a standard of exchange, Aigina must have accumulated wealth, and silver itself, in the form of state revenues, not just private profit.[16] A recent review of Greek numismatic chronology proposes to restore an early date for Aiginetan coinage, which would contribute to the picture of wealth in seventh-century Aigina.[17] A second major exchange commodity seems to have been slaves: Aristotle credits Aigina with the incredible number of 470,000 slaves, a population that the island could never support.[18] All efforts to emend the figure to a more likely population are reduced to an alternative interpretation: that the figure represents the volume of slaves bought, sold, or kidnapped by enterprising Aiginetans, but not necessarily permanent residents of the island.

Within Greece, Aigina developed a special status in commercial relationships. Dependent on timber from high inland forests for shipbuilding, Aigina established a

---

13. On Greek Geometric pottery overseas, see Coldstream, *Geometric Greece*, 55–58 on Athens and Lefkandi, 191f. on Euboea; Boardman, *The Greeks Overseas*, 39–48, 162–68; M. Popham and L. H. Sackett, *Lefkandi I: The Iron Age* (London: British School at Athens, 1980), 355–69, on the activity of Euboea; Diane (Daniela) Saltz, "Greek Geometric Pottery in the East: The Chronological Implications" (diss., Harvard University 1978). Greek pottery in the West: Boardman, *The Greeks Overseas*, 36–38, 44–46.

14. Jeffery, *Local Scripts*, 109–10 (cf. above, 2.7); Figueira, *Aegina*, chap. 4.

15. Ephorus *apud* Strabo (8.8.16) says the island was settled in succession by Argives, Cretans, Epidaurians, and Dorians; Figueira, *Aegina*, chap. 3, B; Buck, "Epidaurians, Aeginetans, and Athenians."

16. C. Kraay, *Archaic and Classical Greek Coins* (London, 1976), 41–49; Figueira, *Aegina*, chap. 2.

17. Kagan, *AJA* 86 (1982).

18. Aristotle, fragment 472 (Rose) *apud* Athenaeus 6.272d, confirmed by a scholiast to Pindar (*Olympian* 8.30); Figueira, *Aegina*, 211–13.

special arrangement with well-forested but landlocked Arcadia, bringing exotic goods (including fish) upland from the port of Kyllene by mule, to ensure a good return in timber.[19] In the eastern Peloponnese, Aigina may have played a similar role for Argos, supplying its citizens with foreign luxuries and sea transport in exchange for military aid (below, 4.3). It has even been suggested that Aiginetan commerce sponsored, if involuntarily, the rise of an Athenian aristocracy in a period culminating in the social inequality which challenged Solon.[20] The tradition attested in Pherecydes which associates the Philaids with the Aiakid dynasty of Aigina suggests a family background appropriate to the Athenian family prominent in early archon lists and distant trade.[21]

Together with the ancient references to Ἀιγινητικά, small trinkets circulated by Aiginetan merchants (above, 2.2), these literary sources make Aigina an important and prosperous carrier of merchandise in the archaic period. This consistent impression of wealth based in trade is substantiated by the archaeological evidence.

Prosperity begins at home, with evidence for contact in the form of archaeological imports to the island. The city sanctuary of Apollo at Kolonna, above the harbor, and the Aphaia sanctuary, remote from the town but the first landfall for ships arriving from the East, both provide evidence of a rich variety of imports.[22]

The pottery in particular reflects the special position of Aigina, surrounded by mainland centers of production, as a comparative chart demonstrates.[23] Argos was the earliest to dominate in imports, appropriate to the role the city played in the island's earliest history (above, n. 15). Corinthian imports appear next, in the ninth century, a period when the Middle Geometric export of pottery from Corinth begins elsewhere, too.[24] Athens plays the role for the longest time, from the eighth to the second centuries, in the history of imports, although the proposed reattribution of the Middle Protoattic

19. Pausanias 8.5.8; Figueira, *CP* 76 (1981): 3, n. 16; Buck, "Epidaurians, Aiginetans, and Athenians," 6, 12. The Arcadian obsession with the sea surfaces in art (fish and ship motifs in the Geometric period: Coldstream, *Geometric Greece*, 156–57) and in cult (Odysseus must have planted his oar there: J. Svoronos, "Ulysse chez les Arcadiens," *Gazette Archéologique* 13 [1888]: 257–80; cf. the number of Odysseus cults mentioned by Pausanias in book 8). The only two coins found at the peak sanctuary on Mount Lykaion in the heart of Arcadia are Aiginetan: K. Kourouniotis *ArkhEph* (1904), 166, 169–70, fig. 5.

20. According to Figueira, "Aegina and Athens," 238–40, the system of enslaving debtors in Attica, coinciding with the growth of the slave market on Aigina, reflects an arrangement to the mutual advantage of ambitious Athenians and Aiginetans.

21. Jacoby, FGH 20, quoted by Marcellinus in his *Life of Thucydides* (2) to show the pedigree of the historian, "φιλαῖος δὲ ὁ Αἴαντος οἰκεῖ ἐν Ἀθήναις," implies that a descendant of Ajax settled in Attica and founded the line prominent in Athenian politics. The two archons named Miltiades in the seventh century B.C. (G. Huxley, "The Date of Pherecydes of Athens," *GRBS* 14 [1973]: 137–43) are fitting ancestors for the Miltiades who explored the Black Sea for profit (Herodotus 6.39–40, 140).

22. Above, 1.2 (excavations); miscellaneous antiquities reported by Welter in his "Aeginetica" series: *AA* 53 (1938): 1–38, 480–540; *AA* 69 (1954): 28–48.

23. Welter, *Aigina*, 129; Kraiker, *Aigina*, for complete publication with comments on imports by Dunbabin, *Gnomon* 25 (1953): 244, and Robertson, *JHS* 73 (1953): 185.

24. Coldstream, *Geometric Greece*, 85.

Black and White style to local workshops reduces the evidence from the seventh century. Other notable imports to Aigina include the splendid Cycladic jug (above, 1.2, n. 18); more distant places such as Rhodes are represented by East Greek bird bowls at both sanctuaries, accompanied by local imitations of the bowls.[25] Other East Greek imports include terracotta figurines such as "Aphrodite" balsamaria and animals, in numbers far exceeding those found on the Athenian Acropolis.[26] Chiote pottery is particularly abundant at the Aphaia sanctuary: fifteen chalices found by Furtwängler have now been increased by recent finds in the Ohly campaigns to over 400 fragments.[27] Many of the cup shapes carry painted dedications in East Ionic letters which illuminate the social and economic circumstances of Aiginetans in the sixth century. Seventy-two kantharoi were double dedications by two Aiginetans, Aristophantos and Damonidas, and the verb form, ἀνέθεταν, is a Doric dual appropriate to Aigina. Aristophantos also dedicated a marble base at the harbor of Aigina and four vases at Naukratis, including two Chiote kantharoi with dipinti.[28] Another wealthy Aiginetan who financed dedications, including Chiote pottery at Naukratis and possibly a monument at Aphaia, was Sostratos, perhaps the same trader active in Italy whose ancestor impressed Herodotus (4.152).[29]

Where the Chiote vases found at Aigina and Naukratis were produced is still an unsettled question. The most recent view favors Chios itself, but the Aiginetan connection with Naukratis makes it more attractive that sixth-century merchants commissioned dedications at Naukratis, if one can accept the theory of a Chian workshop at Naukratis, working with imported clay.[30]

Other artifacts from Aigina point to the Egyptian connection, notably faience objects from both sanctuaries as well as from tombs in the town.[31] These faience objects—figurines of musicians, Egyptian gods, and animals; vessels such as aryballoi in the shape of human heads; and the more common scarabs and pendants—were once assumed to be of genuine Egyptian manufacture and imported from Naukratis, where a

25. Kraiker, *Aigina*, nos. 103–05 (from the necropolis); Pallat, *AthMitt* 22 (1897): 272, fig. 7 (from Kolonna); recent Rhodian finds from Kolonna: *Deltion* 25 (1970), pl. 107d, f.

26. Furtwängler, *Aphaia*, 379–81, pl. 110; cf. the largely handmade terracottas from archaic Athens: Higgins, *Greek Terracottas*, 42–45 (the infrequency of East Greek terracottas on the Acropolis has been noted by R. V. Nicholls, according to a personal communication by Jamie Uhlenbrock).

27. Furtwängler, *Aphaia*, 455–56, pl. 129:2; Ohly and Schwandner, *AA* 86 (1971): 522–26, figs. 11–12; D. Williams, *AA* (1982): 67–68, fig. 6, and *AA* (1983): 155–86.

28. Williams, *AA* (1983): 184, nn. 48–54; R. M. Cook and A. G. Woodhead, *BSA* 47 (1952): 159–70.

29. Williams, *AA* (1983): 185, nn. 61–63; Boardman, *The Greeks Overseas*, pp. 122–24, fig. 139. On Sostratos in Italy, see below, nn. 55–56.

30. Williams, *AA* (1983): 181–82 (Chios); Boardman, *BSA* 51 (1956): 55–62 (Naukratis), and *The Greeks Overseas*, pp. 123–24; other locales proposed in scholarship and reviewed by Williams include Thasos and Erythrae.

31. Furtwängler, *Aphaia*, pls. 108, 118; Pendlebury, *Aegyptiaca*, nos. 278–86 (from Kolonna); U. Köhler *AthMitt* 4 (1879): 366–68, and Webb, *Archaic Greek Faience*, nos. 398, 412, 456, 800, 888, 923–924 (faience from Aigina in Europe, plus 13 from Aphaia); *Deltion* 19:B (1964): 74–79, pl. 77, for figurines from a recently salvaged tomb.

faience scarab factory was discovered in the nineteenth century.[32] More recently, a faience workshop in operation on Rhodes, before the foundation of Naukratis, has been identified.[33] The consequent process of distinguishing true Egyptian from Egyptianizing artifacts is still in progress; according to one estimate, over half the faience objects from Aigina are Greek imitations rather than Egyptian imports.[34] The distinction carries implications for chronology as well as provenance, since the factory on Rhodes was producing in the seventh century, before Naukratis was established. An additional consideration is whence Aigina acquired these faience objects: Rhodes, Egypt, or both? Given the presence of Rhodian imports on the island (above, n. 25) and such factors as the Rhodian influence on the Ram Jug Painter (above, 3.2), the earlier Egyptianizing imports could represent contact with Rhodes, rather than with Egypt. Thus even when the exact origin—Greek or Egyptian—of faience objects from Aigina is established, it may be most prudent to include them as evidence for both Egyptian and East Greek imports.

From farther east are imports to Aigina from Cyprus; they include white painted and bichrome pottery found at both sanctuaries, and terracotta figurines and jewelry from the Aphaia site.[35] Again, however, the source is ambiguous: Gjerstad suggests these objects reached Aigina via the island of Rhodes, a heavy importer of Cypriote material.[36] A similar reservation should be applied to Near Eastern imports to Aigina, such as tridacna shells and North Syrian seals, distributed from the Levantine coast. *Tridacna squamosa*, a species native to the Red and Indian seas, produces scoop-shaped shells which were decorated with incised floral and figural designs by craftsmen in Syria or Phoenicia; the shells, perhaps used for cosmetics, are found at East Greek sites and at Naukratis, but Aigina is the only homeland site where these exotic trinkets turned up.[37] Seals of several different types are found on Aigina, including archaic Greek "island gems" and the North Syrian stone scaraboids known as Lyre Player seals.[38] This last group was made in North Syria or Cilicia in the late eighth century and probably introduced to Greece by the Euboeans, who also took them west; as usual they are rare in Greece except on Aigina. Minor trinkets of the same Oriental provenance are Phoenician

32. W. M. F. Petrie, *Naukratis* (London, 1886), 1: 5, 36–37, 40; Webb, *Archaic Greek Faience*, 1–4.

33. Webb, *Archaic Greek Faience*, 5–10.

34. These figures were shared with me by Nancy Skon, a specialist on Egyptian(izing) objects in Greek contexts who has demonstrated both generosity with her research and patience with my ignorance.

35. Cypriote pottery from Aphaia: Furtwängler, *Aphaia*, pl. 120, no. 102, pl. 127, no. 4; from Kolonna: Aigina Museum inv. 1360 (Gjerstad, *Swedish Cyprus Expedition*, IV: 2, 269, n. 1); *Deltion* 25 (1970), pl. 107, e. Cypriote terracottas: Furtwängler, *Aphaia*, 378–79, fig. 309, pl. 110:1, with the promise of "noch bessere grössere Stücke" from Kolonna (478). Cypriote jewelry: fibulae (Furtwängler, *Aphaia*, pl. 116, nos. 25, 25a) and spiral earring (Furtwängler, *Aphaia*, pl. 116, no. 50).

36. Gjerstad, *Swedish Cyprus Expedition*, IV:2, 464–65, 470 (Boardman, *The Greeks Overseas*, 77).

37. Furtwängler, *Aphaia*, 427–30; tridacna shells discussed by Boardman, *The Greeks Overseas*, 71, and by R. A. Stucky, *Engraved Tridacna Shells*, Dedalo 19 (Sao Paulo, 1974).

38. Greek seals: Boardman, *Island Gems*, nos. 7, 76, and 270 from Aigina; G. Buchner and J. Boardman, *JdI* 81 (1966); cf. Furtwängler, *Aphaia*, pl. 118:2–6, 25.

glazed vases, an occasional find on Aigina.[39] Whether all these imports reflect direct contact with the Levant or simply with an intermediate port (again, Rhodes?) is debatable; but Aigina was at least the main market for them at home, and probably the most successful importer.

In addition to these Oriental imports, one should cite local versions of them as reproduced by Aiginetans. For example, terracotta plaques of a Daedalic fertility goddess, based on an Eastern type, were dedicated at both sanctuaries on Aigina as mold-mates from an identical form.[40] Cylinder seals, so characteristically Near Eastern but rarely imitated in Greece, appear in native versions on Aigina.[41] Imitations of Rhodian pottery were cited above (n. 25). Finally, the allusions to Oriental motifs in the local Black and White style (above, 2.6) complete the evidence of local exposure to Eastern novelties.

Imports to Aigina suggest that the island participated in a network of trading which spanned the Aegean and provided mainland Greece with foreign specialties. The list of trinkets, however, represents only a minor aspect of a larger transport industry in major commodities. Precious metals, grain (wheat and barley), linen and wool, and papyrus were the products which rewarded long sea voyages, and Aigina seems to have monopolized the supply of such commodities to the mainland for a time.[42] These perishable or convertible items cannot be documented in their imported form of raw material but should be emphasized as the chief cargo in profitable trade, the source of the wealth that sponsored successful athletes and lavish building programs.

A final symbolic dedication to Aphaia belongs here: a large ivory eye of the type that adorned ships' prows.[43] The exotic material is an import to Greece in any form; as a votive version of an actual ship's eye it is as appropriate a dedication for a rich merchant as the anchor of Sostratos (below, n. 55).

Most of the imports assembled here belong to the sixth century rather than to the seventh. But the literary sources indicate activity beginning in the seventh century, while the sixth-century manifestations such as coinage, architecture, sculpture, and athletics suggest wealth accumulated over a longer period of time. A contribution to the evidence for early prosperity has emerged in recent investigations in the harbor of Aigina: a

39. Boardman, *The Greeks Overseas*, 71, n. 142.

40. Stais, *ArkhEph* (1895), pl. 12 (Kolonna), and Furtwängler, *Aphaia*, 384, pl. 111:2–3; cf. Higgins, *Greek Terracottas*, 24, 49 (interpreted as local, ca. 660 B.C.).

41. Boardman, *Island Gems*, 77 (no. 334), 135 (no. K1).

42. M. M. Austin, *Greece and Egypt in the Archaic Age* (1970), 35f.; Boardman, *The Greeks Overseas*, 129; Figueira, *Aegina*, chap. 4.

43. Furtwängler, *Aphaia*, 426, fig. 333, found in 1811 inside the temple by Cockerell, who thought he had found "the eye of Jupiter" (according to his daybook entry, cited by Furtwängler). On votive ships' eyes, all other examples of which are in marble, see Chr. Saatsoglou-Paliadeli, "Marmarinoi ophthalmoi apo ton Peiraia," *ArkhEph* (1978): 119–35.

massive built breakwater has been identified as an installation of the seventh or sixth century, contemporary with the alleged prosperity of sea trade.[44]

In tracing complementary evidence for Aiginetan enterprise, found outside the island, one can begin by suggesting her role in imports to the Saronic Gulf. Oriental imports to Athens, such as Chiote chalices or Egyptian faience, could reflect distribution through Aigina.[45] The sanctuary of Apollo at Sounion, at the southeastern tip of Attica, would have been the first landfall for any Saronic ship returning from an Eastern trade voyage; for Aigina, especially, Sounion could have played the same role that Perachora did for Corinth. The early votives piously buried when the sanctuary underwent classical renovations are best known for the fragments of the spectacular marble kouroi.[46] Smaller objects from the same context have been neglected but represent an important selection of early and Eastern material. They include forty-eight faience scarabs and figurines, of both Greek and Egyptian manufacture, jewelry of gold, silver, and glass paste, island gems and sea pebbles worked into gem forms, miniature and full-sized weapons and tools, and curios such as a North Syrian storm-god figurine.[47] The context pottery is predominantly Corinthian rather than Attic, including some thirty painted votive plaques as well as pointed and spherical aryballoi and plastic vases.

These finds are unusual for early archaic Attica, at least when compared with Athens itself. Egyptian (or Egyptianizing) finds in particular are scarce in Athens: only two scarabs are known, two unguent jars from the Agora, and a single Egyptian bronze from the Acropolis—nowhere near the usual quantity of scarabs and figurines one would expect, given contemporary finds at Perachora, Sounion, and the Argive Heraion.[48]

44. Knoblauch, *BonnJbb* 169 (1969); *Deltion* 27:A (1972); Figueira, *Aegina*, 189–91.

45. Brann, *Agora VIII*, 105–06, pl. 41, nos. 653–56, which reached Athens "probably via Aigina" (Boardman, *BSA* 51 [1956]: 59–60).

46. For the excavations and dedications from the bothros in the Athena sanctuary and two pits near the Poseidon temple site, see Stais, *Praktika* (1897): 16–18; *ArkhEph* (1900): 112–50; *Praktika* (1907): 102–04; *ArkhEph* (1917): 178–97. For the kouros fragments from two pits, B. Ridgway, *The Archaic Style in Greek Sculpture* (Princeton, 1977), 52.

47. Hanfmann, *Hesperia* 31 (1962), the first appreciation of the riches among smaller votives, until the selective studies of gems by Boardman (*Island Gems*, 123–27, on the "Sunium Group") and the faience figurines in Webb, *Archaic Greek Faience* (nos. 483–84).

48. Three scarabs from the Agora: *Hesperia* 29 (1960): 406, no. 8, pl. 89 (G 198); no. G 124 and MC 147 from undated contexts are noted but not described or illustrated; the two unguent jars: Brann, *Agora VIII*, 58, nos. 236–37, pl. 13. Add a faience falcon amulet from the Agora: *Hesperia* 27 (1958): 151, pl. 42f (= Webb, *Archaic Greek Faience*, no. 509) and a fragment of a "pilgrim flask" from the north slope of the Acropolis: *Hesperia* 7 (1938): 187, 252 (Webb, *Archaic Greek Faience*, 70–71). Egyptian/Egyptianizing material of the eighth century is more plentiful (e.g., Coldstream, *Geometric Greece*, 349, nn. 1, 2; 361, n. 7), and even the Harpokrates figurine from the Acropolis could be eighth century (A. de Ridder, *Catalogue des bronzes trouvés sur l'Acropole d'Athènes* [Paris, 1896], 280, fig. 269, no. 756), according to Boardman, *The Greeks Overseas*, 112–13. The tantalizing graffito which could read ΨΑΜΑΤΙΧΟΣ should also be included here (Brann, *Agora VIII*, 54, no. 194, pl. 10; Cook, *Gnomon* 34 (1962): 823; Boardman, *The Greeks Overseas*, 142, n. 114).

Although no direct comparisons can be made between the types of Orientalia dedicated at Sounion and those which made their way to Aigina, the Sounion sanctuary belongs to **100** the cultural landscape of the Greek islands, as has been suggested from the evidence of gems and sculptures.[49] As in the Early Helladic period, it seems the east coast of Attica was more readily exposed to Eastern and Cycladic influences. The legend of the pirates from Crete who left Demeter at Thorikos and the variety of foreign imports at Brauron suggest that trade routes initiated by the Euboeans continued to be active in the early archaic period, possibly in the hands of Aigina.[50] In the Saronic Gulf, at least, the tradition of the Kalaureian Amphictyony seems to reflect a trade league of the southern Argolid and the Saronic islands, and Orientalizing imports dedicated at the sanctuary of Poseidon on Kalaureia speak for the success of such a league in the seventh century.[51]

How formal a monopoly Aigina enjoyed in the Saronic Gulf cannot be demonstrated, but both literary sources and the archaeological picture from the island and her neighbors are persuasive.

To trace the foreign evidence which complements imports and wealth in Greece is a more tentative process. First, it must be recognized that the island, poor in resources, had no major export item but functioned as a carrier for other Greek products. As a market for mainland states, Aigina transported their products abroad as well as brought foreign commodities to Greeks. Attic and Corinthian pottery, either the vessels themselves for their quality or as containers of Attic olive oil and Corinthian perfume, might have been the main cargo of ships from Aigina headed for foreign ports. Thus a combination of Attic and Corinthian pottery at a foreign site where history suggests Aigina had an interest may well be a means of recognizing the passage of an Aiginetan merchant.

An ideal case is Naukratis, which provides all three categories of evidence: a historical reference to the presence of Aiginetans, imported Attic and Corinthian pottery, and reciprocal Naukratite objects in Aigina. Athens and Corinth had no recorded trading interests in Egypt in the late seventh century; Attic pottery of this period found at Naukratis reflects the recovery of Athenian wares to a level worth export by Aiginetan

49. Recent interpretations of the Sounion kouroi as products under Naxian influence and appropriate to the Cycladic cult of Apollo: Ridgway, *Archaic Style*, 52–53, 71–72; J. Pedley, "Cycladic Influence in the Sixth Century Sculpture of Attica," in *Athens Comes of Age: From Solon to Salamis* (Princeton, 1978), 55–57. On the Cycladic connections of the Sounion gems: Boardman, *Island Gems*, 123–27.

50. The landing of Cretan pirates at Thorikos is recorded in the *Homeric Hymn to Demeter* (lines 122–29). The Brauron material is only partially published: I. Papadimitriou, *Praktika* (1949): 79–81, figs. 8, a–g (faience scarabs, other seals, and beads); *Ergon* (1961): 31, fig. 31 (early stone seal; Boardman, *Island Gems*, 120, C 15); unusual early protomes among the terracottas (Higgins, *Greek Terracottas*, 44, fig. 13).

51. Kelly, *AJA* 70 (1966): 113–21; Figueira, *Aegina*, 185–88. Griffin protome from the Kalaureia sanctuary discovered in the early excavations: Wide and Kjellberg, *AthMitt* 20 (1895), pl. 10. If the Orchomenos included in Strabo's list of the league cities represents Arcadian (rather than Boeotian) Orchomenos, the trade agreements between Aigina and Arcadia attested in Pausanias (above, n. 19) would have a legitimate basis as well.

merchants. Even the Athenian and Corinthian coins found in Egypt have been interpreted as an "indirect interest in the trade there by issuing cities," and hence could speak for Aiginetan presence.[52]

A second area of Aiginetan interest abroad is in the Levant, where a change in Greek imports to trading posts such as Al Mina seems to correspond to a decline in Euboean activity. In its place, a combination of East Greek bowls and jugs, Attic SOS oil amphorae, and Corinthian aryballoi and cups replaces the predominantly Euboean and Cycladic imports of earlier centuries.[53] Juxtaposed with the Eastern evidence from Aigina—direct imports such as Lyre Player seals and the Euboean alphabet—plus indirect influence through motifs reflected in Black and White style pottery (above, 2.6), the early archaic Greek pottery in the Near East might represent the Eastern terminus of an Aiginetan trading expedition with stops at Cyprus and Rhodes. To protect this Eastern trade route whose ultimate destinations were Egypt and Phoenicia, Aigina insured herself against pirates and rivals with a station on Greek soil at Kydonia, in western Crete.[54]

In the West, one looks for the same telltale presence of Attic, Corinthian, and East Greek pottery at a site where other sources suggest Aiginetan activity. Such a combination of imports has turned up frequently at colonial sites in Sicily, southern Italy, and Etruria, without suggesting exclusive carriers. At Gravisca (Porto Clementino) on the coast of Etruria, the port of Tarquinia and Caere, such archaic imports did not attract attention until the recognition of an unusual phenomenon. Built into a classical sanctuary to Hera were archaic stone anchor stocks, one of which bore an archaeologist's dream of an inscription. The anchor had been dedicated to "Aiginetan Apollo" by "Sostratos the son of . . . ," who signed ΕΠΟΙΕΣΕ before the stone breaks off. It would seem that a merchant of Aigina named Sostratos, possibly a relative of the prosperous native admired by Herodotus, dedicated his anchor stock to his hometown god, in gratitude for a successful business trip. The number of other anchors from the same site suggest such dedications were a regular custom, although one cannot assume that any of the others (uninscribed) were left by Aiginetans. The one inscription, however, provides a clue to the anonymous identity of the Greeks who brought East Greek, Attic, and Corinthian pottery to Etruria.[55] Moreover, Sostratos of Aigina may be connected

52. Boardman, *The Greeks Overseas*, 125. See the evidence from the Asyut hoard: M. Price and N. Waggoner, *The Asyut Hoard* (London, 1975); Figueira, *Aegina*, 251–64.

53. Boardman, *The Greeks Overseas*, 46f., assembles this evidence from the Levant, with the conclusion, "I suspect the Aiginetans" (49).

54. Herodotus 3.59; Strabo 8.6.16; Figueira, *Aegina*, 281–82. Aiginetan coins and inscriptions in Crete: Figueira, *Aegina*, 133–36, 278–80; Jeffery, *Local Scripts*, 112.

55. Torelli, *ParPass* 26 (1971): 56–57 (on the inscribed *cippo* [*sic*], not yet identified as an anchor); D. Ridgway, *Archaeological Reports* 1973/74, 50, fig. 9; P. A. Gianfrotta, "Le Ancore votive di Sostrato di Egina e di Faillo di Crotone," *ParPass* 30 (1975): 311–18 (identifies as anchor); Harvey, *ParPass* 31 (1976); Figueira, *Aegina*, 237–51.

with the many "SO" dipinti and graffiti on late sixth-century Attic vases from Etruria, as a merchant who controlled much of the export in Greek vases to the West.[56]

The onset of Aiginetan traffic with Etruria presumably begins with the demise of the Euboean monopoly after 700 B.C., as in the East, and the rich Oriental material in Etruscan tombs could be adduced as evidence. These Orientalia include faience (the Bocchoris vase, Egyptian amulets, dozens of small figurine-vases and animals), raw and carved ivory of both Eastern and local workmanship, bronze protome cauldrons and stands from North Syria, Phoenician silver bowls, tridacna shells and ostrich eggs, and gems such as North Syrian Lyre-Player seals.[57] The distribution of similar artifacts follows a route from East to West with findspots on Cyprus and the East Greek islands, at central Greek sanctuaries (Olympia, Delphi, and Delos), and in the Greek West.[58] Many of these exotica, or objects which show their influence, have been found around the Saronic Gulf and especially on Aigina. In the West, such Oriental luxuries may have reached inland Etruria through coastal stops made at places like Gravisca by Aiginetans attracted to the iron-rich Italian district.

The eastern coast of Italy along the Adriatic may also have attracted merchants of Aigina. Strabo (8.6.16) mentions an Aiginetan colony in Umbria, a reference which prompts a review of imported pottery at sites such as Adria and Spina. Attic pottery found there, once attributed to Athenian agency, actually carries dedications in Aiginetan graffiti and non-Attic letters on SOS trade amphorae.[59] Even more intriguing are cases of the name "Omrikos" (the Umbrian), named on a Corinthian vase exported to Caere but also a dedicant (as "Ombrikos") of a sixth-century Attic vase at Gravisca.[60] A slave named Ombrikos also appears in a bronze manumission inscription from the sanctuary of Apollo at Bassae in Arcadia, suggesting slaves were among the foreign goods imported to Arcadians by Aiginetans.[61] The other "Umbrian" names on vases may also be slaves, and it is tempting to connect them with Aiginetan enterprise. Deities honored at Adria— Apollo and Hera—are the same ones whose names appear in Graviscan graffiti.[62] The evidence combines to suggest Aiginetan presence on both coasts of Italy, presumably in

56. Johnston, *ParPass* 27 (1972); Figueira, *Aegina*, 242–46.

57. A useful summary of this evidence by Annette Rathje, "Oriental Imports in Etruria in the 8th and 7th c. B.C.: Their Origins and Implications," in *Italy before the Romans: The Iron Age, Orientalizing and Etruscan Periods*, ed. D. and F. Ridgway (London, 1979), 145–83.

58. References for these artifacts and their distribution in Boardman, *The Greeks Overseas*, above, nn. 31–51.

59. Colonna, *RivStordell'Ant* 4 (1974); A. W. Johnston, "An Athenian Rho in the Adriatic," *ZPE* 35 (1979): 277–80. L. Braccesi, *Grecità Adriatica* (Bologna, 1977): 128–34.

60. "Omrikos" as a Corinthian dipinto: Payne, *Necrocorinthia*, p. 122, n. 3, p. 316 (no. 1178: Louvre E 632, from Caere); "Ombrikos" at Gravisca: M. Torelli, "Il Santuario Greco di Gravisca," *ParPass* 32 (1977): 406–08; Boardman, *The Greeks Overseas*, 228.

61. IG V² 429 (Frederick A. Cooper, "Two Inscriptions from Bassai," *Hesperia* 44 [1975]: 224–33, pl. 50d).

62. Apollo at Gravisca: above, n. 55, with Torelli, *ParPass* 26 (1971), on Hera at Gravisca; for Hera and Apollo graffiti at Gravisca, see n. 59; Figueira, *Aegina*, 250–51, on the connection between slaves and pottery.

search of metals and slaves. An early interest in copper, tin, and iron would provide a natural advantage in gaining access to the material in which the sculptors of Aigina distinguished themselves in the late archaic period.[63]

A fourth area of possible Aiginetan evidence is the Black Sea coast. The grain ships intercepted by Xerxes (Herodotus 7.147) and the literary references to such delicacies as "Aiginetan barley cakes," mullet from northern waters, and prostitutes named "Sinope" available on Aigina suggest the island was a busy market.[64] Again, the only substantial support for the presence of Aigina around the Black Sea would be Attic and Corinthian pottery, although it could point to Megarians. One recent report identifies the presence of Aiginetans at Olbia in southern Russia, at the mouth of the Dniepr river.[65] The proposed evidence includes imported Corinthian pottery, transport amphorae stamped with a turtle, and architectural terracottas identified as Aiginetan. The roof tiles and simas called "Aiginetan" look like local imitations, and the turtle stamp merely illustrates the popularity of the device, through the spread of Aiginetan coinage. Such evidence is indirect, at best, but encourages extending the criteria for identifying Aiginetan activity to include artifacts influenced by her wares.[66]

Thus through a cautious comparison of archaeological and literary evidence from Aigina and the remote areas of her commercial interest, one can experiment with a means of identifying the presence of a Greek population without characteristic attributes. A commercial enterprise which may have developed from a form of legalized piracy made the islanders the Phoenicians, or παντοπῶλαι, of the Greek world.[67] Only in the late archaic period did the island become a powerful enemy of Athens rather than just a rival, when the foundation of Kydonia, the dissemination of silver "turtles," and hostilities between the two neighbors represent a more formal phase of competition. In the early archaic period, the seventh century, historical phenomena are barely documented, but the role of a developing Aigina can be perceived from the evidence of artifacts.

63. Pliny, NH 34.5.11 on Aiginetan sculptors; a list of known sculptors and their works in Welter, Aigina, 98–101; Figueira, Aegina, 235–36, on sculpture and metal trade.

64. A lament for Aiginetan μᾶζαι, presumably made or purchased on Aigina, in a fragment of Old Attic comedy (Cratinus apud Athenaeus 6.267e); on mullet (κεστρεύς from Abdera or Sinope?) sold on Aigina, see Athenaeus 7.307 D; the courtesan named Sinope (known as Abdera in her old age, probably a political joke) in Athenaeus 13.586, 595.

65. Brašynski, Archeologia 19 (1968): "L'importation des produits éginètes à Olbia a probablement commencé dès la première moitié du VI. siècle av. n. è. (éléments architectoniques en terre) pour durer jusqu'au milieu du Vᵉ siècle. On importait également de petites quantités d'huile d'olive éginète."

66. Aigina may have specialized in the development and distribution of the tile roof, for both the date and the tile stamps associated with the earliest Greek temple roofs place Aigina in an early and important group: Williams, AA (1982): 63–64 (above, 2.4). R. C. S. Felsch, "Boiotische Ziegelwerkstätten," AthMitt 99 (1979): 1–40, has compiled the stamped tiles from Aigina and Boeotia which suggest an organized industry in roof tiles for export.

67. According to scholiasts to Pindar (Olympian 8.29b), 'Αιγινοπῶλαι was a synonym for παντοπῶλαι, and τὸν ἐπὶ μεταβολῇ φόρτον was called 'Αιγινητικόν.

2. EARLY ATHENS

104

The effect of a new emphasis on Aigina is a reduced role for Athens in this period. History already leads one to expect minimal activity abroad; there are no recorded Athenian colonies before the sixth-century interest in the Black Sea.[68] While other Greek states were developing commercial or colonial settlements abroad, the reluctance of Athens is surprising, especially after the activity of the preceding centuries.[69] Internal colonization has been suggested as the Attic alternative in this period: Athenians moved out into rural Attica to relieve population pressures, instead of emigrating abroad.[70] However, this theory presumes that colonization was motivated exclusively by overpopulation, without the positive incentive of commercial enterprise. Nor does internal colonization explain the lack of import and export activity for Athens in the seventh century, which must reflect other factors.

Attic exports abroad in this period are as rare as Athenian colonists. The limited distribution of Protoattic pottery was considered earlier (above, 2.1). The only significant product marketed abroad by Athens in the seventh century seems to have been olive oil, judging by the wide distribution of SOS amphorae.[71] The transport and sale of these amphorae reached North Africa, Spain, France, Italy, Egypt, and the Levant, but distribution must have been the responsibility of non-Athenians and probably Aiginetans. The limitation of Attic exports to olive oil was attributed in antiquity to the reforms of Solon (Plutarch, *Solon* 24). Like his encouragement of foreign craftsmen as immigrants to Athens, his economic reforms reflect seventh-century, not sixth-century, conditions,[72] for export of oil and immigration of craftsmen begin earlier. Within seventh-century Attica, the conditions of poverty implied by the archaeological record and by the conspicuous absence of prominent historical figures or events suggests that the economic problems tackled by Solon had their origins as much as a century earlier. The concentration of wealth in the hands of a few, the alienation of land from small farmers, and the slavery into which debt forced impoverished citizens were at least a generation old by the time of Solon. His lament for citizens enslaved abroad who no longer spoke their native Attic dialect indicates the length of time they had spent in exile.[73]

Archaeological evidence for this poverty is the absence of significant architecture,

68. Boardman, *The Greeks Overseas*, 264–66, on Greeks in the Black Sea; Drews, *JHS* 96 (1976). The two earliest Athenian colonies are Sigeion (Herodotus 6.34–37) and Elaious (J. Chamonard, E. Dhorme, and F. Courby, *BCH* 39 [1915]: 135–240, for the excavation of the necropolis), on the Hellespont.

69. Jeffery, *Archaic Greece*, 84–85, on the enterprise of Geometric Athens.

70. Coldstream, *Geometric Greece*, 132–37.

71. Johnston and Jones, *BSA* 73 (1978).

72. The conflict between literary and archaeological evidence on oil export was interpreted as an "inconsistency" by Johnston *BSA* 73 (1978): 140; many of the "historical" accomplishments of Solon are a later amalgam of developments in early archaic Athens (Jeffery, *Archaic Greece*, 90–94, 106–07).

73. Solon, fragment 24 (Diehl), lines 8–15 (quoted by Aristotle, *Ath. Pol.* 12).

sculpture, or bronze workshops on the scale found in the Peloponnese or the islands. The major Attic art form of the seventh century, the Black and White style, has been reattributed to Aigina in this monograph; in cultural history, poets were not attracted to Athens as they were to Sparta or Delos until the efforts of Peisistratos. Historical sources are equally silent: "Athens' history before 600 is almost a blank," primarily because "she did not colonize and had no revolution."[74] The names of a few archons and two athletes are all that is known of early Athens before the conspiracy of Kylon, the earliest event whose consequences are preserved in the papyrus of Aristotle's *Constitution of Athens* and an incident important to later Athens.[75]

The revisionist view, beginning with Thucydides, suggests that foreign interests were as influential in the Kylon affair as were internal catalysts toward the inevitable (in other Greek states) phase of tyranny. Kylon married the daughter of the tyrant of Megara, Theagenes, a typical alliance for an aspiring archaic aristocrat. With the military support of his father-in-law and the encouragement of the Delphic oracle, which rarely backed a loser, Kylon attempted to seize the Acropolis. However, the coup backfired on him, thanks to a rally by the population of Attica, who "flocked in, one and all, from the country" to blockade the rebels on the Acropolis (Thucydides 1.126, Crawley translation).

It is unlikely that this united resistance demonstrates the fierce devotion of the Athenian people to their constitution (whatever form it actually took at this date), which they rushed to defend from a potential tyrant. The circumstances suggest instead that an ambitious neighbor tried to take advantage of Athens in a weak moment—that Megara, or Theagenes, had designs on expanding their territory eastward in the late seventh century.[76] A contemporary struggle between Athens and Megara over the island of Salamis, offshore and crucial to both states, adds a cause for hostility to the Kylon incident.[77] The early history of these small Greek states is better viewed in terms of such struggles among ambitious aristocracies than as stages in constitutional history; private, not public (polis), interests dominated even such political events as the Ionian revolt until the Persian wars.[78] Thus Kylon's conspiracy, thwarted by a homicide with lasting

74. Burn, *The Warring States of Greece*, 73.

75. Archons: Marmor Parium (*FGH* 239), discussion and bibliography in Ch. Fornara, *Archaic Times to the End of the Peloponnesian War* (Baltimore, 1977), no. 1, pp. 1–3; T. J. Cadoux, "The Athenian Archons from Kreon to Hypsichides," *JHS* 68 (1948): 70–123. The athletes are Pantakles (696 and 692 B.C.) and Stomas (644 B.C.): L. Moretti, *Olympionikai* (Rome, 1967), nos. 25–27, p. 63; no. 54, p. 65. On Kylon, Olympic victor in 640/639 B.C.: Moretti, *Olympionikai*, no. 56, p. 65; Herodotus 5.71; Thucydides 1.126–27; Plutarch, *Solon* 12; Jeffery, *Archaic Greece*, 87–89; Lang, *CP* 62 (1967).

76. Thus Jeffery, *Archaic Greece*, 87, 156; R. Legon, *Megara* (Ithaca: Cornell University Press, 1981), 93–94, 98–102.

77. Plutarch, *Solon*, 8–10; B. Aratowsky, "Notes on Salamis," *Studies . . . Robinson* 2: 789–96.

78. Dunbabin, *BSA* 37 (1936/37): 201; D. Rocchi, "Motivi economici e pressioni sociali nelle origine dell'espansionismo ateniense," *RendIstLomb* (1971): 523–72; Figueira, "Aegina and Athens," 220f.; A. Lintott, *Violence, Civil Strife and Revolution in the Classical City State* (Baltimore: Johns Hopkins University Press, 1980), chap. 1.

punitive action, may reflect a vulnerable phase in the existence of Attica, not a crisis in internal constitutional history. The attempted coup suggests that Athens, a prosperous leader in Geometric times, was weak enough by the later seventh century to invite a confident attack by her neighbors, supported by the Delphic oracle. Such an interpretation of Kylon's coup increases the evidence for economic distress in seventh-century Athens, but it still leaves unexplained the origins of her poverty. A single and secure reason may be beyond the powers of the meager evidence, but several significant causes have been proposed and should be considered.

The most recent solution is a drastic but welcome one, in that it admits the archaeological evidence and presses for a simple answer from natural causes. An investigation of the history of the Athenian water supply produced statistics on wells in the Agora which suggest that a drought struck Athens in the late eighth century.[79] Both the number of wells closed and the depth to which they were dug, often without ever reaching the water table, are such that only "a prolonged, severe drought in the second half of the 8th c. B.C." could explain these conditions.[80] The author then compared statistics on the numerous Late Geometric graves in Attica with an "interesting gap" in the early seventh century: "Where are all these people in the first half of the 7th century?"[81] If a drought and its inevitable successor, epidemic disease, decimated a major portion of the Athenian population, it would explain neatly a series of problems. In a climate of irregular rainfall, an unexpected bad year would mean a sustained period without a decent harvest and the subsequent consumption of seed stores. Famine and epidemic would alleviate the population pressure—hence no colonization; the decline in wealth would account for the low number of merchants, poets, athletes, and tyrants. Evidence from cemeteries supports the epidemic aspect: the high number of infant burials for this period, and of multiple burials (two children inhumed in a single pithos), suggests increased infant mortality.[82] A drop in the population at the infant level would have an effect through the next generation, so that recovery from the drought would be delayed until the population reached a level sufficient to demand and produce commodities. A country weakened by drought might also be attractive to the ambitions of a neighbor like Megara. The famine associated with the cult of Demeter at Eleusis, as commemorated in the *Homeric Hymn to Demeter* (lines 305–33), may be of particular relevance to an

79. John McK. Camp, *Hesperia* 48 (1979). This theory originated as a casual suggestion by Brann in her conclusions on the topography of the early Agora, as acknowledged by Camp, 379, n. 2, citing Brann, *Agora VIII*, 108.

80. Camp, *Hesperia* 48 (1979): 401.

81. Ibid., 400.

82. Soteriades, *Praktika* (1934): 29–38, in reporting on the excavation of Marathon's exclusively infant necropolis, concluded: "Ὡς φαίνεται, ἐπιδημία τις . . . κατὰ τὸν ὄγδοον αἰῶνα π. Χ. ἥρπασεν ἀπὸ τὰς ἀγκάλας τῶν γονέων τῶν τοὺς μικροὺς τούτους." The cemeteries at Phaleron (K. Kourouniotis, *ArkhEph* [1911]: 246–51; *Deltion* [1916]: 27ff.) at Thorikos (Jean Servais, *Thorikos* 1963, p. 47), and at Eleusis (Mylonas, *O protoattikos amphoreus*, 269) are also predominantly infant burials in this period, with small, poor, and often mass graves.

early drought in Attica. A final irony in the tradition of the drought involves Aigina: the cult of Zeus Panhellenios on Aigina had its origins in a Panhellenic drought relieved by the intervention of Aiakos.[83] It is possible that the legend commemorates an occasion when Aigina saved her neighbors (with an emergency grain shipment?); in any case, dedications left by grateful Greek states on the island, in memory of the action of Aiakos,[84] were still on view in Roman times.

107

Objections to the theory of a drought will undoubtedly find many a voice.[85] Literary corroborations are difficult to pinpoint in time when interpreting legends of droughts, famines, and divine miracles that attend the origin of cults. From a scientific point of view it is difficult to explain a shortage of rainfall in the very area where an abundance was localized in the Late Bronze Age, according to a celebrated theory.[86] In terms of ceramic evidence, the drought might explain the decline of a flourishing industry from over twenty workshops to three painters after 700 B.C. (above, 1.3). However, this explanation from natural causes would leave unsolved the problem of a single eccentric workshop a quarter of a century later, the subject of this monograph. As was admitted in the defense of the drought, "a handful of magnificent individual pieces from this time survives"—but why are most of them on Aigina?[87] Drought and conspiracy enclose a period in which Aigina enters the picture, and the seventh-century struggles of Athens made her vulnerable to the expansion of her neighbors.

3. AN "OLD HATRED"

It was Brann, the original author of the drought theory, who also suggested a second possible explanation for the condition of the Agora wells: an early war between Athens and Aigina, attested only in Herodotus.[88] Its effects survived into the classical period only as the memory of an ἔχθρη παλαιή (old hatred) between the two states which influenced classical history.

In 506 B.C. Aigina responded to the Theban request for aid against Athens with eagerness for revenge on her old enemy, sending ships to harass the coast of Attica around Phaleron while Athens was occupied at the Boeotian border (Herodotus 5.81). A long digression follows in the account by Herodotus, to explain the origins of this "old

83. Ancient sources collated by Camp, *Hesperia* 48 (1979): 403, n. 27. For a modern analogy in rain cult, J. Penrose Harland, "An Ancient Survival in Modern Aigina," in *Studies in Honor of Ullman (The Classical Bulletin,* St. Louis University, 1960), 17–18.

84. Pausanias 2.29.6.

85. Figueira, *Aegina*, 223, n. 54, calls the drought "possible" but "ill-founded."

86. Rhys Carpenter, *Discontinuity in Greek Civilization* (Cambridge, 1977).

87. Camp, *Hesperia* 48 (1979): 401.

88. Brann, *Agora VIII*, 108. T. W. Dunbabin, "Ἔχθρη παλαιή" (*BSA* 36 [1936/37]: 83–91); Buck, "Epidaurians, Aeginetans, and Athenians," is the most recent and detailed analysis.

hatred." It began when Aigina carried off statues of Damia and Auxesia from her mother city, Epidauros, marking the island's independence from the mainland state. The statues were of olive wood obtained from Athens in exchange for an annual sacrifice by Epidauros to Athena Polias and Erechtheus. Once the statues were stolen by Aigina, Epidauros refused to pay for the sacrifice, and Athens demanded the restoration of the statues. The islanders refused, and the Athenians answered this challenge with a warship.

108

The details of the ensuing conflict were confusing, even to Herodotus, who was obviously informed by elaborate and contradictory Athenian, Argive, and Aiginetan accounts. Biases were further complicated by etiological and religious explanations, miraculous earthquakes, and exaggerated consequences.

An important factor is the intervention of Argos on behalf of Aigina, in the form of military reinforcements sent to the island (Herodotus 5.86). Whether the Argive response was motivated by rivalry with Athens and Epidauros or by alliance with Aigina is not made clear, but Argos also joined Aigina in the religious prohibitions against Athens after the war (below). The alliance between Argos and Aigina was an old one: in the heroic past the island belonged to the Argolid kingdom of Diomedes, while archaic Argos was associated with Aigina through the tradition surrounding Pheidon and through cult.[89] The Argive efforts to cut off the Athenians from their ship(s) must have met with at least partial success, for only one survivor returned to Attica, to meet a gruesome death. As for the statues, the Athenians attempted to remove them by violent means, damaging them and committing a violation of the sacred temenos.

The outcome of this conflict left Aigina and Athens bitter enemies who formalized their grievances in certain religious oaths. The Athenian survivor was stabbed to death with dress pins by the wives of those who had failed to return; as a result, the Doric pinned peplos was replaced by the Ionic buttoned chiton to punish the Athenian women. Accordingly, the Argives and Aiginetans adopted even longer dress pins and made them the principal dedication to Damia and Auxesia. Furthermore, all Attic objects were barred from the sanctuary of the two offended goddesses, including pottery, which had to be local.

Herodotus's account probably reflects an actual confrontation among the states around the Saronic Gulf, remote enough for the names of participating personalities to be forgotten but recent enough for the memory to rankle in many breasts. There does not seem to have been a major naval engagement, nor was the territory of Attica or Epidauros threatened. The exact details of this war and its date are difficult to determine from the historical sources alone. Modern attempts to date it, using a variety of methods, have produced a variety of conclusions. Analysis of Herodotus alone suggests dates ranging from the eighth to the sixth centuries. One recent investigation, for example,

---

89. *Iliad* 2.559–67; Figueira, *Aegina*, 170–80; Buck, "Epidaurians, Aeginetans, and Athenians," 7.

argues for a date in the sixth century, between the careers of Solon and Peisistratos, on the analogy of other early sixth-century conflicts such as the dispute over Salamis and the First Sacred War.[90] However, the conspicuous absence in Herodotus of any historical events or figures of the sixth century suggests a remoter date. Evidence such as the absence of Corinthian intervention implies a date before Periander conquered Epidauros, and perhaps even earlier, when Procles ruled Epidauros as a dependency of Corinth. Such was an argument that concluded: "On the whole the narrative seems to fall best into the first half of the seventh century."[91] A detailed reconstruction proposed recently arranges fourteen historical events involving Aigina and her neighbors between the tenth and fifth centuries, with the main stages of the early war falling between 640 and 625 B.C.[92]

The nature of the seventh century and the methodology necessary to understand its protohistorical conditions limit a strictly historical reconstruction of this early war. For example, a figure who may or may not have an effect on the date, when argued from history alone, is Pheidon of Argos, the hereditary monarch who behaved like a tyrant and was called τύραννος by Herodotus.[93] Like Solon, he was credited with a number of contributions to early Greece, including the introduction of standards of weight, measure, and coinage. A late source (Ephorus) even claims that Pheidon invented coinage on Aigina, an important tradition that links the two states.[94] Pheidon's life is variously dated in ancient sources: as ninth-century by Ephorus and the Marmor Parium, eighth-century by Strabo and Pausanias, seventh-century by Aristotle, and sixth-century by Herodotus.[95] An early seventh-century date has been most effectively defended and most widely accepted as the one which best satisfies the conflict of the sources.[96] Thus, if Pheidon were involved in the Argive intervention in the early war, the early seventh century would be the most appropriate date for the ἔχθρη παλαιή.

However, a glaring and often neglected fact is the conspicuous absence of Pheidon in the account of the war by Herodotus, the only source for the war. Elsewhere in

90. Figueira, "Aegina and Athens," 211–31; Aegina, 67, n. 4.

91. Ure, The Origin of Tyranny, 167.

92. Buck, "Epidaurians, Aeginetans, and Athenians," reaches these conclusions through a series of assumptions about the biographies of historical figures and interstate relations marginal to the Aigina war. Although his argument is plausible, it ignores archaeological evidence.

93. Herodotus 6.127.3; Aristotle, Politics 5.8.4, 1310b, reconciles inheritance and character by calling Pheidon a king who became a tyrant.

94. Ephorus apud Strabo 8.6.16, echoed in the Etymologicum Magnum 3.613.13; a recent vindication in Kagan, AJA 86 (1982): 359 (cf. Kagan, "Pheidon," TAPA 91 [1960]: 124–25).

95. Ancient sources collected by Fornara, Archaic Times, 6–7, no. 4.

96. Argued by A. Andrewes in "The Corinthian Actaeon and Pheidon of Argos," CQ 43 (1949): 70–75, and CAH² III. 3 (1982): 372; accepted by Burn (Lyric Age of Greece [London, 1960], 176–79) and Jeffery (Archaic Greece, 134–36); Salmon, JHS 97 (1977): 92, Buck, "Epidaurians, Aeginetans, and Athenians," p. 7, n. 8, p. 12 (680–65 B.C.); Figueira, Aegina, 67, n. 3.

Herodotus, Pheidon's son is a suitor of Agariste, daughter of Kleisthenes of Sikyon, suggesting a possibly late seventh-century for Pheidon.[97] Although Pheidon's name is associated with early developments such as the invention of coinage and the hoplite reform, none of this is securely dated in modern times, and introducing Pheidon to the Aigina war does not provide it with a date.[98]

110

Another approach to the early war between Athens and Aigina presses archaeology into service, whereby most scholars have reached a similar consensus on the war's date—the early seventh century. The specific consequences of the war—change in dress, size of dress pin, and ban on imports—have been the focus of attempts to document the war through its impact on the material record.

The story of the change in Athenian dress suggests an *aition*, a late invention to explain a traditional practise. In the absence of preserved garments, representations are of little help in demonstrating the use or absence of pins in female dress. Thus Ionian dress was certainly in fashion by the late sixth century, according to the series of korai from the Acropolis, whereas a belted dress is worn in the early seventh century on representations by the Analatos Painter.[99] In between these periods, the François vase is still the earliest representation of pinned peploi; the "sleeves" painted by the Polyphemus Painter are worn by both men and women, so presumably they cannot represent pinned peploi (Pls. 6–8).[100]

Rather than trying to press evidence from pictures whose purpose was not to represent realism, one might consider the actual remains of pins from Argos, Aigina, and Athens. The evidence from Athens is striking in the absence of bronze pins from both sanctuaries and graves of the archaic period: "Their absence among the dedications on the Acropolis is sufficiently remarkable to call for an explanation."[101] If the dedication of garments were not an Athenian custom one might expect a lack of pins, but even at sanctuaries such as that of Artemis at Brauron, where the dedication of female garments is attested in inscriptions, no pins are in evidence.[102] Nor have pins been found in Athenian graves later than the Geometric period, or in other seventh-century contexts

97. Herodotus 6.127; a sixth-century date is argued by Kelly in *A History of Argos*, 109–11, but the association with Kleisthenes is typical of the historian fond of staging unlikely encounters (e.g., Solon and Croesus).

98. Snodgrass, *JHS* 85 (1965); Kelly, *A History of Argos*, 85–86; Jeffery, *Archaic Greece*, 134; Salmon, *JHS* 97 (1977). On Pheidon and coinage, see Kraay, *Greek Coins*, 41, 313–16; Figueira, "Aegina and Athens," 63, n. 2 (343–45); Kagan, *AJA* 86 (1982).

99. Harrison, *JWalt* 36 (1977). B. Ridgway, "Of Kouroi and Korai—Attic Variety," pp. 123–24, nn. 32–34, in *Studies in Athenian Architecture, Sculpture, and Topography Presented to Homer A. Thompson, Hesperia* suppl. 20 (1982).

100. See discussion by Paul Jacobsthal in *Greek Pins*, "Representations of Pins on Vases," 105–19.

101. Dunbabin, *BSA* 37 (1936/37): 86; cf. Jacobsthal, *Greek Pins*, 96. A single fibula from the Acropolis has been interpreted as the dedication of a foreigner (Blinkenberg, *Lindiaka V: Fibules Grecques et Orientales* [Copenhagen, 1926], no. 149).

102. IG, *editio minor*, vol. 2, part 1, 1514–1531 from Brauron include garments among the inventoried dedications, but no mention of pins, nor are any known from the (largely unpublished) excavations.

exposed by excavation. However, early archaic Attica is generally poor in imported or local metals, whether jewelry, weapons, or vessels, compared with earlier and later times; a paucity of pins could reflect a general lack of evidence, not a prohibition against peplos or pin.

At sanctuaries associated with Argos and Aigina, on the other hand, an impressive number of pins were dedicated to the female deities in residence. The Argive Heraion produced some three thousand bronze pins; the old excavations at the temple of Aphaia on Aigina recovered all varieties of pins and fibulae, in keeping with the predominantly feminine function of most of the dedications.[103] The typologies of the pins from Aigina and Argos even resemble one another, so that Aigina could be classified as a "Peloponnesian outpost" in terms of her pins.[104] Thus the evidence of actual pins lends substance to Herodotus's account of their absence in Attica and their popularity, though not change in size, in her enemy cities.[105]

Even more appropriate to the war recorded in Herodotus is a fifth-century inventory of the sanctuary of Mnia (Damia?) and Auxesia, in an inscription built into an ancient aqueduct southeast of the town of Aigina.[106] The inventory dates to the Athenian settlement of the island after 431 B.C., and the Attic letter forms agree with this historical context (the Aphaia sanctuary inventory, IG IV 39, represents the same Athenian reorganization). In the opisthodomos the inscription lists 120 iron pins, 5 pins παρὰ τοὺς πέπλους (line 12), and 6 fragments of pins; the area sacred to Auxesia contained 180 iron pins, 8 pins πρὸ τῷ (or πρώτῳ) πεπλῷ (line 41), and 5 pin fragments. Thus in the sanctuary involved in the early war and associated with dedications of dress pins, pins were dedicated with garments as well as alone.

This inscription is the sole archaeological evidence for the sanctuary of Damia and Auxesia on Aigina, whose site and cult are still unknown. The shrine was located by Herodotus in the interior of the island, twenty stades from the town at a place called Oia, and was visited by Pausanias, who does not provide further topographical directions.[107]

Evidence for a related cult of the same goddesses at Epidauros and Troizen strengthens the connection between the island and the southern Argolid and suggests that cult as well as statues were transported to Aigina with the first Dorian settlers.[108] Pausanias and Zenobius record a duplication in cult practises and epithets with the Eleusinian cult

103. Waldstein, *The Argive Heraeum* 2: 300–23; Furtwängler, *Aphaia*, 397–416, pls. 114–16. Killian, *ZPE* 31 (1978): 219–22, on votive pins from archaic sanctuaries.

104. Jacobsthal, *Greek Pins*, 12.

105. Ibid., 90; Dunbabin, *BSA* 37 (1936/37): 87.

106. IG IV, 1588, first published by Furtwängler in *PhilWoch* (1901): 1595–99; discussed in detail by Jacobsthal, *Greek Pins*, 97–100.

107. Herodotus 5.83; Pausanias 2.30.4 (mentions Herodotus's account).

108. IG IV, 1010 (Epidauros); Pausanias 2.32.2 (Troizen); Jacobsthal, *Greek Pins*, 97–100; Figueira, *Aegina*, 170–80.

of Demeter; although this could be a late religious contamination, it is probable that some form of fertility goddess(es) local to the southern Argolid is the ancestor of the cult on Aigina.[109]

112

However, even the evidence for pins from the sanctuary named by Herodotus does not greatly substantiate his account of the early war. The cult of one or more fertility goddesses is likely to have inspired dedications of female garments (after childbirth, as at Brauron?) or of related objects such as women's dress pins. Nor does the classical inscription indicate a date for the votive pins inventoried; they are probably archaic but cannot be dated precisely or used as chronological evidence for the war and its effect on dress pins.[110]

With reluctance, one must admit that the account in Herodotus of a change in dress could represent an elaborate *aition* for the fashion rather than a historical occasion for a deliberate change in custom. Even the change in the size of the pins, a phenomenon which Herodotus records as if its results were still manifest, is hard to reduce to specific statistics, especially with the confusion over Argive standards, pins, and spits.[111] However, history and antiquities at least do not contradict each other, and may both reflect a situation which gave rise to them.

Finally, one turns to the last of the three consequences of the war between Athens and Aigina: the prohibition of Attic products in the sanctuary of the two offended goddesses. The fact that the sanctuary in question has yet to be discovered has not discouraged those in search of archaeological proof, as the opening sentence in Dunbabin's article demonstrates:

> The passage in Herodotus which above all others is written as if to provide a test on their own ground of the historical application of archaeological discoveries is v, 88,2: Ἀττικὸν δὲ μήτε τι ἄλλο προσφέρειν πρὸς τὸ ἱρὸν μήτε κέραμον, ἀλλ' ἐκ χυτρίδων ἐπιχωριέων νόμον τὸ λοιπὸν αὐτόθι εἶναι πίνειν.[112]

The passage does not explicitly apply the prohibition (νόμος) to any other sanctuary, on or off the island, yet scholars have looked eagerly for a timely absence of Attic pottery at likely sites. When the Argive Heraion pottery was studied, Hoppin seized on a noticeable gap (some seventy years) in Attic pottery imports in the sixth century, with

---

109. Pausanias 2.32.2 (with Frazer's commentary); Zenobius, *Cent.* 4.20. The description in Herodotus 5.86 of the damage done to the statues by the Athenians, who knocked the figures to their knees, suggests kneeling statues of fertility goddesses giving birth (e.g., from Sparta: U. Häfner, *Das Kunstschaffen Lakoniens in archaischer Zeit* [diss., Münster/Westphalia, 1965], 161–63); A. Andrewes, *CAH²* III. 3 (1982): 372.

110. Jacobsthal, *Greek Pins*, 98–99, argues that iron pins are most appropriate to the Protogeometric period and therefore the pins and the cult date to the tenth century. However, iron pins turn up in later contexts on Aigina, e.g., in a sixth-century grave: Welter, *AA* 53 (1938): 507–08, fig. 24.

111. Dunbabin, *BSA* 37 (1936/37): 86–88; Jacobsthal, *Greek Pins*, 90; Jeffery, *Archaic Greece*, 135–36, n. 1; Kraay, *Greek Coins*, 313–16; Figueira, *Aegina*, 72–75.

112. Dunbabin, *BSA* 37 (1936/37): 83. The Herodotus passage is also cited by Athenaeus (11.502).

the presumption that the prohibition was enforced by Argos as well as Aigina.[113] In 1922, before the quantity of Protoattic pottery from Aigina was publicized, Percy Ure pointed out a lack of such pottery from the island.[114] To be sure, all that was known from the early seventh century was the pottery published by Pallat in 1897 (above 1.2), plus what was on display in the museum. Since the Ram Jug had been declared local and no new Protoattic finds had yet been announced (e.g., by Furtwängler or Karo), Ure could cite only Pallat's and Loeschke's promise of Attic pottery, with his misgivings. On historical grounds, Ure's inclination was to date the war in the early seventh century, and he was satisfied by the fact that "both in Argos and Aegina there does appear to be an abrupt cessation of Attic imports early in the seventh century."[115]

Thus, in Ure's day, historical probability and archaeology argued for a date in the early seventh century for the war between Athens and Aigina. When the Berlin collection and its companion pieces from Aigina appeared as Protoattic, they invalidated Ure's argument. Even before the major publication of these Attic vases, the next scholar, Thomas Dunbabin, tackled the subject of the war. With dismay, Dunbabin could no longer report a convenient gap in the early seventh century, although his historical instincts persuaded him the war belonged in that period. He maintained that date in his article, concluding that the embargo simply would not have been perceptible as a gap in imported pottery, and consoled scholars with the unexplored sanctuary of Damia and Auxesia:

> Were it to be dug, one would expect to find quantities of the unpainted hand-made pottery such as was used not only at the Aphaia temple . . . but also at Tiryns, where little other pottery was found, at the Argive Heraion, Corinth, and Perachora: especially drinking-vessels, as Herodotus expressly says πίνειν.[116]

What Dunbabin probably meant was the handmade "Argive monochrome" ware which appears at those sanctuaries. These small lekythoi and pyxides with incised decoration were popular in graves and as offerings from the ninth through the seventh centuries, thus bearing no particular relationship to a specific war, and certainly not a fabric for drinking cups or χυτρίδες.[117] What Dunbabin should have noted is a much more significant type of pottery from Aigina, more likely to be local. The sanctuary of Aphaia did produce a tremendous quantity of coarse and handmade ware, mostly do-

113. Hoppin in Waldstein, *The Argive Heraeum*, II, 174–76. This is the only archaeological evidence invoked by Buck, "Epidaurians, Aeginetans, and Athenians," 12–13, hence his date of 625–480 B.C. for the ban.

114. Ure, *The Origin of Tyranny*, 318–19, in an appendix on the early war.

115. Ibid., 168.

116. Dunbabin, *BSA* 37 (1936/37): 85.

117. "Argive monochrome" has its origins in ninth-century "Pie Ware," develops characteristic shapes and fabric in the eighth century, and is picked up in local imitations in Athens and Corinth, lasting into the seventh century (Jan Bouzek, *The Dark Age Incised Ware* [*Sbornik* 28, 1964]). Cf. the lekythos found with the Eleusis amphora (above, chap. 1, n. 54).

mestic vessels for cooking and serving food (spouted bowls, covered dishes, pitchers, serving trays, tripod cookers, hearth-burnt pots).[118] In the Aphaia publication Thiersch noted this coarse ware, for him an "involuntary reminder of the half-joking designation of Aigina in antiquity as χυτροπῶλις."[119] More such pottery has emerged at Aphaia in the recent Munich excavations, and there are a few fragments of it among the unpublished miscellanea from Aigina in Berlin. However, the nature and context of the pottery suggest that it filled a normal function as coarse and cooking ware (a specialty of the island: above, 2.2) for use at the sanctuary in festivals. The buildings associated with the temple include baths, an "amphipoleion," and probably facilities for cooking and shelter during festivals.[120] The date of the coarse ware which also served such festivals is archaic, as are all finds from the fill for the late archaic terrace and temple. That the pottery was an emergency issue in respect of the prohibition seems less likely than that it was intended for standard use; even if it represents the conditions after the war, the coarse ware provides no precise stratigraphic date.

Since Dunbabin's assignment of the war to the early seventh century, in spite of the rich imports in Protoattic pottery, the most recent attempt to date the war follows Brann's second suggestion (above, n. 88): the late eighth century. In his major publication of Greek Geometric pottery, Nicholas Coldstream introduced the war to explain a lacuna in Attic exports to Aigina in his Late Geometric Ib phase.[121] Later, in a general history of Geometric Greece, he explored the war more fully, calling in Pheidon as an eighth-century figure with the testimony of Pausanias and supported by archaeological evidence from Argos.[122]

Coldstream's argument rests on two assumptions: that Pheidon's career necessarily coincides with, if not accounts for, the wealthiest period in Argive archaeology and that Pheidon was definitely involved in the war with Aigina. The difficulty in associating Pheidon with archaeological evidence was admitted above, and the spotty record of seventh-century Argos (due to lack of publication) may exaggerate the impression of eighth-century wealth.[123]

Coldstream also presumes the role of Argive warships in the rescue of Aigina, but Herodotus suggests rather that troops were ferried over from Epidauros for a defense on land (5.86: διαβάντες ἐς τὴν νῆσον). Indeed, it is far more likely that the Argive alliance with Aigina involved dependence on ships from Aigina, as a friendly base in

118. Furtwängler, *Aphaia*, 441–46, pls. 122–24; Ure, *The Origin of Tyranny*, 320.

119. Thiersch in Furtwängler, *Aphaia*, 441 (on χυτροπῶλις see above, 2.2).

120. Furtwängler, *Aphaia*, 481–91, on minor buildings; cf. D. Ohly, *Tempel und Heiligtum der Aphaia auf Aegina* (Munich, 1978), 32–34.

121. Coldstream, *Greek Geometric Pottery*, 361, n. 10.

122. Coldstream, *Geometric Greece*, 135, 154–56.

123. As admitted by Kelly, *A History of Argos*, 176, n. 16.

the Saronic Gulf, in exchange for a mainland ally for the island.[124] Most important, Pheidon is not mentioned in connection with the war, as emphasized above. To introduce him at all, as Coldstream does, is a measure of interpretation, not proof.

The third objection to Coldstream's hypothesis is his identification of the gap, in a stylistic phase he defined as "the later and less inspired products of the Dipylon workshop (LG Ib: ca. 750–735 B.C.)."[125] It could be possible that this minor aspect of Dipylon influence was simply not exported to Aigina; instead, vases by the Hirschfeld Painter are found throughout rural Attica and represent the Athenian "colonization" of Attica.[126]

Furthermore, Coldstream's selection of a gap leaves unexplained the closing of the Agora wells and the general poverty of Attica in the seventh century; in fact, he presumes a quick recovery of the Attic industry and a resumption of Attic imports to Aigina in LG II that continues through the seventh century.[127] Thus Coldstream's theory avoids the peculiar Protoattic phenomenon analyzed in this study by assuming that the Middle Protoattic pottery found on Aigina represents the recovery of steady imports. Instead, that very pottery could have filled the gap brought on by embargo, as the conclusion to this chapter sets forth.

4. CONCLUSION

To summarize the archaeological evidence against its historical background already points to a likely solution. This monograph has identified a talented workshop resident on Aigina, producing "Attic" pottery for local funerary purposes. The leader of the workshop, the Polyphemus Painter, was a native of Aigina; he and his colleagues combined Attic, Corinthian, and Oriental inspirations in a style eccentric to contemporary Athenian tradition. Historically, this workshop coincides with a period when one would expect a conspicuous absence of Attic pottery on Aigina, according to the most widely accepted date for a war between the two states.

This coincidence need not necessarily be a contradiction, as Dunbabin decided in frustration. As a local manifestation of taste for Attic pottery, the Black and White style could represent a local substitute industry to compensate for the prohibition. Even

124. Jeffery, *Archaic Greece*, 136: "Argos was never a sea power"; Figueira, "Aegina and Athens," 215, 231, 269, 289, 291; Kelly, *A History of Argos*, 74.

125. Coldstream, *Geometric Greece*, 114.

126. Coldstream, *Greek Geometric Pottery*, 399–403, under Aigaleos, Analatos, Anavyssos, Eleusis, Laurion, Menidi, Phaleron, Spata, and Vari for LG Ib from rural Attica (cf. Buck's objections: "Epidaurians, Aeginetans, and Athenians," 9).

127. Coldstream, *Geometric Greece*, 135 (cf. *Greek Geometric Pottery*, 361, n. 10).

116 without the war, one could imagine Greek craftsmen being attracted to the prosperous island, at a period when Athens suffered a depression. But the concentration of the eccentric vases on Aigina, simultaneous with an absence of other Athenian pottery, is unusual, and the embargo suggests a reason for this temporary reorientation of workshops.

The attractive simplicity of this theory cannot hide the weakness inherent in all interpretations of early archaic history, which rely on a network of hypotheses. Only if the identity of the workshop as local is recognized, and if the early seventh-century date for the war is accepted, can the two configurations support each other. In terms of methodology, therefore, the theory is no sounder than Coldstream's solution (if the role of Pheidon in the war is necessary, if the Pausanian chronology for Pheidon is accepted, and if the definition and date of LG Ib are recognized, they would agree on an eighth-century date for the war). However, flexible applications of such methods of argument are not only appropriate but necessary to the reconstruction of protohistoric events.[128] With the acknowledgment of the limitations on such arguments, one can consider a reasonable scenario in which the Aigina workshop fits the tradition of the war.

As admitted above, the growth in prosperity on Aigina and the decline in demand for pottery among Athenians might be sufficient to explain the relocation of a group of artisans to the island, importing the Attic clay they preferred. Moreover, the Middle Protoattic artists now identified as Aiginetan are not the earliest ceramic craftsmen on the island (above, 2.2, 3.5), and the island's success in the middle of the seventh century could be the result of centuries of ceramic experience. By the late seventh century, once the Athenian economy picked up again, Athens would again have attracted a wider ceramic industry and thence dominated it for centuries.

However, the opportunity for a simultaneous solution to the workshop mystery, the poverty of Athens, and the date of the war, all with a single body of evidence, is too good to neglect. With all the hesitation due any such conclusion in early Greek history, one can suggest a date in the early seventh century for an encounter between Aigina, a nascent naval power, and Athens, perhaps weakened by drought or at least dependent on grain imports. The resulting embargo on Attic pottery to the island encouraged a substitute industry on Aigina, now wealthy enough for dependable customers.

The artists active on the island could have been natives trained in Athens, like the Polyphemus Painter, who shows clear influence from Athenian painters (above, 2.1) and who also seems to be a leader of the workshop. His followers had more varied backgrounds: the Ram Jug Painter and the Oresteia Painter are relatives who both have an early piece from Athens while their later work is from Aigina (see catalogue). The

---

128. A typological parallel in methodology for the Aigina war is the Lelantine War, where references in Hesiod and Archilochus, the abandonment of the site of Lefkandi, and the decline of Euboean pottery overseas all supposedly reflect the same event, at a date around 700 B.C.: for a summary see Jeffery, *Archaic Greece*, 64–67, 69–70; Popham and Sackett, *Lefkandi* 1: 11, 368–69, 425–27.

Checkerboard Circle was a more provincial group; their training must have taken place on Aigina, for their exposure was limited to the Polyphemus Painter and the New York Nessos Painter. As a workshop the Aigina craftsmen do not develop a generation of successors; by the Late Protoattic period they disappear, and their only relative, the Painter of Berlin A 34, is absorbed in the Athenian recovery of leadership in production and export. Whether the embargo was lifted, or retained only in the sanctuary mentioned by Herodotus, cannot be extracted from any evidence. If the prohibition applied only to that sanctuary, it is at least reflected at the other sites explored: there is no Middle Protoattic from Aphaia, and the only two "Attic" vessels from Kolonna are both of local fabric (Pls. 10, 22: 484). If private burials were exempt from the prohibition, aristocratic families nevertheless patronized the local workshop, according to the abundance of local Black and White style vases from the Aigina necropolis (above, 1.2).

Outside of Aigina there was little demand for this pottery. Trips to Attica for clay may have been the occasion for a few sales, and how the lone customer from Eleusis acquired his vessel is unknown (by boat, Aigina would be as close as Athens to Eleusis). The single dedication at the Argive Heraion (Pl. 17) could represent a visitor from the allied state, or even a souvenir from Aigina; since Argos participated in the boycott, she may have had access to the same substitute "Attic" pottery.

The connection between Argos and Aigina, emphasized through the tradition that Pheidon first minted coinage on the island, is reinforced through a comparison of other votives from the Heraion with those found on Aigina. The similarities begin in the Geometric period with Argive imports in pottery and seals to Aigina (above, 4.1), at a time when the Dorian island was still a dependency of the Argolid. Particularly striking are the Late Geometric offering trays found at both locales, which confused the early excavators of the Argive Heraion (who conducted microscopic comparisons of the fabric of the trays, to determine whether they were from Argos or Aigina).[129] Egyptian and Egyptianizing objects are also found in large quantity at the Argive Heraion, without any record of Argive activity in Egypt; such imports must have reached Argos through merchants supplying the eastern Peloponnese, and Aigina is the most likely candidate for such a role.[130] Connections such as the Gorgon common to both an ivory seal from the Heraion and the amphora by an Aiginetan painter (above 3.1, n. 33) suggest that both Argos and Aigina participated in the same cultural milieu. The quantity of Protocorinthian pottery found at both sites once caused both Argos and Aigina to be considered possible provenances for it.[131] The similarity in number, size, and type of metal pins

129. Waldstein, *The Argive Heraeum* 2: 64–67, 116; cf. Courbin, *La Céramique géomètrique de l'Argolide*, 552.

130. Waldstein, *The Argive Heraeum* 2: 367–74 (discussion of "Egyptian or Graeco-Egyptian" objects by Lythgoe).

131. Ibid., 64–67, n. 9; 119f. on the "Argive Style" [*sic*].

dedicated at Argos and Aigina adds itself to other duplications in votive material: Rhodian bird bowls, for example, are an import common to both states.[132] The only evidence missing is coinage; one would expect to find Aiginetan "turtles" at the Heraion to support the association between Pheidon and Aiginetan coinage.[133] Finally, at least two inscriptions in Aiginetan letters indicate an ΑΡΓΕΙΟΣ who presumably died or resided on the island.[134] This variety of evidence could reflect a cooperative agreement between Argos and Aigina in the archaic period—perhaps based on the exchange or sharing of naval and infantry resources.

One cannot press a political alliance from the evidence of similar dedications at two sanctuaries where female deities were worshiped. However, the general resemblance in votives makes reasonable the single stand found at the Argive Heraion (Pl. 18) and suggests a cultural, if not a political, connection between Argos and Aigina. The coincidence, in subject and style, of the single well-known seventh-century Argive vase painting with the Polyphemus Painter's name vase suggests a substantial connection between these two Orientalizing styles.[135] Thanks to the recent revival of an early date for the first Greek coinage,[136] the military collaboration against Athens implied by Herodotus is supported by a picture of economic and cultural alliance.

Ceramic and historical evidence can now be brought into a single focus, illuminating the art and activity of the Orientalizing period. Within the history of Athenian vase painting, the Middle Protoattic period has been recast as a phase of specialization and simultaneous experiment in different directions for different purposes. One direction was Aigina, always a reliable customer for Attic pottery and also an imitator, but now a more prosperous city than Athens and one that could capture the exclusive attention of the finest artists. The imbalance in wealth may be related to an actual defeat of Athens by Aigina, producing a change in the pattern of imports for a generation, perhaps a readjustment to hostile conditions if not an explicit prohibition. After the middle of the seventh century, this exclusive workshop dies out and Athens recovers her previous economic security and ceramic monopoly. The successful suppression of Kylon's attack on the Athenian state thus coincides with the recovery of Athenian confidence and prosperity.

132. Compare the bird bowls from the Heraion (Waldstein, *The Argive Heraeum* 2: 135–36) with those from Aigina cited above (4.1).

133. However, one might mention that Argive spits and Aiginetan turtles have been found together in an Argolid temple, at Halieis: M. Jameson, "The Excavation of a Drowned Greek Temple," *Scientific American* 231:4 (1974): 116–17.

134. Jeffery, "IG I² 1007: An Aiginetan Grave Inscription."

135. For the Argive Polyphemus krater, see Courbin, *BCH* 79 (1955). Scraps of contemporary figural painting from Argos promise more of a local school, if only the material were more systematically excavated and published. For a figural fragment, see Courbin, 26, fig. 16 (Inv C 306); a Proto-Argive cult scene is published by Bommelaer, *BCH* 96 (1972).

136. Kagan, *AJA* 86 (1982).

Within the wider context of the Orientalizing world, the reattribution of an innovative workshop is appropriate to a period active in local enterprise. Panhellenic sanctuaries attracted bronze workers, while ivory and metal production was localized at Sparta and Corinth; gem cutting was a specialty of the Cyclades, faience had its own workshop on Rhodes, and pottery apparently was manufactured at most places. In ceramics, especially, local workshops developed at colonial and provincial sites as well as at major mainland exporting cities such as Corinth (above, 3.5). On Aigina the brilliance of the Black and White style encourages a new consideration of the island's productivity in earlier periods, whose local Geometric styles have been overlooked in the focus of scholarship on Athens. Finally, in addition to restoring to Aigina the place she deserves in vase painting, the results of this study cast a new light on Athens in the Orientalizing period. In this active century Athens experienced a brief recession in both political and cultural development. The Athenocentric approach to Greek history, and art history, has avoided the irregularity of evidence in Athens during this period; what has been called the finest painting in early Greek art actually belongs to a city far more able to sponsor it—Aigina.

CATALOGUE

THE POLYPHEMUS PAINTER (ca. 670–640 B.C.)

1. **Metropolitan amphora (Pl. 1)**

   New York, Metropolitan Museum of Art, 1949.101.17a–q, anonymous gift (no provenance).

   Neck-handled amphora with banded body, in fragments. P.H. of neck: 0.288 m. Flying eagles (neck panel, Pl. 1): applied white eye, reserved eye, reserved head. Ornaments: dotted cable strand, hatched triangles, meander cross.

2. **Horses krater (Pl. 2)**

   West Berlin, Antikenmuseum, A 35, from Aigina (necropolis).

   Kotyle krater on stand, with lid. H. 0.575 m. Grazing horses with ladder manes (stand and lid). Black and white rosettes, stuffed rosette, radiate dot rosette, lozenge star, meander square, trefoil (under handle).

   CVA Berlin 1, A 35, pls. 35–36, p. 7 ("Pferde-Maler"); Mylonas, *O protoattikos amphoreus*, pp. 109–10.

3. **Munich krater (Pl. 3)**

   Munich, Staatliche Antikensammlungen, 6090, from Aigina.

   Ovoid krater, probably with stand (broken below belly). P.H. 0.44 m. Animal fights on obverse and reverse (lions and deer). Elaborate floral ornament, much incision.

   CVA München 3, 6090 (1350), pls. 131:2, 133:2; *CVA Berlin 1*, p. 7 ("Pferde-Maler," no. 2); Mylonas, *O protoattikos amphoreus*, p. 110.

4. **Cheiron krater (Pl. 4: 544, 581, 583, 587)**

   Aigina Museum, from Aigina (necropolis).

   Fragments of rim, handle area, and lower body of ovoid krater. Centaur (Cheiron?) carrying animals from branch. Lavish black and white ornaments: cable, leaves, spiral rays and florals; painted bands separated by incision.

   Kraiker, *Aigina*, nos. 544, 581, 583, 587; Brann, *Agora VIII*, no. 558 (attribution of Aigina 583); restored by E. Walter-Karydi (unpublished).

5. **Agora amphora, horses (Pl. 5, *below*)**

   Athens, Agora, P 16991, surface find near Areopagus cemetery.

   Neck-handled amphora (?), fragmentary. P.H. 0.315 m. Grazing horses with ladder manes (belly); black and white rays, meander square (shoulder); black and white pendent tongues, rosettes, and floral ornament (belly).

   Young, *Hesperia* 20 (1951): 86, pl. 37:c. J; Brann, *Agora VIII*, no. 558, pp. 35, 94–95.

6. **Agora amphora, cock (Pl. 5, *above*)**

   Athens, Agora, P 4950, disturbed levels near Tholos cemetery.

   Amphora neck with cock, painted white; dotted cable strand, rosette.

   Young, *Late Geometric Graves*, B 69, pp.

132–33; attributed by Mylonas, *O protoattikos amphoreus*, p. 111; Brann, *Agora VIII*, no. 560.

7. Fragment with mule
Athens, Agora, P 22691, well O 12:1 (Brann, *Hesperia* 30 [1961]: 322–46, third quarter of seventh century B.C.).

Head and neck of mule; incised teeth, anatomy.

Brann, *Hesperia* 30 (1961): 326–27, F 8; Agora VIII, pl. 35, no. 562.

8. Eleusis amphora (Pl. 6)
Eleusis Museum, from West Cemetery, Eleusis.

Neck-handled amphora, missing side below right handle; openwork handles. P.H. 1.42 m. Perseus and Gorgons, Athena (belly); bird (right handle); lion and boar (shoulder); blinding of Polyphemus (neck). Black and white rosette, pomegranate rosette; lavish white paint.

Mylonas, *O protoattikos amphoreus*.

9. Menelas stand (Pl. 7)
Once East Berlin, Antiken-Sammlung, A 42, from Aigina (necropolis).

Conical stand with flaring bowl (rim missing). P.H. 0.68 m. Menelas (dipinto) and warriors, marching right (lower stand); cavalry riders (upper stand); couchant sphinxes (torus molding); animal (lion and deer) fights (upper rim). Stuffed rosette, multiple lozenge; incision, white?

CVA Berlin 1, A 42, pls. 31–33; add Kraiker, *Aigina*, no. 553 (cf. Pl. 4: 555,

556); Mylonas, *O protoattikos amphoreus*, p. 108.

10. Flowery Ornaments stand (Pl. 8)
East Berlin, Antiken-Sammlung, A 41, from Aigina (necropolis).

Conical stand with wide bowl. H. 0.63 m. Marching warriors (lower stand); fighting hoplites, three-quarter shields (upper stand); feeding roosters (torus molding); women carrying protome cauldrons (upper rim). Floral ornaments; much incision, little white.

CVA Berlin 1, A 41, pls. 30, 34:2, p. 7 ("Maler der blumigen Ornamente").

11. Spouted bowl (Pl. 8, *upper right*)
West Berlin, Antikenmuseum, A 44, from Aigina (necropolis).

Dinos with two loop handles, spout. P.H. (near handle) 0.09 m. Chariots and hoplites (bowl). Much incision (incised rosette), no white.

CVA Berlin 1, A 44, pl. 36:1, p. 7 ("Maler der blumigen Ornamente").

12. Fragments, possibly from a stand
Athens, National Museum, from Acropolis.

Fragment with lion's mane (white paint), starburst; fragment drapery; two fragments with faces.

Graef and Langlotz, *Vasen von der Akropolis*, nos. 347a–b (faces), 377 (lion); Cook, *BSA* 35 (1934/35): 194, n. 2; *CVA Berlin 1*, p. 7 ("Maler der Widder-Kanne," no. 14).

THE RAM JUG PAINTER (ca. 660–640 B.C.)

1. Acropolis stand (Pl. 11: 357a, b; 370a, b)
Athens, National Museum, from Acropolis.

Fragments of conical cauldron stand. Grazing horses (?) (lower stand); running dogs, meander cross, outline cable ornament (torus molding); alternate black and white rosettes between cable strands (flat molding); grazing deer, boar, pendent dot-

ted triangles, meander square (rim). No incision (added white lines).

Graef and Langlotz, *Vasen von der Akropolis*, nos. 357a–b, 370a–b; DAI photo "Akropolis Vasen 13" (unnumbered fragment); *CVA Berlin 1*, p. 7 ("Maler der Widder-Kanne," no. 14); Cook, *BSA* 35 (1934/35): 194, nn. 3–4.

2. Lions dinos (Pl. 12, *right*)
West Berlin, Antikenmuseum, A 43, from Aigina (necropolis).

Dinos with round base, imitation ring handles. H. ca. 0.185 m. Pacing lions, floral ornaments in field (belly).

CVA Berlin 1, A 43, pls. 34:1, 35, p. 7 ("Maler der Widder-Kanne," no. 6).

3. Peleus amphora (Pl. 12, *left*)

West Berlin, Antikenmuseum, A 9, from Aigina (necropolis).

Neck-handled amphora, body in fragments. Peleus and Achilles (side A); Cheiron (side B); floral ornament on neck.

CVA Berlin 1, A 9, pl. 5, p. 7 ("Maler der Widder-Kanne," no. 10).

4. Ram Jug (Pl. 10)

Aigina Museum, from Aigina (Kolonna sanctuary).

Imitation Rhodian oinochoe; non-Attic fabric. D. 0.255 m. Odysseus and companions escaping from cave of Polyphemus (body); black and white leaves (neck). Ornaments in field: black spiral rays, dot rosette, multiple lozenge, dotted triangle; white paint, no incision.

Pallat, *AthMitt* 22 (1897), pl. 8; Cook, *BSA* 35 (1934/35): 189–95; Kraiker, *Aigina*, no. 566, pls. 44–45.

5. Hoplites bowl (Pl. 11: 584, 585)

Aigina Museum, from Aigina (Kolonna sanctuary).

Dinos, everted rim; spout (or handle?). Hoplites arming (side A); mounted archers, flautist (side B). No ornaments in field; much incision.

Archaeological Reports 1945–47, pl. 7:b, attributed in *CVA Berlin 1*, p. 7 ("Maler der Widder-Kanne," no. 4); Kraiker, *Aigina*, pl. 42, nos. 584, 585.

6. Fragment of Horses bowl (Pl. 11: 577)

Aigina Museum, from Aigina.

Fragment of bowl with flat rim. P.H. 0.044 m, P.W. 0.092 m. Team of horses, incised manes; pendent spiral.

Kraiker, *Aigina*, no. 577, pl. 42, p. 89.

7. Acropolis face (Pl. 11, unnumbered fragment)

Athens, National Museum, found under Acropolis Museum.

Convex fragment with head (of male?) facing left, swallow.

Archaeological Reports 1951, pl. 6:4b; Karouzou, *ArkhEph* (1952), pl. 9:3.

THE ORESTEIA PAINTER (ca. 660–650 B.C.)

1. Centaurs krater (Pl. 14)

Athens, Kerameikos Museum, 98, from mid-seventh century mound in Kerameikos.

Deep krater with steep inturned rim, missing most of lower body. D. ca. 0.40 m. Black and white centaurs marching right, with branches. No incision; few ornaments (ray rosette, stacked zigzag).

Kübler, *Kerameikos VI, 2*, no. 35, pl. 29.

2. Oresteia krater (Pl. 13)

Once East Berlin, Antiken-Sammlung, A 32, from Aigina (necropolis).

Ovoid krater on stand with bull's-head handles, missing fragments from reverse. H. 0.66 m. Capture scene, with black warrior seizing white man, two white women mourning (side A); Apollo and Artemis (?) (side B); Oriental monsters under handles. Incision and white paint; bird and grasshopper ornaments.

CVA Berlin 1, A 32, pls. 18–21, p. 7 ("Maler der Widder-Kanne," no. 3).

3. Fragment with sphinx.

Aigina Museum, from Aigina (necropolis).

Fragment of large open shape (krater?). P.H. 0.088 m. Head of sphinx repainted over white; incised hair.

Kraiker, *Aigina*, pl. 43, no. 582, pp. 89–90.

THE NEW YORK NESSOS PAINTER (ca. 650–640 B.C.)

124 1. New York Nessos amphora (Pl. 15)
New York, Metropolitan Museum of Art, 11.210.1, said to be from Smyrna.

Neck-handled amphora, missing fragments from belly. H. 1.085 m. Herakles, Nessos, and Deianeira, charioteer (?), running figure under handle (belly); lion attacking deer (neck); grazing horses (shoulder). Much incision and white; misfired red patches.

Richter, *JHS* 32 (1912): 370–84, pls. 10–12.

2. Iphigeneia krater (Pl. 16)
Boston, Museum of Fine Arts, 6.67, anonymous loan.

Ovoid krater in fragments (missing most of lower body), with double handles. P.H. 0.52 m. Sacrifice (of Iphigeneia?) on belly, bearded figure under handles.

White and misfired red; elaborate floral ornament under handles.

Vermeule and Chapman, *AJA* 75 (1971), pls. 69–71.

3. Agora fragments with animals, ornaments
Athens, Agora:
P 26201 (mixed deposit near early wells) = Brann 463;
P 25725 (C–G 13:16) = Brann 464;
P 25323 (seventh-early sixth-century level between Metroon and Great Drain) = Brann 465;
P 459 (debris from votive deposit, 700–650 B.C.) = Burr *Hesperia* 2 (1933), no. 132; Brann 466;
P 25327 (disturbed fill near Tholos) = Brann 467.

Brann, *Agora VIII*, pl. 34, nos. 463–67.

THE CHECKERBOARD PAINTER (ca. 650 B.C.)

1. Ovoid kraters with lids, from Aigina (necropolis):
   a. West Berlin, Antikenmuseum, A 21 (Pl. 19)
   Man and centaur (Herakles and Nessos?). H. 0.21 m.
   b. East Berlin, Antiken-Sammlung, A 22 (Pl. 20)
   Lions and deer. H. 0.62 m.
   c. Once East Berlin, Antiken-Sammlung, A 24.

   Animals. P.H. 0.535 m.
   d. East Berlin, Antiken-Sammlung, A 25.
   Animals. P.H. 0.145 m.
   e. Once East Berlin, A 23.
   Lid with lion and deer. D. 0.29 m. Sprawling brushwork, copious white; no incision. Debased Black and White Style ornaments.

CVA Berlin 1, A 21–25, pls. 10–15, 37:3, p. 7 ("Schachbrett-Maler").

NEAR POLYPHEMUS PAINTER (?)

1. Conical stand (Pl. 18)
West Berlin, Antikenmuseum, A 40, from Aigina (necropolis).

Conical stand. P.H. 0.52 m. Warriors in spear and sword combat, Oriental goblin (lower stand); couchant sphinxes with floating eyes, bird and worm (upper

stand); alternating black and white rosettes between cable strands (torus molding). (Rim fragment, sphinx, from separate stand by Polyphemus Painter?)

CVA Berlin 1, A 40, pls. 28–29; Cook, "Protoattici vasi," p. 501 (early Polyphemus Painter).

PLATES

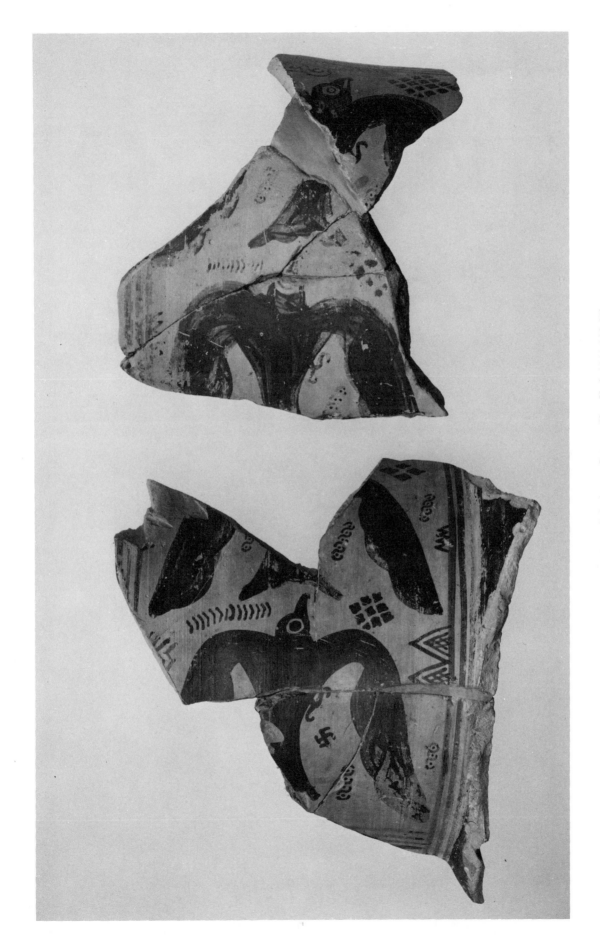

1. Metropolitan amphora, Polyphemus Painter (New York 1949.101.17)

2. Horses krater and lid, Polyphemus Painter (West Berlin A 35)

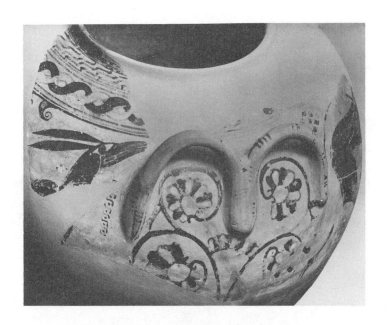

3. Munich krater and detail near handle, Polyphemus Painter (Munich 6090)

556

581

555

587

544

581

583

4. Cheiron krater and other fragments, Polyphemus Painter (Aigina Museum)

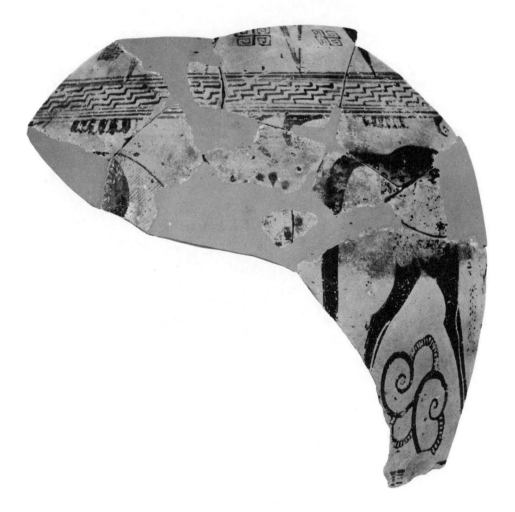

5. Neck amphoras, Polyphemus Painter (Athens, Agora P 4950, *above*, P 16991, *below*)

6. Eleusis amphora and details, Polyphemus Painter (Eleusis Museum)

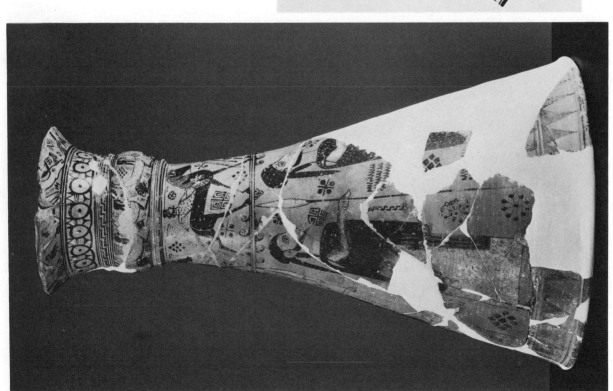

7. Menelas stand and drawing of reverse, Polyphemus Painter (once East Berlin A 42)

8. Flowery Ornaments stand with detail (East Berlin A 41) and bowl (West Berlin A 44), Polyphemus Painter

9. Ovoid krater, Woman Painter (West Berlin A 34)

10. Ram Jug (Aigina Museum 566)

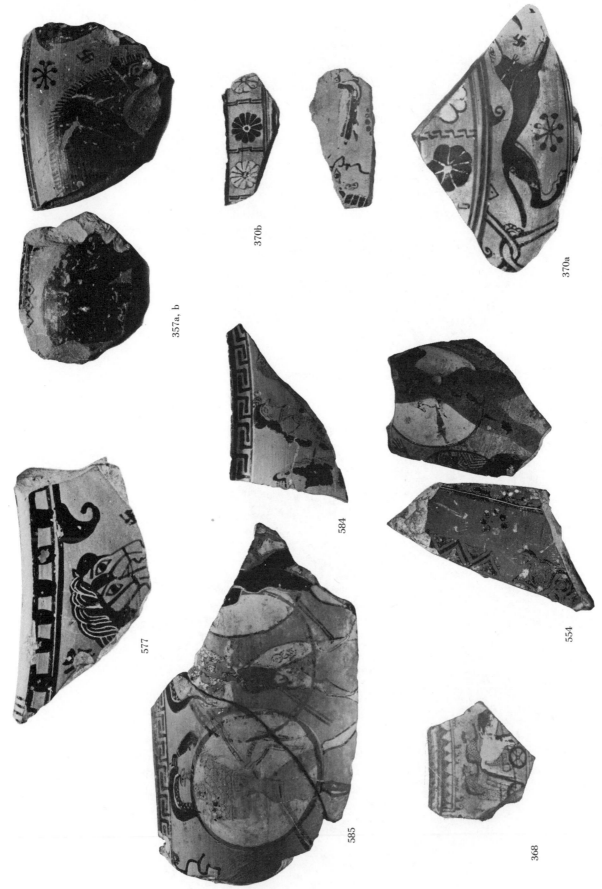

357a, b

370b

370a

584

577

554

585

368

11. Fragments from Athenian Acropolis and Aigina, Ram Jug Painter and others (Athens, National Museum, and Aigina Museum)

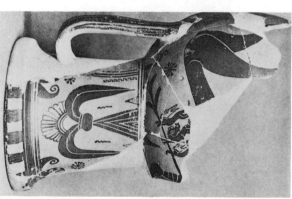
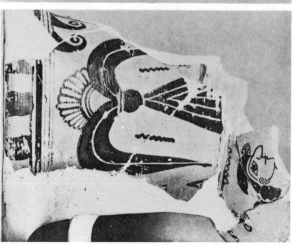

12. Peleus amphora, lions dinos, Ram Jug Painter (West Berlin A 9, A 43)

13. Oresteia krater (drawing), Oresteia Painter (once East Berlin A 32)

14. Centaurs krater, Oresteia Painter (Athens, Kerameikos Museum 98)

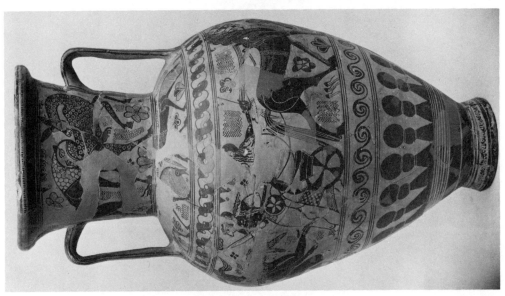

15. New York Nessos amphora (New York 11.210.1)

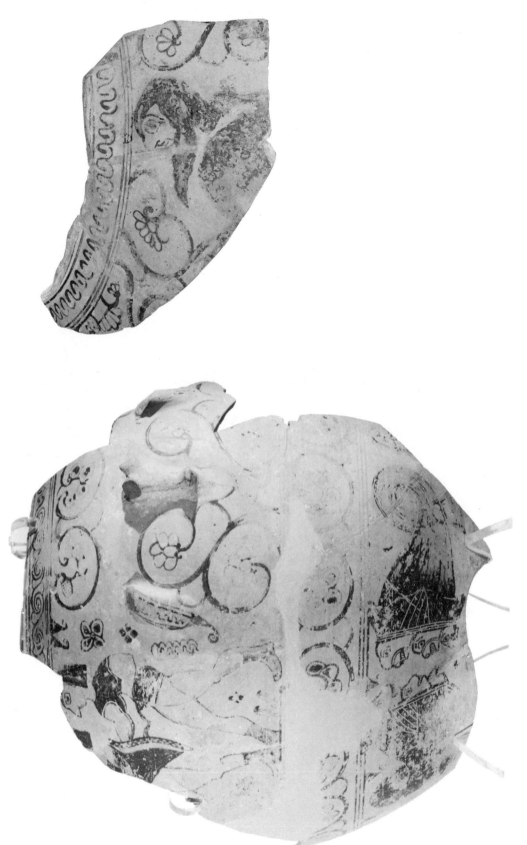

16. Iphigeneia krater and detail, New York Nessos Painter (Boston 6.67)

17. Argive Heraion stand (Athens, National Museum)

18. Conical stand and drawing, near Polyphemus Painter (West Berlin A 40)

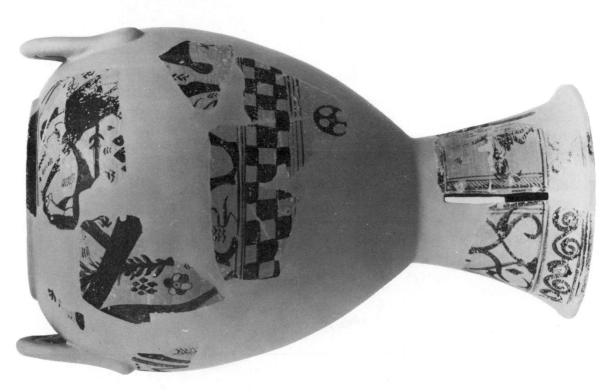

19. Ovoid krater and detail of reverse, Checkerboard Painter (West Berlin A 21)

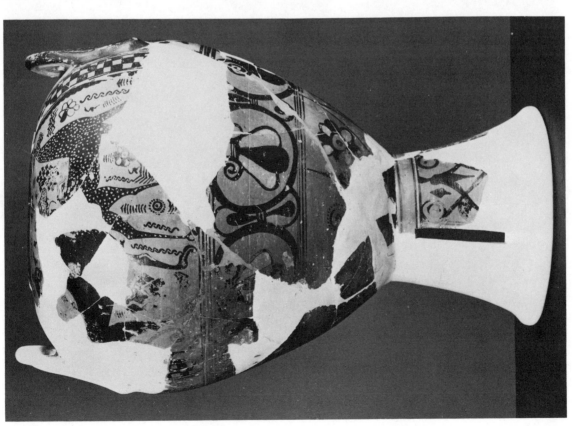

20. Ovoid krater and details, Checkerboard Painter (East Berlin A 22)

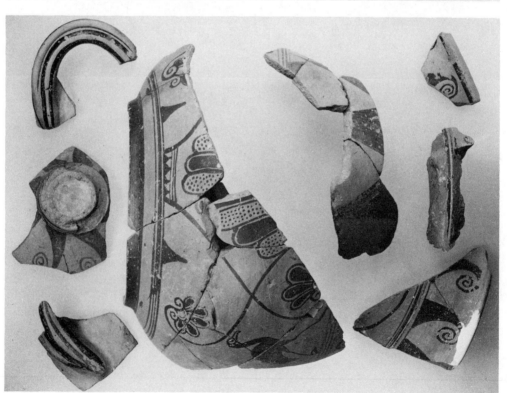

21. Ovoid kraters from Aigina (East Berlin A 31, *left*, West Berlin A 33, *right*)

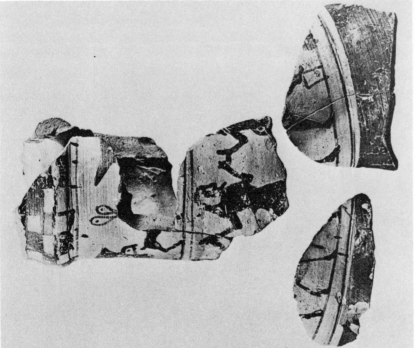

22. Local vases from Aigina (West Berlin A 46, *above*, Aigina Museum 484, *right*)

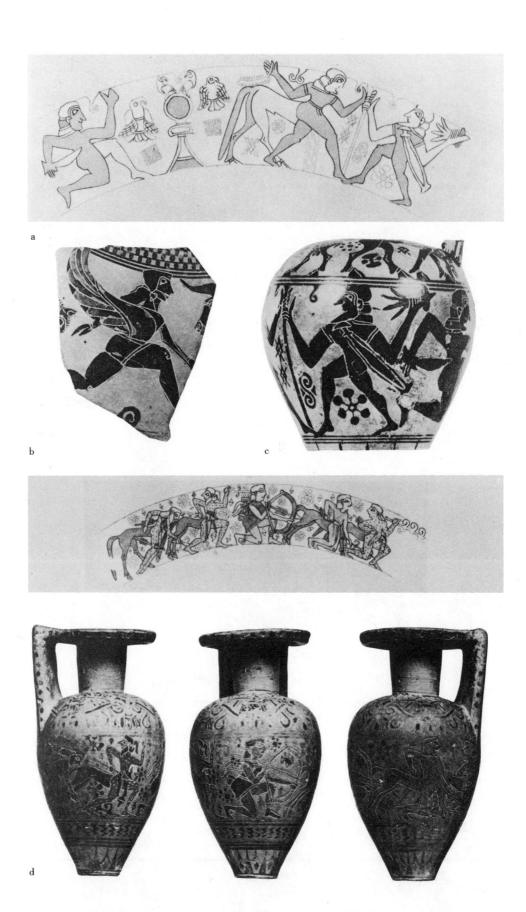

23. Middle Protocorinthian pottery:
      Ajax Painter: *a*, *b*, drawing and detail of aryballos from Corinth (Boston 95.12); *c*, oinochoe (Aigina Museum 265)
      MacMillan Painter: *d*, aryballos from Corinth (Berlin 2686)

24. Chigi vase, MacMillan Painter (Rome, Villa Giulia Museum)

25. Protocorinthian kotylae (Aigina Museum 191, *left*, and 253 [Bellerophon Painter], *right*)

26. Kerameikos mugs (Athens, Kerameikos Museum 73, *left*, 1280, *right*)

27. Kotyle kraters (Athens, Kerameikos Museum 130, *above*, 151, *below*)

BIBLIOGRAPHY

Andrewes, Anthony. "The Corinthian Actaeon and Pheidon of Argos." *CQ* 43 (1949): 70–75.

Barnett, R. D. "The Amathus Shield-Boss Rediscovered and the Amathus Bowl Reconsidered." *RDAC* 1977, pp. 157–69.

Beaumont, R. L. "Greek Influence in the Adriatic Sea before the Fourth Century B.C." *JHS* 56 (1936): 159–204.

Beazley, John Davidson. "Groups of Early Attic Black-Figure." *Hesperia* 13 (1944): 38–57.

————. *The Development of Attic Black Figure*. Berkeley: University of California Press, 1951.

Benson, Jack L. *Die Geschichte der korinthischen Vasen*. Basel: Schwabe, 1953.

Beyer, Immo. "Die Datierung der grossen Reliefgiebel des alten Athena-Tempels." *AA* (1977): 44–74.

Blegen, Carl W. "Inscriptions on Geometric Pottery from Mount Hymettos." *AJA* 38 (1934): 10–28.

Boardman, John. "Pottery from Eretria." *BSA* 47 (1952): 1–48.

————. "Painted Votive Plaques and an Inscription from Aigina." *BSA* 49 (1954): 183–201.

————. "Early Euboean Pottery and History." *BSA* 52 (1957): 1–29.

————. *Island Gems: A Study of Greek Seals in the Geometric and Early Archaic Periods*. London: Society for the Promotion of Hellenic Studies, suppl. paper no. 10, 1963.

————. "Island Gems Aftermath." *JHS* 88 (1968): 1–12.

————. *Athenian Black Figured Vases: A Handbook*. London: Thames and Hudson, 1974.

————. *The Greeks Overseas*. 3d ed. London: Thames and Hudson, 1980.

Böhlau, J. "Frühattische Vasen." *JdI* 2 (1887): 33–66.

Bommelaer, J.-Fr. "Nouveaux documents de céramique Proto-Argienne." *BCH* 96 (1972): 229–51.

Borell, Brigitte. *Attisch geometrische Schalen: Eine spätgeometrische Keramikgattung und ihre Beziehungen zum Orient*. Heidelberg, 1978.

Brann, Eva. "Seventh Century Sherds from the Olympieion Area." *Hesperia* 28 (1959): 251–52.

————. "Protoattic Well Groups from the Athenian Agora." *Hesperia* 30 (1961): 305–79.

————. *Agora VIII: Late Geometric and Protoattic Pottery*. Princeton: American School of Classical Studies at Athens, 1962.

Brašynski, J. "Nouveaux documents pour l'étude des contacts céramiques d'Olbia aux VI.–V. siècle av. n. e." *Archeologia* 19 (1968): 45–60.

Brein, Friedrich. *Der Hirsch in der griechischen Frühzeit*. Vienna: Notring, 1969.

Brokaw, Clotilde. "Concurrent Styles in Late Geometric and Early Protoattic Vase Painting." *AthMitt* 78 (1963): 63–73.

Brückner, A., and E. Pernice. "Ein attischer Friedhof." *AthMitt* 18 (1893): 73–191.

Buchner, Giorgio, and John Boardman. "Seals from Ischia and the Lyre-Player Group." *JdI* 81 (1966): 1–62.

Buck, R. J. "Epidaurians, Aeginetans, and Athenians." in *Classical Contributions: Studies in Honor of Malcolm Fr. McGregor*, edited by Gordon S. Shrimpton and David J. McCargar, pp. 5–13. Locust Valley, N.Y. J. J. Augustin, 1981.

Burke, Susan. "A Protoattic High Standed Bowl in Buffalo." *AJA* 78 (1974): 63–65.

Burn, A. R. "The So-Called 'Trade Leagues' in Early Greek History and the Lelantine War." *JHS* 49 (1929): 14–57.

————. "Early Greek Chronology." *JHS* 69 (1949): 70–73.

————. *The Warring States of Greece*. London: Thames and Hudson, 1968.

Burr, Dorothy. "A Geometric House and a Proto-Attic Votive Deposit." *Hesperia* 2 (1933): 542–640.

128

Cadoux, T. J. "The Athenian Archons from Kreon to Hypsichides." *JHS* 68 (1948): 70–123.

Callipolitis-Feytmans, Denise. *Les Louteria attiques*. Athenes, 1968.

———. *Les Plats attiques à figures noires*. Paris: De Boccard, 1974.

Camp, John McK. "A Drought in the Late Eighth Century B.C." *Hesperia* 48 (1979): 397–411.

Canciani, Fulvio. "Coppe 'fenice' in Italia." *JdI* 90 (1978): 1–6.

Caskey, J. L., and Pierre Amandry. "Investigations at the Heraion of Argos, 1949." *Hesperia* 21 (1952): 162–221.

Coldstream, Nicholas. *Greek Geometric Pottery*. London: Methuen, 1968.

———. *Geometric Greece*. London: Methuen, 1977.

Coleman, John. "Archaic Pottery from Pylos in Elis." *AAA* 1 (1968): 285–88.

Colonna, G. "I Greci di Adria." *RivStordell'Ant* 4 (1974): 1–21.

Cook, John M. "Protoattic Pottery." *BSA* 35 (1934/35): 165–219.

———. "Athenian Workshops around 700." *BSA* 42 (1947): 139–55.

———. "Protoattici vasi." In *Enciclopedia dell'Arte Antica*, vol. 6, Rome: Istituto dell'Enciclopedia Italiana, 1965, pp. 495–504.

Cook, Robert M. "The Distribution of Chiote Pottery." *BSA* 44 (1949): 154–61.

———. "Die Bedeutung der bemalten Keramik für den griechischen Handel." *JdI* 74 (1959): 114–23.

———. *Greek Painted Pottery*. 3d ed. London: Methuen, 1972.

———. "Archaic Trade: Three Conjectures." *JHS* 99 (1979): 114–23.

———, and A. G. Woodhead. "Painted Inscriptions on Chiot Pottery." *BSA* 47 (1952): 159–70.

Courbin, Paul. "Un Fragment de cratère protoargien." *BCH* 79 (1955): 1–49.

———. *La Céramique géométrique de l'Argolide*. Paris: De Boccard, 1966.

CVA Athènes 2: Musée National 2 (Grèce 2). Edited by Semni Karouzou. Paris: Librairie Ancienne Honoré Champion, 1954.

CVA Berlin 1 (Deutschland 2). Edited by Richard Eilmann and Kurt Gebauer. Munich: Beck, 1938.

CVA Cambridge 1 (Great Britain 2). Edited by Winifred Lamb. Oxford: Oxford University Press, n.d.

CVA La Haye 2: Musée Scheurleer 2 (Pay-Bas 2). Edited by C. W. Lunsigh Scheurleer. Paris: Librairie Ancienne Honoré Champion, 1931.

CVA Mainz 1 (Deutschland 15). Edited by R. Hampe and E. Simon. Munich: Beck, 1959.

CVA München 3 (Deutschland 9). Edited by R. Lullies. Munich: Beck, 1952.

Davies, Mark. "Thoughts on the Oresteia before Aeschylus." *BCH* 93 (1969): 214–60.

Davison, Jean. "Attic Geometric Workshops." *Yale Classical Studies* 16 (1960).

Delivorrias, A. "Amphoreas protoattikos." *Deltion* 20: A (1965): 65–74.

Dontas, George. "Local Imitations of Corinthian Vases." *Hesperia* 37 (1968): 331–37.

Drews, R. "The Earliest Greek Settlements on the Black Sea." *JHS* 96 (1976): 18–31.

Ducat, Jean. "L'Archaisme à la recherche de points de repère chronologiques." *BCH* 86 (1962): 165–84.

Dunbabin, T. J. "Ἔχθρη παλαιή." *BSA* 37 (1936–37): 83–91.

———. "An Attic Bowl." *BSA* 45 (1950): 193–202.

———. "The Chronology of Protocorinthian Vases." *ArkhEph* 1953–54, pp. 247–62.

———, and Martin Robertson. "Some Protocorinthian Vase-Painters." *BSA* 48 (1953): 172–81.

Fellmann, Berthold. *Die antiken Darstellungen des Polyphem*. Munich: Fink, 1972.

———. "Zur Deutung frühgriechischer Körperornamente." *JdI* 93 (1978): 1–29.

Figueira, Thomas. "Aegina and Athens in the Archaic and Classical Periods: A Sociopolitical Investigation." Diss., University of Pennsylvania, 1977. Ann Arbor: University Microfilms.

———. "Aeginetan Membership in the Peloponnesian League." *CP* 76 (1981): 1–24.

———. *Aegina: Society and Politics*. New York: Arno Press, 1981.

Fittschen, Klaus. *Untersuchungen zum Beginn der Sagendarstellungen bei den Griechen*. Berlin: Hessling, 1969.

Furtwängler, Adolf. "Schüssel von Aegina." *AZ* 40 (1882): 197–208.

———. *Aegina: Das Heiligtum der Aphaia*. Munich: Königliche Bayerliche Akademie der Wissenschaften, 1906.

Geroulanos, Johannes. "Grabsitten des ausgehenden geometrischen Stils im Bereich des Gutes Trachones bei Athen." *AthMitt* 88 (1973): 1–54.

Gjerstad, Einar. "Decorated Metal Bowls from Cyprus." *OpusAth* 4 (1946): 1–18.

———. *The Cypro-Geometric, Cypro-Archaic and Cypro-Classical Periods.* Vol. 4:2 in *The Swedish Cyprus Expedition.* Stockholm: The Swedish Cyprus Expedition, 1948.

———. *Greek Geometric and Archaic Pottery Found in Cyprus.* Stockholm: Paul Åstrøm, 1977.

Graef, Botho, and Ernst Langlotz. *Die antiken Vasen von der Akropolis zu Athen.* Berlin: W. de Gruyter, 1909–25.

Hackl, R. "Zwei frühattische Gefässe der Münchner Vasensammlung." *JdI* 22 (1907): 78–105.

Hammond, N. G. L. "The Seisachtheia and the Nomothesia of Solon." *JHS* 60 (1940): 71–83.

Hampe, Roland. *Ein frühattischer Grabfund.* Mainz: Römisch-Germanisches Zentralmuseum, 1960.

———, and Adam Winter. *Bei Töpfern und Zieglern in Süditalien, Sizilien und Griechenland.* Mainz: Römisch-Germanisches Zentralmuseum, 1960.

Hanfmann, George M. A. "A Syrian from Sounion." *Hesperia* 31 (1962): 236–37.

Harrison, Evelyn B. "Fragments of an Early Attic Kouros from the Athenian Agora." *Hesperia* 24 (1955): 290–304.

———. "Notes on Daedalic Dress." *Essays in Honor of Dorothy Kent Hill, JWalt* 36 (1977): 37–48.

Harvey, F. D. "Sostratos of Aegina." *ParPass* 31 (1976): 206–214.

Higgins, Reynolds. *Greek Terracottas.* London: Methuen, 1967.

Holwerda, A. E. J. "Korinthisch-attische Vasen." *JdI* 5 (1890): 237–68.

Humphreys, S. C. "Family Tombs and Tomb Cult in Ancient Athens: Tradition or Traditionalism?" *JHS* 100 (1980): 96–126.

Hurwit, Jeffrey. "Image and Frame in Greek Art." *AJA* 81 (1977): 1–30.

Jacobsthal, Paul. *Greek Pins and Their Connexions with Europe and Asia.* Oxford: Clarendon, 1956.

Jeffery, Lillian H. "Comments on Some Archaic Greek Inscriptions." *JHS* 69 (1949): 25–38.

———. *The Local Scripts of Archaic Greece.* Oxford: Oxford University Press, 1961.

———. "IG I² 1007: An Aeginetan Grave Inscription." In *Phoros: Tribute to Benjamin Dean Meritt*, edited by D. W. Bradeen and M. F. McGregor, pp. 76–84. Locust Valley, N.Y.: J. J. Augustin, 1974.

———. *Archaic Greece: The City-States c. 700–500 B.C.* London: Methuen, 1976.

Johnston, Alan. "The Rehabilitation of Sostratos." *ParPass* 27 (1972): 416–23.

———, and R. E. Jones. "The SOS Amphora." *BSA* 73 (1978): 103–14.

Kagan, Donald. "The Dates of the Earliest Greek Coins." *AJA* 86 (1982): 343–60.

Kahil, Lilly Ghali-. "Quelques vases du sanctuaire d'Artemis à Brauron." In *Neue Ausgrabungen in Griechenland. AK* supplement 1 (1963): 5–29.

Kardara, Chrysoula. "On Mainland and Rhodian Workshops." *AJA* 59 (1955): 51–54.

———. *Rhodiake angeiographia.* Athens: Archaeological Society, 1963.

Karo, Georg. "Menelas auf einer frühattischen Vase." *26. Hallisches Winckelmannsprogramm*, Halle, 1928, pp. 10–14.

———. *An Attic Cemetery.* Philadelphia: Oberlaender Trust, 1943.

Karouzos, Christos. "Eine Naxische Amphora des früheren 7. Jahrhunderts." *JdI* 52 (1937): 166–97.

Karouzou, Semni Papaspyridi-. "Archaïka mnemeia tou Ethnikou Mouseiou." *ArkhEph* (1952): 149–66.

———. *Angeia tou Anagyrountos.* Athens: Archaeological Society, 1963.

Kelly, Thomas. "The Calaurian Amphictyony." *AJA* 70 (1966): 113–21.

———. *A History of Argos to 500 B.C.* Minneapolis: University of Minnesota Press, 1977.

Kemp-Lindemann, Dagmar. *Darstellungen des Achilleus in der griechischen und römischen Kunst.* Archäologische Studien no. 3. Frankfurt am Main: Peter Lang, 1977.

Killian, Imma. "Weihungen an Eileithyia und Artemis Orthia." *ZPE* 31 (1978): 219–22.

King, Cynthia. "More Pots by the Mesogeia Painter." *AJA* 80 (1976): 79–82.

Knoblauch, Peter. "Neuere Untersuchungen an den Hafen von Aegina." *BonnJbb* 169 (1969): 104–16.

———. "Die Hafenanlage der Stadt Aegina." *Deltion* 27 (1972): 50–84.

Knox, Mary. "Polyphemos and His Near Eastern Relations." *JHS* 99 (1979): 164–65.

Kraiker, Wilhelm. *Aigina: Die Vasen des 10. bis 8. Jh. v. Chr.* Berlin: Gebr. Mann, 1951.

Kübler, Karl. *Altattische Malerei.* Tübingen: Wasmuth, 1950.

———. *Kerameikos VI, 1: Die Nekropole des späten*

130

8. bis frühen 6. Jahrhunderts. Berlin: de Gruyter, 1959.

————. *Kerameikos VI, 2: Die Nekropole des späten 8. bis frühen 6. Jahrhunderts.* Berlin: de Gruyter, 1970.

Lang, Mabel. "Kylonian Conspiracy." *CP* 62 (1967): 243–49.

Langdon, Merle. *A Sanctuary of Zeus on Mount Hymettos. Hesperia,* supplement 16. Princeton: American School of Classical Studies, 1976.

Loeschke, G. "Vase aus Aegina." *AthMitt* 22 (1897): 259–64.

Lorimer, H. L. "The Hoplite Phalanx with Special Reference to the Poems of Archilochus and Tyrtaeus." *BSA* 42 (1947): 76–138.

Matz, Friedrich. *Geschichte der griechischen Kunst.* Vol. 1: *Die geometrische und früharchaische Form.* Frankfurt am Main: Klostermann, 1950.

Mertens-Horn, Madeleine. "Beobachtungen an dädalischen Tondächern." *JdI* 93 (1978): 30–65.

Moustakas, Charidemos. "Kimolos." *AthMitt* 69–70 (1954–55): 153–58.

Mylonas, George. *O protoattikos amphoreus tes Eleusinos.* Athens: Archaeological Society, 1957.

————. *To dutikon nekrotapheion tes Eleusinos.* 2 vols. Athens: Archaeological Society, 1975.

Pallat, Ludwig. "Ein Vasenfund aus Aegina." *AthMitt* 22 (1897): 265–333.

Papastamos, Dimitrios. *Melische Amphoren.* Münster/Westphalia: Aschendorff, 1970.

Payne, Humfry. "Cycladic Vase Painting of the Seventh C." *JHS* 46 (1926): 203–18.

————. *Necrocorinthia: A Study of Corinthian Art of the Archaic Period.* Oxford: Clarendon, 1931.

————. *Protokorinthische Vasenmalerei. Bilder griechische Vasen,* 7. Berlin: H. Keller, 1933. Reprint. Mainz: Zabern, 1974.

————. *Perachora I: The Architecture, Bronzes and Terracottas.* Oxford: Clarendon, 1940.

————, et al. *Perachora II: Pottery, Ivories, Scarabs and Other Objects from the Votive Deposit of Hera Limenia.* Edited by T. J. Dunbabin. Oxford: Clarendon, 1962.

Pendlebury, J. D. S. *Aegyptiaca: A Catalogue of Egyptian Objects in the Aegean Area.* Cambridge: Cambridge University Press, 1930.

Pernice, Ernst. "Bruchstücke altattischer Vasen." *AthMitt* 20 (1895): 116–26.

Pfuhl, Ernst. *Malerei und Zeichnung der Griechen.* Munich: F. Bruckman, 1923.

Price, Martin, and Nancy Waggoner. *Archaic Greek Coinage: The Asyut Hoard.* London: Vecchi, 1975.

Richter, Gisela M. A. "A New Early Attic Vase." *JHS* 32 (1912): 370–84.

Ridgway, Brunilde. *The Archaic Style in Greek Sculpture.* Princeton: Princeton University Press, 1977.

Robertson, C. Martin. "Excavations in Ithaca." *BSA* 43 (1948): 1–124.

————. *Greek Painting.* New York: Skira, 1959.

————. *A History of Greek Art.* London: Cambridge University Press, 1975.

Roebuck, Carl. "Pottery from the North Slope of the Akropolis." *Hesperia* 9 (1940): 141–260.

————. "The Grain Trade between Greece and Egypt." *CP* 45 (1950): 236–47.

————. "The Organization of Naukratis." *CP* 46 (1951): 212–20.

Ruckert, Anne. *Frühe Keramik Boeotiens: Form und Dekoration der Vasen des späten 8. und frühen 7. Jhr. v. Chr. AK* supplement 10, 1976.

Rumpf, Andreas. *Malerei und Zeichnung der klassischen Antike.* Munich: Beck, 1953.

Salmon, John T. "Political Hoplites?" *JHS* 97 (1977): 84–101.

Schefold, Karl. *Die Griechen und ihre Nachbarn.* Berlin: Propyläen, 1967.

————. *Myth and Legend in Early Greek Art.* New York: Abrams, 1967.

Schiering, Wolfgang. *Werkstätten orientalisierender Keramik auf Rhodos.* Berlin: Gebr. Mann, 1957.

Schiffler, Birgit. *Die Typologie des Kentauren in der antiken Kunst vom 10. bis zum Ende des 4. Jhr. v. Chr.* Archäologische Studien no. 4. Frankfurt am Main: Peter Lang, 1976.

Schilardi, Dimitrios. "Anaskaphe pros ta Makra Teiche kai e oinochoe tou Taurou." *ArkhEph* 1975, pp. 66–149.

Smith, Cecil. "A Proto-Attic Vase." *JHS* 22 (1902): 29–45.

Snodgrass, Anthony. *Early Greek Armour and Weapons from the End of the Bronze Age to 600 B.C.* Edinburgh: Edinburgh University Press, 1964.

————. "The Hoplite Reform and History." *JHS* 85 (1965): 110–22.

————. *Archaic Greece: The Age of Experiment.* London: Dent, 1980.

————. "Towards the Interpretation of the Geometric Figure Scenes." *AthMitt* 93 (1980): 51–58.

Strøm, Ingrid. "Some Groups of Cycladic Vase-Painting from the 7th Cent. B.C." *ActaA* 33 (1962): 221–78.

Torelli, Mario. "Il Santuario di Hera a Gravisca." *ParPass* 26 (1971): 44–67.

Touloupa, Evi. "Une gorgone en bronze de l'Acropole." *BCH* 93 (1969): 862–64.

Tréziny, Henri. "Megara Hyblaea X: Une série de cratères subgéometriques de types attiques." *MEFR* 91 (1979): 7–62.

Ure, Percy. *The Origin of Tyranny*. Cambridge: Cambridge University Press, 1922.

Vanderpool, Eugene. "A Relief Pithos Fragment from Attica." *AAA* 4 (1971): 75–76.

Vermeule, Emily, and Suzanne Chapman. "A Protoattic Sacrifice?" *AJA* 75 (1971): 285–93.

von Freytag, Bettina. "Neue frühattische Funde aus dem Kerameikos." *AthMitt* 90 (1975): 49–81.

von Steuben, Hans. *Frühgriechische Sagendarstellungen in Korinth und Athen*. Berlin: Hessling, 1968.

Walberg, Gisela. "A Bichrome V Bowl with Wavy Sides." *RDAC* 1979, pp. 276–80.

Waldstein, Charles. *The Argive Heraeum*. Vol. 2. Boston: Houghton Mifflin, 1905.

Walter, Hans, ed. *Alt-Ägina II, 1*. Mainz: Zabern, 1982.

Walter-Karydi, Elena. "Zwei Giebel-Figuren des Apollon-Tempels auf Aegina." *AA* 1979, pp. 481–87.

Webb, Virginia. *Archaic Greek Faience: Miniature Scent Bottles and Related Objects from East Greece, 650–500 B.C.* Warminster: Aris and Phillips, 1978.

Weinberg, Saul. "What Is Proto-Corinthian Geometric?" *AJA* 45 (1941): 30–44.

———. *Corinth VII, 1: The Geometric and Orientalizing Pottery*. Cambridge: Harvard University Press, 1943.

———, ed. *The Aegean and the Near East: Studies Presented to Hetty Goldman on the Occasion of Her Seventy-Fifth Birthday*. Locust Valley, N.Y. J. J. Augustin, 1956.

Welter, Gabriel. "Ausgrabungen." *Gnomon* 5 (1929): 415.

———. "Ausgrabungen." *FuF* 1931, pp. 181–82, 261–62.

———. "Aiginetische Keramik." *AA* 52 (1937): 19–26.

———. "Aeginetica I–XII" and "Aeginetica XIII–XXIV." *AA* 53 (1938): 1–33, 480–540.

———. *Aigina*. Berlin: Gebr. Mann, 1938.

———. *Troizen und Kalaureia*. Berlin: Gebr. Mann, 1941.

———. "Aeginetica XXV–XXXVI." *AA* 69 (1954): 28–48.

Wide, Sam, and L. Kjellberg. "Ausgrabungen auf Kalaureia." *AthMitt* 20 (1895): 267–327.

Williams, Dyfri. "Aegina, Aphaia-Tempel IV. The Inscription Commemorating the Construction of the First Limestone Temple and Other Features of the Sixth Century Temenos." *AA* 1982, pp. 55–68.

———. "Aegina, Aphaia-Tempel V. The Pottery from Chios." *AA* 1983, pp. 156–86.

Wolters, Paul. "Vasen aus Menidi." *JdI* 14 (1899): 103–35.

Young, Rodney. "Pottery from a Seventh Century Well." *Hesperia* 7 (1938): 412–28.

———. *Late Geometric Graves and a Seventh Century Well in the Agora*. Hesperia, supplement 2, 1939.

———. "Graves from the Phaleron Cemetery." *AJA* 46 (1942): 23–57.

———. "Sepulturae Inter Urbem." *Hesperia* 20 (1951): 67–134.

INDEX